INDIAN NATIONAL ARMY

A Documentary Study

INDIAN NATIONAL ARMY

A Documentary Study

(In 5 Volumes)

Volume-III

(1943-1944)

T. R. SAREEN

GYAN PUBLISHING HOUSE
NEW DELHI - 110002

INDIAN NATIONAL ARMY—A DOCUMENTARY STUDY

Rs. 4,500/-

ISBN : 81-212-0833-5 (Set)
ISBN : 81-212-0846-7 (Vol-3)

Published in 2004 in India by
Gyan Publishing House
5, Ansari Road, Daryaganj
New Delhi-110 002
Phones-23282060, 23261060, Fax-23285914
Email : gyanbook@vsnl.com
Visit our Website at : http//www.gyanbooks.com

Lasertype Setting by: Tact Computer Graphics, Delhi
Printed at: Chawla Offset Press, Delhi

To
Dr. Lata Singh

List of Documents

Introduction

The documents in this volume deal with the most momentous events in the history of the Indian National Army (I.N.A.). They cover mainly 1944 when I.N.A. alongwith the Japanese forces crossed the Indo-Burma border and carried the armed struggle on the Indian soil.

They came very close to success. The Japanese—I.N.A. offensive consisted of two campaigns in Arakan and Imphal. Two I.N.A. battlions and two Bahadue units joined the Japanese forces from the very beginning of the campaign, two other regiments of No. 1. I.N.A. Division under Col. M.Z. Kiani joined them in April and May, 1944. Between February and May, I.N.A. fought on the Indian side in the Arakan Secter and in Imphal. The inital success in the Arakan caused much enthusiasm and Bose as the Supreme Commander of the I.N.A. in a special order of the day referred to the glorious and brilliant actions of the brave forces of "Azad Hind Fauj" (Doc. 8)

This was immediately followed by a proclamation urging the Indian people to cooperate with the I.N.A. and its allied forces for ousting the British from India (Doc. 16)

The news of the welcome by the people of Manipur and their cooperation with the I.N.A. and Japanese were not mere propaganda (Doc. 19). These were supported by the reports from the Political Agent Manipur and how the people were punished for their cooperation. The prospects of initial success made it necessary for the Provisional Government of Azad Hind to prepare for taking over the civil administration of the liberated territories. A party of civil administrators trained also in the military discipline called the Azad Hind Dal was organized. A detailed scheme was drawn up for the civil administration of the liberated areas and even proclamation was issued informing the local people about the Provisional Government of Azad Hind. They were requested to cooperate with it. Even the Japanese Prime Minister gave full promise and declared in the

Diet that the liberated areas would be placed under the Azad Hind Government (Doc. 17, 31).

British were fully aware of the activities of the I.N.A. as is clear from the notes prepared by the military intelligence. (Doc. 12, 25). On the basis of the information received from their agents, counter-measures were taken to frustrate the designs of I.N.A. These measures included strict secrecy about the I.N.A., and creation of special "Josh group". In all the official documents. I.N.A. was labelled as J.I.F. (Japanese Inspired Force). Safe conduct passes were issued to those, who were still loyal to the British army (Doc. 27.)

By press statements, interviews, promotion and even special orders of the Day, Bose kept up the spirit of the I.N.A. very high. But there were number of administrative difficulties, which the I.N.A. had to face while fighting in Imphal and Kohima sectors. These were pointed by Col. M.Z. Kiani. Steps were taken to solve these difficulties, to some extent (Docs. 45, 46)

The failure of the Imphal campaign was a very significant event for the I.N.A. It definitely minimised the chances of success for the I.N.A. to liberate India.

Bose tried to thwart British propaganda and appealed to Indian leaders and people regarding the sincerity of Japan and the need for outside help for the liberation of India (Doc. 38)

Bose went to Tokyo for exchanging views with the new Japanese Premier. His speeches and statements during the time show as to how his mind was working about the liberation of India. His speech at the Tokyo Imperial University is very important to understand his views about the fundamental problems of India.7

Bose was also aware of the fact that the congress leaders in India had written off chances of a Japanese victory after the failure of the Imphal campaign and were ready to come to terms with the British. Bose was against the partition of India and gave a warning in his broadcasts that the Indain leaders should not play into the hands of Britain.

The Appendices dealing with this period throw a good deal of light on the activities of the I.N.A. and the Provisional Government of Azad Hind. Especially important are some notes prepared by the British Military Intelligence on the training schools run by the I.N.A. British had full details about the despatch of I.N.A. agents in India and could take prompt action against them. They were aware of the working of the Hikari Kikan, the Japanese liaison agency dealing with the Indian National Army. From these documents, it is evident that the British had prior knowledge about the I.N.A.'s activities and was prepared to take adequate action on the basis of the information.

The documents are arranged in the chronological order and have been drawn from various archival repositories in India and abroad. I am specially thankful to Netaji Subas Chander Bose Academy. Japan for their help and providing me with the photocopies of documents included in this volume

T.R. Sareen

1

British Military Intelligence on Spy Training Schools of I.N.A[1].

2 January, 1944

Swaraj Young Men's Training Institute

1. This was last referred to in W.I.S. No. 95 dated 13 Aug 43, part III, para 12 (e). There is very little to add to what has already been published. The first course known to have taken place at this Institute started in Nov. 43 and consisted of some 60 students. These were disbanded and returned to their homes on the arrival of a batch of some 40 (not 96 as previously reported) students for the second course, which opened about the middle of Dec 45. Training continued at this Institute, on the lines already ascribed, until March or April 43, when the Institute was finally closed down and students who completed the course were issued with certificates. They were returned to their homes and told to be prepared to be called up at any moment. It appears that this Institute was intended chiefly to serve as a holding centre, for some of its students who were later identified at the Swaraj Young Men's Training Institute at Kanbe and Thingangyun. The need for such holding centres probably disappeared when intelligence agents under training were concentrated at Kanbe in the middle of 1943.

Biren Roy's School, Rangoon

2. This school was in the Neogy Building, Sparke Street, Rangoon, and was run by Biren Roy, an ex-detenu of Dacca and an important I.I.L.

1. British had an elobuate system of getting information from their agents. Number of Notes on the Indian National Army and its activites were prepared and circulated in weekly intelligence summary. The name I.N.A. was hardly used in these notes. I.N.A. was described as J.I.F.C. (Japanese Inspried Fifth Columnist) F. No. 601/7378/H.S. Ministry of Defence.

organizer in Burma, sometimes between the end of Aug. and Dec. 42. Roy and his assistants recruited about 32 students, all Bengalis, in various parts of Burma. There appears to have been no regular, staff apart from Roy himself, but N.K. Banerji of the Thingangyun Institute and some of the senior students delivered lectures.

3. **Training.** Instruction in the use of fire-arms was given on the roof of the building. Apart from this there was no regular syllabus and "training" was confined to informal discussions between Roy and the students on the aims and objects of the I.I.L. The main theme of these discussions was anti-British and pro-Japanese propaganda and the "liberating" role of the I.N.A. Students were strictly confined to the building and their presence there was kept secret.

4. **Instructions.** Biren Roy's professed object was to train students to cause internal chaos in India during the advance of forces. True to the Bengali terrorist tradition, N.K. Banerji instructed the students to resort to "money-actions" when in need of funds, to sabotage telegraph wires and railway lines, students were sent off for infiltration purposes in India with revolvers and small amount of cash in (forged) Indian currency notes. They were told that their arms were to be used in self defence if attempts were made to arrest them, and if arrested they were to commit suicide in order to avoid disclosing their mission.

5. **Summary.** The school is now defunct. It appears to have been more of an informal secret group rather than regular training centre, the majority of its members being diseffected Bengalis who were willing to engage in terrorist activities under Biren Roy's leadership.

Baba Amar Singh's School, Rangoon and Mawlaik

6. This was last referred to in G.H.G.W.I.S. No. 93 dated 13 Aug. 43, part III, para 12(j). Baba Amar Singh, the old Ghadrite conspirator whom the Japanese took to Burma form Bangkok to organise intelligence activities, started a training school for about 25 students in Feb. or Mar. 43. His staff seens to have consisted only of 2 "chief recruiters" named Chanda Singh and Ram Lekha. The agents he selected were of a poor type and were given little useful training. There appears to have been no particular syllabus, emphasis being laid on propaganda. Later the school was moved to Mawlaik, and there

some elementary training in bomb-making and the use of small arms was given.

7. Full details of the instructions given to agents sent from this school are not yet available, but a number of them were dispatched to Manipur State to contact the ex-Royal family on behalf of the Japanese and to engage in sabotage, espionage and propaganda against Indian troops and Government employees. As far as is known on success attended these efforts, all the agents who were sent out being arrested before they had approached their tasks. One feature peculiar to Baba Amar Singh's school is that the secret parties whom he had sent out were provided with guides, residents of the Indo-Burman frontier area, who had been through the same training as the agents themselves. Some of these guides were intended to provide the means of communication between the agents and the enemy in Burma.

2

Bose's Broadcast from Burma after Visiting Andamans, Announces the Appointment of A.D. Loganandan as Chief Commissioner of the Islands[1]

6 January, 1944

"FRIENDS! I shall now give you a very interesting peace of news-namely, that before I arrived in Burma, I was able to visit the Andaman and Nicobar Islands. You will remember that on the 6th November, 1943 at the assembly of Greater East Asiatic Nations held in Tokyo, His Excellency Premier General Hideki Tojo made an historic declaration to the effect that the Government of Nippon would transfer the Adaman and Nicobar Islands of the Provisional Government of Azad Hind. Following that declaration I had conversations with the Nippon Authorities on the subject both in Tokyo and in Shonan. After these conversations, the Nippon Authorities arranged for my visit to these islands in which I was accompanied by members of my Government and of my personal staff I have now come here after completing that trip. The object of the journey to the Andaman Islands was to discuss with the local Nippon authorities the preparatory measures necessary for effecting the transfer of the Andaman and Nicobar Islands to the Provisional Government of Azad Hind. In pursuance of the discussions that were held there, I can now announce that I have appointed Lt.-Col A.D. Loganadan, a high ranking officer of the Indian National Army, as the Chief Commissioner of the Andaman and Nicobar Islands. As soon as Transport arrangements are made, the newly appointed Chief Commissioner will proceed to the above Islands with his staff.

"During this visit, I and the other members of my party had the unique experience of our lives when we stood on the soil of free India for the first time. It was an unforgettable event for us to see our tri-colour

---

1. *Greater Asia*, 8 Jan, 1944. A.D. Longananden was appointed as Chief Commissioner of Andamans and Nicobar Islands. Which Japanese had accopied in 1942. Logananden was in Andamans from Feburary 1944 till September, 1944. After his departure Alvi acted as Chief Commissioner till July 1945.

national flag fluttering in the air, over the former British Chief Commissioner's residence in Rose Island. During our stay there, we occupied the former British Chief Commissioner's residence and we wonder all the time how the wheels.

History was now moving in India's favour. The sight of our national flag flying over the Chief Commissioner's house made all of us think of the day when the same flag would be hoisted over the Viceroy's house in New Delhi.

"My countrymen will remember that since August last year, I have been giving expression to my hope and belief that before the end of 1943 we would stand on the soil of Free India. That this dream has actually been fulfilled before the 31st December 1943 has given me the greatest happiness.

"While we were in the Andaman islands, we visited the notorious Cellour Jail in Port Blair and paid silent homage to those patriotic countrymen of ours who suffered indescribable persecution and torture in the past and some of whom even laid down their lives as victims of British tyranny and brutality. We were informed by the Superintendent of the Jail that the last batch of political prisoners constisting of about 200 court-martial prisoners were transported back to India along with some British officials shortly before the Nipponese occupation of the Islands.

"During my visit to the Island I was able to study conditions there and to get acquainted with the local population. I found that they were all happy that the British had been expelled from the place and their joy knew no bounds when they heard the declaration of the Government of Nippon regarding the Islands in November last. A strong national awakening was visible among the people and they were determined to become good and patriotic citizens in future.

"In the mass meeting that was held I told the people that since they had suffered so much at the lands of British Imperialism in the past, it has pleased Providence to give them the first taste of freedom and happiness. Consecuently, they should now forget their unhappy past, become worthy citizens of Free India and work hard in order to create a bright and happy future for themselves.

"From what I have seen of the Islands and of their natural resources, I am confident that as a part of Free India the Andaman and Nicobar Islands will become a place fit for free, cultured and progressive men and women to live in.

"I am sure that if, in future, the British attempted to reconquer the Islands, they will meet with the fierce and stub-born oppositiion of the people there."

3

Japanese Orders for the Treatment of I.N.A. and Handling of Indian Army Soldiers, who would Join them (Extract)

1 February, 1944

1. Policy—When handling Indian prisoners the object is to reinforce the Indian National Army and thus facilitate Japanese Army operations. Prisoners are to be won over to allegiance to the Imperial Army by concrete evidence of the sincerity of our intentions. Hence, except for those who are hostile to us, no Indian prisoner will be killed or treated harshly for any reason.

2. Procedure in handling—Indian prisoners captured at the front (including deserters) are to be separated from white prisoners and treated warmly. They are to be won over to cooperation with our army by kindling their sentiments for independence from GREAT BRITAIN and resistance against GREAT BRITAIN and the UNITED STATES.

Indian prisoners are classified into three categories based upon their military qualifications and their attitude regarding independence from GREAT BRITAIN. Methods of handling should be determined by these classifications:

Class A—	Men strongly anti-British and favouring independence, who are fit for fighting, are immediately inducted into the Indian National Army.
Class B—	Men not physically equal to those in class A, but fit for work, are inductedd into labour units.

1. South East Asia Translation and interrogation Bulletine No 23. A memographed copy of these orders was captured by the British. Though undated, these must have been issued before the I.N.A. and Japanese forces crossed the Indo-Burma, border" in Feb 1944

Class C— Men who are anti-Japanese and pro-British, or unfit for either combat or labour, are handled according to the general regulations for treatment of prisoners.

It is a basic rule that the above classification is to be done by the Replacement Department of the Indian National Army (INDOKOKUMINGUN HOJUBU); under the direction of branches of the HIKARI Agency (HIKARI KIKAN BUNHAKIKAN) as directed by Army supreme command. (TN: the HIKARI KIKAN is the special service organization of the Japanese Army in charge of espionage, propaganda and subversion in BURMA, FRENCH INDO-CHINA, PHILIPPINES and DUTCH FAST INDIES. It is now know as "Southern Area Guerrilla Unit" (NAMPO YOUGEKITAI).

The presence of subversive elements among Indian prisoners should be anticipated. Each unit will take all measures for its own security. Such prisoners should not be killed indiscriminately, but branches of the Mieari Agency or the replacement Department of the Indian National Army will take appropriate measures for their elimination.

The HIKARI Agency is to be given preference in the selection of personnel for agents.

As regards rations, Indian prisoners of even class C should be treated much better than white prisoners.

3. Reports—Reports on type and number of prisoners taken are required.

Supplement 2 Handling the ordinary Indian in the Theater of Operations.

1. Policy—The policy in treatment of the ordinary Indian in the theater of operations is to make him respect and obey the Imperial Army and cooperate in operations against INDIA.

2. Procedure in Handling—Prohibitions and precautions to be observed.

3. Reports—Reports on Indian willingness to cooperate in the theater of operations are required.

Supplement 3 Handling the Indian National Army.

1. Policy—The Indian National Army is to be inculcated with complete faith in and respect and friendliness for the Imperial

Army, and then allowed to cooperate in military activities. To this end its ambition for independence end its hostility to GREAT BRITAIN is to be encouraged, and its officers imbued with enthusiasm. The mistake must not be made at any time of adopting a superior or arrogent attitude toward it, nor will there be harsh treatment or insults in word or action.

2. Procedure—The Indian National Army will be treated as the military force of an allied nation, since it is under the jurisdiction of the Free India Provisional Government and is cooperating with the Imperial Army against a common enemy. The right of command of the Indian National Army is to be respected. When it is attached to the Japanese Army, the command will be given to a Japanese officer of a rank lower than the former Indian National Army officer, and care will be taken to preserve the original organization. Furthermore, the execution of command will be carried as much as possible through the Hikari Agency. The key to the employment of the Indian National Army is to keep firm control of its highest commander, to permit him to exert command, while retaining full responsibility ourselves, and to give him a clear and concrete mission.

   Care will be taken to see that the Indian National Army carries out its own counter espionage measures. Rewards and punishments for the Indian National Army will be promulgated by the Area Army, to whom the units will submit cases.

3. Reports—Reports are required on all aspects of the situation.

Supplement 4 Handling Indian (Soldier) Agents (INDIAN HEIKOSAKUIN)

1. "Special activities" (TOKUMU KOSAKU) (TN: espionage, propaganda; and subversive activities) against INDIA will be perfected if we develop in the Indian (soldier) agents a spirit of sacrifice for the nation which will enable them to infiltrate boldly into enemy territory and perform "special activities", and if we do everything possible to facilitate their work.

2. Procedure—Care should be taken against given away agents, indentities, and againsts maltreating or killing them on their return from enemy territory through failure to indentify them.

To prevent their revealing information to the enemy if captured or being used by the enemy against us, they will not be given information about our own troops or the Indian National Army.

Supplement— Tables of rations and clothing issued to officers and men of the Indian National Army.

Supplement— Method of Identifying the Indian National Army in Forward Areas.

1. Method of Identification during Infiltration of Enemy Territory— Until crossing the most advanced front line of our forces, an identity certificate, issued by units concerned or by the HIKARI Agency, will be carried. This will be destroyed upon crossing that line.

2. Method of Indentification at Time of Return from Enemy Territory—All persons returning from enemy territory will establish their identity by repeating "HIKARI KIKAN" (IN;HIKARI Agency) and "INDOKOKUMINGUN" (TN: Indian National Army), and by showing the "T". symbol sewn somewhere on their garments. Persons in enemy territory, such as those who, even though they are not in the Indian National Army, have received the necessary certification from the Indian National Army which has infiltrated into the area, will follow the above method of ilndetification for liaison with the Japanese Army. However, these will not show a "T" symbol. Persons returning from anemy torritory will not be harmed, but will be turned over to an official of the HIKARI Agency.

Notes—Persons wearing the uniform of the Indian National Army will not carry indentity certificates.

4

Announcement about the Advance of I.N.A. and Japanese Forces Towards Arakan[1]

7 February, 1944

The Spokesmen of the Nippon Army in the Burma sector declared a second "Tragedy of Arakan" is what lies ahead of enemy forces as a result of our new operations in the Burma-India sector launched since last Friday.

He said the present operations are featured by active participation by troops of the Indian National Army, who with their Nippon comrades-in-arms are surging ahead, with the capture of Chittagong, enemy stronghold in Bengal, as the first objective of their historic advance into Indian territory.

The Spokeman recalled that all the enemy's attempts to recapture Burma have ended in miserable failure involving heavy losses to the enemy. He pointed out that the enemy's counter offensive aimed at the recapture of Burma last spring met with disaster at the hands of our forces, resulting in what is known as "The Tragedy to Arakan".

He added that the enemy High Command made another unsuccessful attempt last Autumn to invade northern Burma from the upper reaches of the Salween River.

He pointed out that the enemy sustained crushing defeats on this occasion, after which enemy activities in this sector had been confined to defence of its positions on the eastern bank of the Salween River.

The Spokesman recalled in this connection that Chen Cheng. Commander of the Chungking forces in the Burma sector, tendered his resignation to Chiang Kaishek in protest against the Anglo-American High Command's attempt to subjugate Chungking troops following their defeat at the hands of our forces.

He futher recalled that the enemy High Command, since it was reorganized under Mountbatten, were launching yet another counter-

1. *The Syonan Shimbun 8 Feb. 1944*. This paper was started by the Japanese after occupation of Singapore.

offensive campaign against Buthidaung with the main force of the British 14th Army supported to tank and heavy artillery corps.

The spokeman pointed out that the enemy's much publicized "recapture of Maungdaw" followed only after our strategical withdrawal from that point which by that time had lost its strategic importance. He added how the enemy is capitalizing on this "recapture of Maungdaw" can be seen from being from the fact that Churchill wired Mounthatten congratulation on that intrinsically insignificant military development.

The spokesman declared that our High Command in the meantime, completed all necessary preparations for the next offensive in close concert with the Indian National Army who had been itching for action to accelerate the advent of the day of complete liberation of their motherland from Anglo-American oppression.

The fact that enemy forces were able to make an advance was the result of part of our strategy to draw the enemy forces close to our positions before dealing a decisive blow to the enemy. He declared last Friday marked the day when our forces, hand in hand with our Indian comrades-in-arms, started on their long awaited march towards India.

He revealed that this onslaught is now being pushed ahead most satisfactorily with our forces surging ahead towards the enemy base of operations in this sector, after, inflicting heavy blows on enemy units. The Spokesman pointed with complete satisfaction to the successful progress being made by units of the Indian National Army, whose first objective in the current operation is believed to be the capture of Chittagong, enemy stronghold in Bengal.

He declared that the hour of the second "tragedy of Arakan" is thus fast approaching the enemy forces, which are bound to perish in a watery grave in the Bay of Bengal. He disclosed that our force simultaneously succeeded in silencing Chungking troops which have been making, nuisance moves in the Hukawng sector in northern Burma. He declared the enemy's much vaunted attempt to reopen the Burma route to aid the isolated Chungking regime will also end in a mere propaganda campaign.

Concluding, the Spokesmen declared that the Nippon Army in the Burma sector launching the present offensive is directing its attack right at Mounthatten's headquarters, with the flag of Free India already flying over Arakan.

5

Bose Statement on the I.N.A. Penetration in Arakan to Crush the British Forces[1]

7 February, 1944

THE GREAT battle which has just begun on the Arakan front for the destruction of the Anglo American forces of aggression and the liberation of India's four hundred million people heralds the decisive phase of the Dai Toa Senso (Greater East Asia War) for the achievement of the ideal of Asia for Asiatics. In the initial stage of the war, the invincible forces of Imperial Nippon dealt the death blow on the Anglo-American-Dutch imperialism in Toa (East Asia), leading of Asiatic people. And now the campaign has started for the crowning achievement of Nippon's noble mission.

It is hardly forty-eight hours since the great news of the beginning of the offensive on the Arakan front was announced by the Imperial Headquarters: But the dispatches that have come in during these hours are extremely gratifying indeed. The joint operations launched by the Imperial Nippon Army and the Indian National Army, have been progressing most favourably. The allied forces of Nippon and Free India have already pierced the enemy lines at several points. The British forces have been pushed back all along the fighting line and their retreat is fast developing into a rout. Judging from these frontline despatches, it is apparent that the British forces are panic-stricken over the second "Arakan Disaster" that now threatens them.

The Indian campaign, now in full swing, is of tremendous significance, not only in the light of the far reaching repercussions it will have on the entire trend of the Dai Toa Senso, but also in view of the active participation in this campaign by the Indian National Army organised in Toa under the supreme command of Subhas Chandra Bose.

---

1. *The Syonan Shimbun 9 Feb. 1944.*

This Army of patriotic Indians in Toa (East Asia) appropriately called the Azad Hind Fauj (India's Army of Liberation)—is at the forefront of the battle, fighting shoulder to shoulder with the Imperial Nippon Army: and the presence of the Indian Army at the battle front is bound to produce the most heartening effect on the people in India, soldiers and civilians alike, Nippon and Indian forces, waging the common war, for the common cause, against the common enemy and for the common goal, have gone into action on the Arakan front, as true comrades-at-arms, grimly resolved to share the hardship and sacrifices of war and the joy of victory as well.

It is this salient aspect of the Arakan campaign which makes it the most outstanding demonstration of Asiatic unity and resolve in the war to crush the Anglo-Americans and to establish an Asia for Asiatics.

Nationalist Indians, in India and abroad, have been convinced that they must take up arms and fight the British if ever their goal of national independence is to be achieved. Free Indians in Toa, under the inspiring leadership of Subhas Chandra Bose have therefore been organising themselves for the battle against the Anglo American enemies in India; and Nippon in pursuance of her policy, has pledged all-out aid to the Indian people in their efforts to win their freedom. Nippon's war aim is a free Asia but there can be no Free Asia without Free India. The expulsion of the Anglo-American forces of aggression, now entrenched in india, is a vital necessity not only for the liberation of India, but also for the safety of Toa and the victory of Nippon and her allies in Toa.

Such is the ideal that has inspired the combined Indian and Nippon forces to battle on the Indo-Burma frontier. It is the beginning of the March to Delhi by the Indian National Army and its Nippon allies. And the outcome of this historic campaign has been best expressed by Subhas Chandra Bose, Head of the provisional Government of Free India, in the following terms:-

"We have full confidence in our own strength. We have complete faith in our allies; and we have unlimited optimism regarding national victory. We shall go on toiling and fighting till our flag is fluttering in India's metropolis."

6

Bose Statement Countering British Propaganda Against I.N.A.[1]

8 February, 1944

The following cable was sent by Netaji Subhas Chandra Bose, Supreme Commander, Indian National Army, to the officer commanding, Indian National Army, Arakan front under date February 8.

All officers and men of the Indian National Army and myself feel happy and proud over the achievements of our troops at the Arakan Front under your command. I am confident that all Freedom-Loving Indians in the world share our feelings. Please accept my warmest congratulations and convey the same to the officers and men under you.

"Since the time that the announcement regarding the formation of the Azad Hind Fauj or the Indian National Army was first made several months ago, enemy propagandists have been trying to tell the Indian people as well as Britian's Indian Army in India that the Indian National Army does not exist and that it is only a propaganda-stunt. In December last, the Headquarters of the Indian National Army opened its own broadcasting Station and from that station officers and men of the Indian National Army began to broadcast regularly in their own names. This made enemy propagandists extremely uneasy and uncomfortable and they, therefore, fell back on a new propagandastic. They put out a false story to the world that I had promised to reach Delhi with my Army before the end of 1943 and on that false story they began to issue radio commentaries everyday saying that I had failed to redeem propaganda-offensive against me was to hide Mountbatten's utter failure to start his much-advertised offensive for re-conquering Burma.

"I have already replied to enemy propagandists saying that I made no promise to them or to their masters—the British Government-and that whatever promise I made to my own countrymen either have been already

1. *Greater Asia, 10 Feb. 1944.*

redeemed or will be redeemed in the fulness of time. I have also declared to the whole world that during the last twelve months, we have been working according to plans that we have been advancing from one success to another. The only thing about which any complaint can be made is that our time-table has been slightly delayed.

When the Headquarters of the Provisional Government of Azad Hind and of the Supreme Command of the Indian National Army were removed from Shonan to Burma in the first week of January, there was nervousness and panic at Delhi. Enemy propagandists thereupon had to discover new methods for hiding their discomfiture. Not being able to deny the existence of the Indian National Army any longer, they started abusing me and my Army and began to assert again that this Army had not been able to advance towards its destination. But, he laughs best who laughs last. The announcement that is being made from Tokyo regarding the Indian National army will tell something about our activities, of the Indian National Army. I shall not say much at this stage but let events speak for themselves. I shall only say this that we are working according to plan and that in the fulness of time we shall redeem our solemn pledge to liberate our Motherland. We have full confidence in our own strength—we have complete faith in our Allies and we have unbounded optimism regarding our final victory. We shall go on toiling and fighting till the Flag that is now fluttering over the Arakan Hills flies over the Viceroy's House and the Red Fortress in India's Metropolis.

7

An Editorial on the Importance of I.N.A. : "March on to Delhi"

9 February, 1944

Free Indians, On to Delhi!

The Battle is on, Warriors of the Indian National Army are in full cry after the enemy who is already beginning to retreat in disorder on the India-Burma front. Confident of the support they will receive from the Imperial Nippon forces who have smashed previous enemy bids to launch counter-offensives in this theatre of war, soldiers of the Indian National Army are dashing forward, convinced of the success that awaits them once they enter their motherland and join forces with the disgruntled British Indian troops who are waiting to turn on the British at the opportune moment.

Today all attention is focussed on the doings of the Indian National Army. The Netaji's battle-cry of "On to Delhi" was no empty rhetoric. It is an inspired slogan, with which the Revolutionary Army will go on to tear down the British flag from the Red Fortress in Delhi and in its stead hoist the National Flag of Free India. Sympathisers with the cause of the people of India are thrilled at the way the Azad Hind Fauj has gone into battle. Everything augurs well for the future; the enemy is already hard pressed.

Already Nippon air units are paying the way for the advances of the ground forces. The enemy's plan of attack has been frustrated, nipped in the bud. Winging their war far over the Bay of Bengal, Nippon Wild Eagles have blasted enemy concentrations and installations at bases in India, dive-bombing the enemy's rear and causing havoc to his communications. A convoy in the Bay was attacked, causing severe loss to the enemy. All this is going to help the task of the Indian Nationalist Army. and hasten their entry into India.

---

1. *The Syonan Shimbun, 9 Feb. 1944.* This paper was published from Singapore and was controlled by the Japanese. Its chairman was Tashio.

Once the Indian Revolutionaries set foot on Indian soil, they will fight with renewed vigour and inspiration, for then will their goal-their long-cherished dream of an India free of alien domination, able to call her soul here own-more realistically appear within their reach. The people of Malai, together with the peoples of the rest of Dai Toa, will earnestly pray for the success of the Indians; campaign.. They have suffered long and patiently. The day of retribution is at hand. The British are on the run and must be swept out of India. There must be no halting, no respite. Free Indians, march to Delhi.

8

Special Order of the Day by Subhas Chandra Bose, Supreme Commander, Azad Hind Fauj, on the Success of I.N.A. in Arakan[1]

9 February, 1944.

The eyes of the whole world are focussed on the Arakan Front, where events of far-reaching consequences are taking place to-day. The glorious and brilliant actions of the brave units of Azad Hind Fauj working in close concert with the forces of the Imperial Nippon Army, have helped to foil attampts by the Anglo-American forces to start counter-offensive in this sector.

I am sure that the brave deeds of our comrades on the Arakan Front will be a great inspiration to all the Officers and men of the Azad Hind Fauj wherever they may be stationed at the present moment. Our long awaited march to Delhi has begun and with grim determination, we shall continue that march until the tricolour National Flag that is flying over the Arakan mountains is hoisted over the Viceregal Lodge and until we hold our victory parade at the ancient Red Fortress of Delhi.

Comrades, officers and men of India's Army of Liberation: Let there be one solemn resolve in your hearts—'Either liberty or death.' And let there be but one slogan on your lips 'Onward to Delhi.' The road to Delhi is the road to freedom. That is the road along which we must march. Victory will certainly be ours.

Inqlab Zindabad : Azad Hind Zindabad.

1. I.N.A. Trial Papers.

8

Special Order of the Day by Subhas Chandra Bose, Supreme Commander, Azad Hind Fauj, on the Success of I.N.A. in Arakan[1]

[illegible]

9

Statement of S.A. Ayer on the I.N.A.'s Success on the Arakan Front[1]

10 Feburary, 1944

Mr. S.A. Ayer, Publicity and Propaganda Minister of the Azad Hind Government comments on the Dai Honyei announcement as follows:-

"A stunning reminder to the British in India that Netaji Subhas Chandra Bose is a man of action and that he means what he says". This was the comment of Mr. S.A. Ayer, Minister of Publicity and Propaganda of the Provisional Government of Free India when a Greater Asia representative interviewed him on the historic announcement of the Dai Honyei to the effect that the Indian National Army is fighting in close unison with the Imprial Nipponese Forces in the Arakan regions, in an effort to crush the British Indian troops once again, in order to bring about the second "Arakan Debacle". This represents, no doubt, the feelings of all freedom-loving Indians in India as well as outside India who are rejoiced at the news that Netaji has at last started his offensive against the Anglo-Americans.

Continuing, the Propaganda Minister said "I would recall Netaji's first words on his arrival in East Asia eight months ago when he said : 'The enemy who has drawn the sword must be fought with the sword."

Mr. Ayer added, "Lately, the British in India have been indulging in the cheap and foolish propaganda that Netaji and his Army are idle. Well, Netaji is content to let events speak for themselves; I would add that events have begun to speak for themselves," the Propaganda Minister concluded.

In co-ordinated action with Netaji Subhas Chandra Bose, 3,000,000 Indian people residing in East Asia rose equal to the occasion to follow him toward Delhi and liberate all Indian people from British tyranny, as an opportunity like this will never come again for centuries.

---

1. *Greater Asia, 10 Feb, 1944*

9

Statement of S. A. Ayer on the I.N.A.'s Success on the Arakan Front

[illegible], 1944[1]

Mr. S. A. Ayer, Publicity and Propaganda Minister of the Azad Hind [illegible] comments on [illegible] [illegible] reminded of the [illegible] Netaji Subhas [illegible] is a man of action and that he means what he says. This [illegible] comment of Mr. S. A. Ayer, Minister of Publicity and Propaganda of the Provisional Government [illegible] a Greater Asia representative interviewed him on the historic announcement of the [illegible] the offensive [illegible] Azad Hind Fauj, fighting in close [illegible] with the Nippon Army [illegible] on the Arakan regions, in an [illegible] the British Indian forces [illegible], in order to bring about [illegible] Arakan Defences. [illegible] proved [illegible] who are engaged at the [illegible] that [illegible]

Continuing, the Propaganda Minister said: [illegible] Netaji's [illegible] his arrival in [illegible] eight months ago when he said: "The [illegible] who has drawn the sword [illegible] with the sword."

Mr. Ayer added: [illegible] the British in India have been indulging in the cheap and foolish [illegible] that Netaji and his Army are idle. Well, [illegible] let them [illegible] speak for themselves. I would add that [illegible] speak for themselves," the Propaganda Minister concluded.

[illegible] Subhas Chandra Bose [illegible] the [illegible] Asia [illegible] equal to the occasion to follow him to [illegible] Delhi and [illegible] of Indian people from [illegible] tyranny so that [illegible] will never come again for centuries.

1. [illegible]

10

Impact of I.N.A. on British Forces in Arakan[1]

21 February, 1944

February, 1944 will long remain one of the most memorable days in the annals of the Indian people—as a day of monumental importance to the Indian race heralding the coming of their national redemption. On this fateful day, the Indian National Army in cooperation with the imperial Japanese Forces began its historic march toward New Delhi over the mountains of Mayu and on the Burma-India border.

In outlining the policies of the Imperial Government, Prime Minister Hideki Tojo on January 21 declared in the Imperial Diet :

"Subhas Chandra Bose is ready to march into India at the head of his National Army. The Imperial Government will give its wholehearted assitance to his attempt to secure Indian Independence.

The Indian National Army has already begun its westward march in India's first armed contest against its hideous master-Britain. And side by side with the army stand the formidable Imperial Forces which are ready to cruch all enemy resistance in their onslught over the Burma-India frontier.

The Indian National Army is marching shoulder to shoulder with the Imperial Japanese Army. In its sacred mission of liberting India. It is now dealing a deadly blow on the British troops which had long been planning to launch an invasion of Burma in its for hold to recover its lost prestige in East Asia. When Mr Bose advanced to Burma at the head of his National Army, it had the effect of fundamentally shaking the very souls of the Indian populaces, who had been groaning under the terrifying mistreatment of British rule. The number of desertions among the Indian soldiers at the front increase steadily, while others will join the Indian National Army as soon as they come into contact with it, and take up arms against the British Troops.

---

1. *Nippion Times, 21 Feb, 1944.*

Dismayed by such stupendous effects, the British authorities in India placed a strict ban on any reports about the army and circulated the falsehood that the exitence of such an army was war propaganda. But such decription has been disproved by the actual fighting of the Indian National Army in colliboration with the Japanese troops in the persents operations around the Muyu region. When the news of this historic event is flashed over India, its people will respond in their surging enthusiaism to overcome British rule. The thick wall which the Indian people had tried vainly to break down in order to secure their freedom is at last being shattered by their brave sons who are marching over the Burma India border. India is on the eve of its emancipation.

11

Bose on the success of the I.N.A. on the battle front[1]

29 February, 1944

"The annihillation of the main fore of the British Seventh Division is really glorious news. Particularly, it is joyful to hear that the Indian National Army has scored a glorious victory in its first battle in the Arakan district, under close cooperation with the Imperial Japanese Forces.

"This fact proves, that the Burma offensive planned by Lord Louis Mountbatten is fated to end in a disastrous result. It is impossible to get around the effect the defeat at Arakan will bring on the fighting spirit of the British forces in India. The army under Lord Mountbatten has now fallen into a death pit. I am interested to learn what excuse Lord Mountbatten will make for his defeat in reporting to Churchill. Stillwell or Chiang Kai-shek.

"Probably Churchill is now regretting that he prematurely sent a telegram of congratulation to Lord Mountbatten on the victory at Maungdaw and thus made himself a laughing stock of the whole world. If he had known that the Seventh Division was unable to gain any success, beyond rushing blindly to his self-destruction, he would have recollected the ancient saying, 'silence is golden'.

"Chaing Kai-shek also must have been disappointed as he believed that the anti-Axis forces in India would gain considerable success by the next rainy season, and the Burma supply route would be reopened. Not only was the Burma route unopened, but the Mountbatten forces have received a decisive blow on the Burma front. No longer can Chiang hope for the materialization of the empty promise given him by Lord Mountbatten to send aid over the reopened Burma route. Stillwell, no doubt, is also disappointed in the strategy and fighting strength of the British troops.

---

1. *Nippion Times*, 1 March, 1944.

For Churchill there will be no further need to send congratulations to Lord Mountbatten.

"The retreat from Burma in June, 1942, the first Arakan tragedy of last spring and the present second defeat at Arakan form links in the total defeat of the British forces. It is a prelude to final collapse of Britain in India.

"The victory gained by the Indian troops on the Burma front has stirred great excitement among the officers and men of the Indian National Army and also among all the Indian residents in Greater East Asia. There is not doubt whatever that our brother in India have been greatly comforted by the fatal blow Britain has suffered on thé Burma frontier.

12

British Intelligence's Assessment of the I.N.A.[1]

10 March, 1944

The Indian National Army

1. Introduction—Unconfirmed reports from several sources have been received recently of the arrival of organised Jif units or formations in the Kalewa area. While little definite is known as yet about the armament, training and morale of the I.N.A. information recently received enables some amplification to be made of the tentative review given in paras 16-24 of W.I.S. part III No. 97 of 1943.

The I.N.A. in Malaya

2. To recapitulate, the first serious attempt to organise the I.N.A. were made after the Bangkok conference in June 42 and, by Nov. the approximate strength in Malaya was estimated at 24,000 concentrated in and around Singapore.

3. A Paper organisation, which may have existed on the ground, was announced as:

(a) Three Guerilla Brigades (Gandhi, Nehru and Azad).

(b) A field Group (Brigade) consisting of a Signal Coy., and Armoured unit, an Ordance unit and a Supply unit.

(c) A Special Service Group (now known as the Bahadur Group).

(d) An Intelligence Group.

(e) A Cadets Training School.

(f) A Provost Units and Detention Camp.

1. War office 203/803 Public Record office, London.

Training was elementary and armament and equipment, mostly from captured British stocks, was issued on a meagre scale.

4. In Nov. 42 a so-called "advance party of the I.N.A" of 400 men left for Burma. In Dec. a quarrel occurred, between the leaders and the Japanese, which resulted in the disarshment of the "army" by the latter. Reorganisation took place about March 43, but it was not until after Subhas Chandra Bose arrived in Malaya that serious steps were undertaken to recruit, organise and train the I.N.A.

5. Of this new "army" little definite is known. Army H.Q. is in Singapore and the following units have been reported:-

(a) A field Force (Gandhi, Nehru and Azad Bdes).

(b) A Guerilla Regiment.

(c) Ancillary Units.

(d) "Crack" Regiment.

(e) Rani of Jhansi Regiment (Women's Regt.)

(f) A Signed Coy.

(g) An I.N.A. Hospital.

6. The Bahadur (hitherto known as the Special Service Group) and Intelligence Groups, a feature of the pre-Bose I.N.A., have moved into Burma. Reports of strengths, training, organisation and morale of these units when in Malaya are still conflicting. Units which had finished their training are reported to have left for Burma on 8 Jan 44 by overland and sea routes.

The I.N.A. in Burma

7. On arrival in Burma the I.N.A. "Advance Party" consisted of 200 picked men from the Gandhi, Nehru, Azad and Field Brigades, and 200 of 'A' coy of the Bahadur Group. Throughout 1943 little was heard of this body, except that the Bahadur Group representatives were being trained as intelligence agents, had been supplemented by a new ('E') company and that many of them were despatched to the forward areas on intelligence tasks in Sep. and Oct. 43. On 29 Oct. 43, 'B', 'C', and 'D' companies of the Bhadur Group arrived in Rangoon. This confirms the forecast made in paragraph 8 of A.I.S.,

8. Simultaneously with the arrival of reinforcements for the Bahadur Group, the Intelligence Group of the I.N.A., totalling 350 men, arrived in Rangoon under the command of Copt. (I.N.A. Lt.-Col.) S.A. Malik, 1st Bahawalpur, Infantry. Since then but 70 to 80 have moved up into Arabun and about 80 (two sections) were seen at the end of Jan in transit to Myitkleyina. Three other sections are said to have moved out to an unknown destination. Personnel from this and the Bahadur Group style themselves I.N.A. They are in fact intelligency agents; the Bahadur Group is intended for deep penetration and the Intelligence Group to carry out a role similar to that of our Battalion Intelligence Sections, and also to carry out espionage tasks in plain clothes.

9. In addition to the Bahadur Group, the Intelligence Group and elements of the Field Force, unconfirmed reports speak of the arival in Rangoon of a detachment of ancillary and other units of the I.N.A. during the letter half of 1943.

Jifs in Arakan

10. The first elements of the Bahadur Group moved up to Arakan in Sep. 43, and others in late October. Captain (I.N.A. major) Misra, 5/17 Dogra Regiment, who commanded 'A' company of the Bahadur Group in Rangoon, left there in Oct. with a detachment and established his H.Q. in Buthidaung, with Lt. (I.N.A. Capt.) Mehar Dac, 3 Lt. A.A. Bty., as his 2nd in command. By 17 Dec. Misra had disposed the Bahadur Group in the Buthidaung and coastal areas. Their duties were chiefly military espionage in forward areas.

11. The Intelligence Group did not arrive in Arakan until the beginning of Feb., although captured document states that 73 men of the Group were to come under command of 55 Div. from 15 Jan. They were to operate under the orders of Capt. Misra through an officer of 143 Regiment. The latter was linked with the Akyab branch of the Hikari Kikan through a small liaison group.

12. An operational order of 20 Jan stated that, in the event of operations, most of the Hikari Kikan personnel would operate on the Buthidaung-Maungdaw front with one section in the upper regions of the Kaladan. Their tasks were "to collect intelligence necessary to conduct operations and look for deserters from British Indian Army

Kaladan. Their tasks were "to collect intelligence necessary to conduct operations and look for deserters from British Indian Army and destroy enemy installations."

13. At the beginning of Feb. all Jifs were ordered to concentrate east of the Malu Range for an operation "whose zero hour had been put forward." During the early stages of the Japanese attack they participated in raids, were used as a screen for an out flanking movement, attempted to cause confusion amongst our troops by shouting in English and Urdu, carried out espionage tasks, and acted as messengers.

14. On 10 Feb. Capt. Misra and capt. Hattori (O.C. of the Akyab branch of the Hikari Kikan) were joined by '3' section of the Intelligence Group (70 men of the 73 referred to in para 11 above) and 110 men of the field force. Personnel of both forces were lightly armed. On 11 Feb., with a detachment of 'A' Company of Bahadur Group and about 50 Japanese, this composite force moved to S.E. of Taung Bazar and dug in. From there mixed patrols of Japanese and I.N.A were sent out.

15. In addition to these purely ex P.W. bodies of Jifs, agents from the Kanbe Swaraj Training Institute also took part in the operations. In Dec. 43 their HQ known as HQ 'J' force, was well forward with a detached HQ of the Bahadur Group. Jif strengths in Arkan forward of Akyab in the latter half of Feb. were approximately:-

Bahadur Group	70
Intelligence Group	70
Field Force	110
Kanbe S.T.I Students	50
Others	110
Total	410

Jifs on other Fronts

16. There are reliable indications that Jifs on other fronts are being reinforced. On the night 2/3 Mar, about 14 miles N.E. of Tiddim, 5 out of a party of 7 Jifs voluntarily surrendered to our troops. They stated that they formed the Intelligence Group of the Nehru Brigade, and

Malik, who as mentioned in para 8 above, is believed to command the Intelligence Group of the I.N.A.

17. From this and other information it seems probable that the Japanese intend using I.N.A troops in 4 Corps area in a more active role than hitherto. The Hikari Kikan has been paying particular attention to the Manipur plain for some time. A pointer may be the recent Japanese broadcast announcing a new organ for smoother liaison in future between the I.N.A., the Japanese army and the B.T.A. "To strengthen the joint strategic operations of the three allies for frustrating the enemy guerilla attempt to re-capture Burma and to draft important offensive as well as defensive operations."

13

Report of A.D. Loganandan on his Taking over as Chief Commissioner of Andaman[1]

12 March, 1944

Having left Syonan on 17th Feb 2604 the party arrived at Port Blair on the 18th mid-day. We were accommodated temporarily in the bungalow of Min Sei Bu-cho (Chief of the Civil Administration). Owing to extreme congestion, with difficulty a small bungalow was ultimately found, to which we shifted on the 11th instant. On the 21st of Feb there was a rally to celebrate the first Provisional Government day, and another rally on the second Saturday to mourn the death of Srimati Kasturba Gandhi, and also to celebrate the Arakan Victory. It is hoped to set up an office a few days hence when the transference of some of the departments will be made, details of which are still under discussion. The packages have not yet arrived, may be they may not have been despatched so far from that end. Attempts may please be made to expedite despatch, as the stationery is urgently required here. Sorry to report that nothing whatever is available here locally, and hence we are seriously handicapped. Crockery and cutilery for a dozen persons if despatched will greatly be appreciated. Dysenterics, amoebic and bacillary are endemic and in equal proportion. It will greatly help if emetine or its equivalent, as much as can be spared, could be sent. There is not a grain of Mag Sulph available here. About 420 lbs. which will last about 3 months may please be also sent. All kinds of food-stuffs are scarce, and the chance of feeding the propulation with a well-balanced diet is remote. Up-to-date no communication has been received from that end, and therefore we are absolutely in the dark as to what is happening outside. Jai Hind.

(Sd.)

A.D. Loganandan, Chief Commissioner,
Admans and Nicobar.

1. I.N.A. Trial Papers.

11

Report of A.D. Loganathan on his Taking over as Chief Commissioner of Andaman

14

Role of Indian Women in the I.N.A.[1]

12 March, 1944

SHONAN. March 12, Miss Swaminathan Lakshimi. Director of the Women's Department of the Rani of Jhansi Regiment, in an interview with a Domei correspondent yesterday, asserted that the Indian women's corps is taking an active part in the fight for the attainment of freedom Lakshimi had just returned from a two months visit to the women's corps at a certain base in Burma, and on returning to Shonan has plunged into the task of training new women recruits.

"Since the Provisional Goverment of Azad Hind took up its headquarters in Burma, a large number of Indian women in Burma have joined our ranks and are training with remarkable ardor and earnstness," remarked Miss Lakshimi. "Wonderful progress has been made by the women's corps and the members in Rangoon are all anxious to advance to the front lines. Every time we see the men of the Imperial Forces march off to the front, the women persistently ask me when they, too, will be allowed to go.

"Although frequently raided by enemy planes, Rangoon, according to members of the women's corps is on longer the line of battle. A firm determination to wrest back their motherland from fetters of British domination burns flercely in their hearts.

"Manifestations of genuine comradeship are evidemt every where between the men of the Japanese Forces and those of the Indian National Army. Once when we were advancing on X.X. a certain Japanese officer was wounded in an enemy air attack. An officer of the Indian National Army immediately carried the wounded Japanese officer on his back to the hospital When the Indian officer visited the hospital, the Japanese officer

1. *Nippon Times*, 14 March, 1944.

on the verge of death, grasped the Indian's hand firmly and with his dying breath shouted 'Jai Hind'. The Indian officer was profoundly moved and vowed that the death of his Japanese comrade would be revenged.

"The Indians who rally to our banners from the British Indian army all express amazement at how well the Provisional Government of Azad Hind and the National Army has been perfected. Also the Indian troops did not know of the famine in Bengal Province. The crafty British Propaganda had kept the Indian masses in complete ignorance."

15

Duties of I.N.A. and the Japanese Forces while Fighting together on Imphal Front[1]

21 March, 1944

1. The Indian National Army, under the leadership of the Provisional Government of Azad Hind, has now massed in force and advanced into a territory of Eastern India as the spearhead for the creation of a free India.

The Indian National Army with the help and cooperation of the Imperial Nipponese Army, has pushed into Eastern India with the object of crushing the Anglo-American forces the common enemy of East Asia: of making India really an India for Indians by liberating her from the shackles of the despotic role under which she has been groaning for ages; of bringing complete freedom and peace and order to three hundred and eighty million of our brothers and sisters in India; and also of driving away the Anglo-American menace from the borders of our neighbours the Independent Burmese.

Brothers and Sisters in India

Be engaged in your daily work without fear; gather wholeheartedly under your Tricolour Flag of Independence hoisted by the Provisional Government of Azad Hind; brace yourselves up for winning Complete Independence by retaking our Motherland from the hands of our enemies, the Anglo-Americans.

The East Indian Territory into which the Indian National Army has advanced with the powerful aid of the Imperial Nipponese Army, as well as the people thereof have now been liberated from the bondage of the Anglo-Americans. The terriroty has become the first free Indian territory on the Mainland of India under the Provisional Government and will serve as tne base for liberating our Motherland. The Imperial Nipponese Army will not

1. I.N.A. Relief and Enquiry Committee Papers.

establish a military administration but will cooperate with and wholeheartedly help the Provisional Government of Azad Hind in maintaining perfect peace and order.

2. If any person fails to understand the intentions of the Provisional Government of Azad Hind and the Indian National Army, or of our Ally, the Nippon Army, and dares to commit such acts as are itemised hereunder which would hamper the sacred task of emancipating India, he shall be executed or severely punished in accordance with the Criminal Law of the Provisional Government of Azad Hind and the Indian National Army or with the Martial Law of the Nippon Army, the application of which has been agreed upon between the two allied Armies, namely the Indian National Army and its Ally, the Imperial Nipponese Army.

Punishable Acts

(i) Rebellious acts against the provisional Government of Azad Hind or the Indian National Army, or our Ally, the Nipponese Army.

(ii) Acts of spying.

(iii) Acts of stealing and taking by force, damaging and destroying war materials which are in the possession of the Provisional Government or belong to our Ally, the Nippon Army.

(iv) Acts of damaging or destroying of valuable material resources controlled or utilised by the Provisional Government of Azad Hind or by the Nippon Army under previous agreement with the Provisional Government.

(v) Acts of destroying various installations or equipment's for traffic, Communication, transportation, broadcasting etc., which are controlled or utilized by the Provisional Government of Azad Hind and the Indian National Army, or by the Nippon Army under Previous agreement with the Provisional Government utilization thereof.

(vi) Violent acts against, intimidation of, killing or wounding of, or doing other harmful acts to those who belong to the Provisional Government of Azad Hind and the Indian National Army or our Ally, the Nippon Army.

(vii) Acts of spreading enemy propaganda or wild and false rumours, and other acts of disturbing and misleading the minds of the inhabitants.

(viii) Acts of disturbing the money circulation and economic organisation or of obstructing the production and free interchange of commodities.

(ix) Any act other than those contained in the above items, that benefits the enemy or is harmful to peace and order, and the well-being of the Provisional Government of Azad Hind and the Indian National Army or our Ally, the Nippon Army.

(x) Acts of attempting, instigating and abetting those acts contained in the above items.

The trial and punishment of such criminals will entirely be at the discretion of the Provisional Government of Azad Hind except when crimes committed are of such a nature as of necessity, owing to war-time emergency, must be dealt with by the Nippon Army as agreed upon between the two Allied Armies.

III. The Nippon Army will maintain strict discipline and protect in the area into which they have advanced the lives and properties of the Indian masses who do not commit any hostile act; and due respect will be paid to the religions, customs and manners of the Indian people.

It is guaranteed that any Nippon soldier that may violate these strict injunctions shall be severely punished in accordance with the Martial Law of the Imperial Nipponese Army.

The Indian National Army will maintain strict discipline and protect, in the area into which it has advanced, the lives and properties of the Indian masses who do not commit any hostile act; and due respect will be paid to the religions, customs and manners of our countrymen.

It is guaranteed that any Indian soldiers that may violate these strict injuctions shall be severely punished in accordance with the Martial Law of the Indian National Army.

THE ABOVE IS SOLEMNLY PROCLAIMED IN THE MONTH OF MARCH IN THE YEAR 1944 BY THE SUPREME COMMANDER OF THE INDIAN NATIONAL ARMY.

[illegible] and the masses [illegible]

(e) [illegible] of spreading such [illegible] wild and false rumours and other [illegible] disturbing the [illegible] of the inhabitants.

(f) [illegible] of disturbing the [illegible] and economic [illegible] of [illegible] and free [illegible] of commodities.

[illegible] other than those mentioned in the above [illegible] that [illegible] the Ending of [illegible] peace and order and the [illegible] of the [illegible] Government [illegible] and [illegible] the [illegible] Army.

[illegible]

The trial and punishment of [illegible] in the [illegible] of the [illegible] where [illegible] shall be [illegible] with [illegible]

(ii) The Indian National Army will [illegible] and [illegible] in the [illegible] they have [illegible] and [illegible] the [illegible] and [illegible]

[illegible]

It is guaranteed that any [illegible] who violate the [illegible] shall be severely punished in accordance with the Martial Law of the Indian National Army.

The Indian National Army will [illegible] strict discipline and [illegible] [illegible] which [illegible] the lives and properties of the [illegible] who do not [illegible] and due respect will be paid to the religions, customs and manners of the [illegible]

It is guaranteed that any [illegible] that may violate these strict [illegible] shall be severely punished in accordance with the Martial Law of the Indian National Army.

THE ABOVE IS HEREBY PROCLAIMED BY THE [illegible] THE [illegible] COMMANDER OF THE INDIAN NATIONAL ARMY

16

Historic Proclamations by Bose that the Azad Hind Fauj had Crossed the Indo-Burma Frontier; Bose also called on all Indians to Extend their Help direct or Indirect to the Armies of Liberation[1]

21 March, 1944

"The Azad Hind Fauj under the leadership of the Provisional Government of Azad Hind and the Imperial Nippon Army, working in the closet co-operation, and fighting shoulder-to-shoulder, when the allied armies of India and Nippon are crossing the frontier and marching into India, the Provisional Government of Azad Hind makes the following proclamation :

"Since the bloody war of 1857 when the armies of Indian were defeated in battle by the invading forces of Britain, the Indian people have never morally surrendered to the British. In spite of inhuman persecution, and in spite of forcible disarmament, they have continued their resistance to British domination. Through propaganda and agitation, through acts of terrorism and sabotage, through armed revolution, and in recent years through satyagraha or passive resistance initiated by Mahatma Gandhi-they have not only kept up the struggle for independence but have also advanced a long way toward the goal of freedom.

"Since the outbreak of the present war, all attempts have been made by the Indian people and their leaders for the achievement of liberty through peaceful settlement with Britain. But all these attempts have failed. More over British has in the course of this war, strengthened her stranglehold over India through ruthless exploration and brutal suppression, and has converted Indian into a gigantic military base for presecuting her imperialistic war.

"In pursuance of this policy, foreign troops namely Australian, American, Chinese and Negro troops—have been imported in to India,

1. *The Syonan Shimbun*, 22 March, 1944.

and owing to the unbearable burden thrown on the shoulders of the already impoverised Indian masses, famine conditions of an unprecedented nature have broken out in large areas of the country.

"In a last desperate attempt to spare India the horrors of war. Mahatma Gandhi advised the British Government to recognise India's demand for independence and quit India. The reply of the British. Government was to throw him into prison along with hundreds of it Thousands of India's patriots. The last act of vandllam committed by the British Government was the virtual murder of Mrs. Kasturba Gandhi in British custody.

"Viewing the worsening situation to India, Indian in East Asia numbering about 3,000,000 made a solemn resolve to participate actively in the fight for the Indian people at home and their national liberation. They organised themselves politically under the Azad Hind Sangh, or Indian independence League. They organized an army and on Oct. 21, 2003 (1943), they set up the Provisional Government of Azad Hind when the Azad Hind Fauj had completed all its preparations, it lanunched the last fight for freedom of its sacred Motherland on Feb. 4. 2604 (1944) in the Arakan region of Burma.

The success achieved in this fight by the allied armies of India and Nippon has now enabled the Indian National Army to cross the frontier of India and continue its march to Delhi.

"Since the outbreak of the war in East Asia, the victories achieved by the armed forces of Nippon, which are unparalled in military history have rended it possible for Indians in East Asia to organise themselves for active participation in India's fight for freedom. The Government of Nippon has repeatedly declared before the whole world that Nippon is fighting not only for her own security but also for the destruction of Anglo-American imperialism in East Asia, and further that Nippons stands for the complete and unconditional independence of India.

"In pursuance of this policy, the Government of Nippon has repeatedly expressed its readiness to give all out aid to India in her struggle for independence—formally recognised the Provisional Government of Azad Hind has decided to hand over the Andamans and Nicobar Islands to the Provisional Government.

"Now the Azad Hind Fauj has launched its offensive and the Azad Hind, with the co-operation of the Imperial Nippon Army, is marching shoulder-to-shoulder in the common fight against the comon foe—the Anglo-American and their allies. Until these foreign armies of rigression are thrown out of India, there can be no freedom for the Indian people, there can be not freedom and security in Toa, and there can be not and to the present imperialistic war of the Anglo-Americans:-

"Nippon is therefore determind to reduces her pledge to keep the Indian people to create an India for the Indian."

"The Provisional Government of Azad Hind hereby proclaims its solemn determination to go on fighting in closet brotherhood with Nippon until India is completely liberated. We call upon Indian people who are the bone of our bone, the flesh of our flesh to ender all help—direct or indirect to our armies of liberation.

"We call upon all patriotic Indians—men, women and children, our brothers and sisters in India, to throw themselves wholeheartedly into this last fight for India's Independence. We call upon every Indian to destroy the Anglo-American war effort in India by systemic sabotage and thereby hasten the successful conclusion of the war for our country's freedom.

"We call upon our brothers, Indian soldiers and officers in Britain's army to refuse to fight any longer for their despotic rulers, and to come and actively join our ranks. We call upon Indians worring in various departments of the British service to render all possible help to us in the sacred fight.

"We solemnly ensure the Indian people our brothers and sisters. That they have nothing whatever to fear so long as they do not help the Anglo-America or their allies in India. We assure them further, that in liberated territory in India, the Provisional Government of Azad Hind will be established and that the Provisional Government will take over the administration of that territory.

We advise the Indian people, our kith and kin, to keep away from the Anglo-American armies, their munltion factorles, their harbours and mullatry inslations, and their war destroyed by us before the enemy can be defeated.

"Sisters and brothers in India! This is the golden opportunity for you to fulfil your long-cherished aspirations for freedom. If you rise to the occasion and do your duty, freedom will be yours before long. In this momentous event Indian expects every one to do his or her duty Jai Hind! Head of state of the Provisional Government of Azad Hind and Supreme Commander of the Indain National Army.

It is only natural with the advance of the Indian National Army that anti-British activities should become more intensified than over. Fearing the possible revolt of the Indian soldiers at the front, the British authorities have been resorting to various objectionable measures to cope with the situation. They recently withdrew the Gurkha soldiers who are said to the faithful watchdogs of British rule to carry out machinations among the upper classes of the Indian populase for the purpose of effecting some compromise concerning protest against British administration in the country. These soldiers are also utilized in dividing up the Indian National Congress members in order to weaken their united resistance. During the past several months, some 30,000 Indian patriots have been placed under arrest because of their alleged complications in plots against the British authorities.

"Minister of State for Indian Army recently declared that a famines no longer exists in Bengal Province because of its good crop this year amounting to 8,300,000 tons of rice. But the annual consumption by this single province is more than 11,000,000 tons.

Moreover India must supply provisions to the Anglo-American forces in that country and the British troops in Western Asia and as a results of these demands, the people are facing a still greater difficulties in securing foodsetuffs. The authorities declared recently that Britain has not been exporting food from India in recent months, but the exports of rice and other foodstuffs from India to Western Asia for the consumption of British troops there are not included in these statistics.

Moreover, Indian has been shouldering a considerable amount of Britain's war burden since the beginning of the present World War. The contribution of 2,100,400,000 rupees for the fiscal year of 1942-43 is 75 per cent of her entire revenue for that year. Britain exploitation of Indian resources has become increasingly unbearable, the total amount of goods supplied to Britain by Indian up to the end of July 1943 being estimated at the vast sum of 37,150,000,000 rupees. It is expected that further increases will be made in present war in respect to both material resources and manpower. The economic exploitation and objectionable administrative measures adopted by the British authorities have led the people of India to become more and more anti-British in their thoughts and activities.

The inactivities of Admiral Mountbatten, who is supposed to recapture Burma. and of viceroy Wavell as well as the misgovernment of Minister of State for India Army have aggravated the unrest in India. Anti-British riots, boycotts, strikes, etc. in the home front and in the industrial field have increased in both scale and internally, whole desertions in the army have been growing in numbers. So serious is the situation throughout India that in such cities as Calcutta, Bombay and Madras dire conditions are prevalent.

To make the situations still worse, friction of a most serious nature has developed among Britain, the Untied States and Chungking over the question of military command, Britian in undertaking various forms of patchwork in order to retrieve the existing situations but its success seems well nigh impossible of statement. Conditions are going from bad to worse, and soon the whole of India will be overrun by a growing anti-British agitation. It was such a situation in India that Ambassador Halifax had in mind when he recently declared in a lecture before a meeting of the National Geographic Society.

"Britain hopes India will remain in the British Commonwealth after the war, but will not block her if India desires to sever Empire connections."

But India will not be swayed by such sweet words and sugar-coated expressions. She is advancing headlong toward her prime objective—independence. Minister of State for India Amery may try to intimidate by declaring that emergency measures might be adopted against the present critical conditions, but such threats will not deviate the Indian masses from their present progress toward their "Fateful Day." The more relentless British oppression becomes the greater will be the zeal and enthusiasm of the Indian patriots to gain their coverted prize which means complete freedom.

17

Japanese Premier's Statement in the Imperial Diet Declaring to Place all Liberated areas under the administrative Control of the Provisional Government of Azad Hind[1]

21 March, 1944

Tokyo, March 22—Regarding the march on Delhi already started by the Azad Hind Fauj in cooperation with Nippon forces, Premier Hideki Tojo, addressing the Imperial Diet which reconvened today, say Nippon aims at expelling enemy influence from India and placing India completely in the hands of Indians.

"It is natural," he asserted "that all areas over which the Azad Hind Fauj marches within India must be placed completely under the administration of Provisional Government."

Premier Tojo reiterated Nippon's firm resolve to surmount all difficulties in order to prosecute the war to a victorious conclusion. He called attention to the further intensified war situation with particular reference to fierce enemy air attacks on the Marshall and Mariana Islands and urged the nation to give its all for the downfall of Britain and the United States.

"This is the only way complete victory can be attained." he declared.

The Premier praised the progress of the emergency administrative measures initiated by the Government at the bond of September last year. In that respect the Premier said the speedy strengthening of the nation's air strength was significant. He suggested importance of adopting decisive war time administrative manual as well as closer liasion between the fighting forces and the civil administration in order to cope with the present situation.

He declared that by adopting decisive wartime measures. Government aims at mobilizing national strength to the maximum extent through total concentration on bolstering the fighting strength , thus guaranteeing the

1. *The Syonan Shimbun*, 23 March, 1944.

attainment of certain victory. He praised the readiness of the Nippon nation to face any difficulty as well as its firm and immutable resolve to overcome all obstacles which, he said, will make certain that Nippon can fight its way to victory.

The Premier said that Government on the strength of the absolute trust and reliance placed in it by the people, is determined to adopt most suitable measures in future in order to ensure victory in the present war.

Commenting on developments within Dai Toa, he asserted that all nations and people of Dai Toa are closely collaborating in the face of all difficulties and marching bravely forward for the destruction of Anglo-American aggressive designs in Asia and for the construction of a new order in Toa.

High tribute was paid by the Premier to the fighting spirit and full co-operation shown by East Asia.

The Premier lauded the gallant fight carried on by Germany in the European theatre of war in the face of all difficulties and the fact that Germany is now about to launch fierce counter-attacks against the Anglo-Americans and his wishes for the success of Germany's war efforts.

Declaring that "India's Independence is the unanimous will of all Asia and the demand of the world's sense of Justice," the Premier reaffirmed Nippon's determination to spare no efforts in extending all possible assistance for India's liberation.

"Nippon's object is to crush enemy influence and leave India completely in the hands of the Indian people", he said. He added that those who, knowing the distress and suffering of India, dare to interfere with the liberation of India "cannot but be regarded as enemies of Justice."

"The Azad Hind Fauj under the command of the head of the Provisional Government of Azad Hind, Subhas Chandra Bose has in co-operation with imperial Nippon forces started its long expected advance into the Indian homeland. It is a matter for sincered congratulations that in the brief period of only half a year since the establishment of the Provisional Government, the Azad Hind forces of the National Army have vigorously embarked upon their march. The joy of the 400 million people of India who have been under in tyranny and prosecution of Britain for many years must surely be beyond our imagination.

"Nippon's object is to crush enemy influence and place India completely in the hands of the Indian people. All territories of India into which the Indian National Army advances will immediately be placed under the administration of the Provisional Government of Azad Hind. We may confidently expect that with the growing patriot fervor of the Indian people who welcome the advance of the National Army, the areas to be liberated will rapidly expand and that India's independence will ultimately be realized.

"It is not difficult," he concluded, "to imagine that the road leading to the complete liberation of India is yet rough, and I wish, therefore, to clarify at this time on behalf of the Nippon Government that while the Nippon Government will not under any circumstances grudge Indian patriots every possible support, it is sincerity hoped that Indian both soldiers and civilians united more than ever before will continue to fight to overcome all obstacles until that final victory is won and secured."

18

Assurance of Japan's Help for the I.N.A.[1]

22 March, 1944

Tokyo, March 22—Assuring that Nippon will extend all-out assistance and support to Subhas Chandra Bose and his Government, Sadao Iguchi, spokesman of Joho Kyoku (Board of Information), in a statement today, expressed the firm conviction that the Azad Hind Fauj will not lay down arms until the British are ousted from India and Indians gain complete freedom.

Mr. Iguchi's statement follows: "The Azad Hind Fauj of the Provisional Government of Azad Hind has crossed the Indo-Burma border as a result of successful joint operations with the Imperial Nippon force. This advance into the home soil of India is a matter of historical significance for the India Independence movement and gives boundless hope to its future.

"Subhas Chandra Bose has stated that India's anti-British independence movement has a long history of more than 100 years. At the time of the First World War, Britain coerced India into the war with a promise of home rule as a reward, but as soon as the war was over. Britain trampled upon her given word. Since then the independence movement has become more intensified.

"It is literally a miracle that though India has been robbed of all weapon, Gandhi and many other Indian patriots as well as a countless number of Indian people have upheld and carried on the Independence struggle in the face of many overwhelming obstacles, staking indeed their very lives, with undying faith in their ultimate victory. This struggle manifests to the world, the noble spirit of India ultimately to win over the brute forces of British injustice.

"The indomitable courage of the Indian people in resisting British pressure to enter the war, the highhanded exactions upon India's man-

1. *The Syonan Shimbun*, 23 March , 1944.

power and resources, the conversion of India into a military base and other policies of force taken by Britain since the beginning of the war contracts sharply with the severity of the Britain measures and moves to stronly. But why in spite of these heroic efforts has the movement for Indian Independence failed so far to succeed and instead has resulted in the imprisonment of Gandhi and tens of thousands of patriots? The foremost reason is to be found in the fact that the people of India have had no means to arm themselves, and thus armed force is the prime requiste in crushing British control and carrying through the independence struggle to its final goal.

"In July, 2603 (1943), three million Indians in Toa (East Asia) united under the Provisional Government of Azad Hind with Subhas Chandra Bose as his head and by creating the Azad Hind Fauj accomplished the first great step towards the arming of Indian people. Crack forces of the Independence Army which had since their formation been polishing their arms and preparing for the day of advance in their homeland, co-operated in our operation against the British in the Arakan region which began on Feb. 4 and succeeded in smashing their sworn enemy, the British army, thus giving concrete proof to their countrymen at home and to the world, of Indian armed power.

"The people of Nippon, sharing as they do the same blood as people of Asia, and fighting as they are in the same cause of crushing British imperialisms cannot withhold their unbounded joy over the reports of this splendid achievement by India's own forces. Inspired with confidence and hope by the success already achieved the Azad Hind Fauj today is on the march, fully conscious that each advance, earn piece of Indian soil they wrest back from the British., brings the Indian people nearer their ultimate goal.

"Since the attitude of India will determine Britain's doom or survival, it is to be expected that the British could not hold India as a military base. But no matter how unscrupulous the measures the British may take, one stern and immovable fact remains—the inde-structibe spirit of the Indian people for independence, and their complete distrust and enmity towards Britain. The greater the oppression the British may apply in their desperation, the greater will become the intensity of India's resistance at home and the fury of the Independence Army now knocking at the gates of India.

"The situation that has been brought about by the enhancement of the anti-British independence spirit, the decline of British military strength, intensification of military participation of the armed revolutionary power of India herself, promises, the days of British control of India will have been completely destroyed from its foundations. The Nippon Government has declared from time to time that the defense of Nippon's existence against Anglo-American control means at the same time the liberation of the people of Toa (East Asia) from the shackles of Britain and America.

"Accordingly Nippon desires to extend all her national assistance and support to Subhas Chandra Bose and his Provisional Government and the Azad Hind Fauj in the firm conviction that through this war India will surely win her freedom and national independence."

19

Welcome by the People of Manipur to the I.N.A. and Japanese Forces[1]

22 March, 1944

UNDISCLOSED BASE ON THE BURMA FRONT. March 22—Shouting "Banzai" as they welcomed the Indian heroes as they crossed the border at a point west of Myinthamin, the Manipuris residing in the Indo-Burmese border area witnessed with great astonishment and profound respect the gallant entrance of the Indian National Army into Indian territory in conjunction with the Japanese Forces.

After having cooperated with the Japanese Forces in the Kabaw Valley, the Indian National Army together with its Unit crossed the Arakan Range and penetrated the Indo-Burmese border west of Myinthamin.

As they set foot on the soil of their motherland, the India troops could hardly express their deep feelings. The Japanese, on their part, shared the joys of the Indians and re-doubled their determination to crush the Anglo-American foe. A narrow precipitous path confronted the advancing warriors. Giant teak trees deprived of their leaves stood in their way.

Laboriously and courageously struggling over the mountains and valleys, the Japanese and Indian troops arrived at a small hamlet. Though the village had been completely demolished, no British-Indian troops were to be found there, thus attesting to the hasty restart of the enemy. It was apparently a common practice of the enemy to burn all foodstuffs, buildings, and everything available before retreating.

The Manipuris and Chins who were treated most cruelly by the British-Indian troops deepened their faith in the Japanese and the Indians when they witnessed how well the latter were disciplined. As a token of hearty welcome, they brought rise, chicken and other foodstuffs to the

1. *Nippon Times*, 29 March 1944.

Japanese. Finding the Japanese very much like themselves in complexion and physique, the Manipuris immediately took to the former, offering their services as guides.

Anticipating the advance of the Japanese Forces, the British-Indian troops had ordered the native villagers to evacuate. Because of such coercive measures, the resentment of the villagers against the British was intensified. The fact was also revealed that the native youths on the border had been compulsorily requisitioned and had been trained in guerrilla warfare by the British.

As soon as they had finished their training, these native youths had been ordered to conceal themselves among the trees with light machine guns and automatic rifles and to fire on the Japanese. However, during a three-day march through the jungle, the Japanese were not attacked even once by these native youths. On the contrary, they volunteered their unlimited services to the Japanese.

Upon advancing into Indian territory, the Japanese Forces witnessed how deeply rooted the Indians' anti-British sentiment is and how ardently they are struggling for the liberation of their motherland.

20

Bose's Message Thanking the Japanese Premier for his Help[1]

27 March, 1944

A telegraph message of gratitude was received on Sunday by Prime Minister General Hideki Tojo form Subhas Chandar Bose, Head of the Provisional Government of Azad Hind and Commander-in-Chief of the Indian National Army, who is now at an undisclosed frontline base commanding the Azad Hind Fauj.

Prime Minister Tojo, sometimes ago, sent a cordial cable to the Netaji congratulating the Indian National Army on its successful drive toward the Indo-Burme border and reaffirming Japan's deterimination, to extend every possible assistance to the Netaji army of liberation until it has achieved its long cherished aspiration of freeing the Indian people from British shackles.

Commander-in-chief Bose's acknowledgement read as follows "I have been profoundly moved by Your Excellency's cordial telegraphic message in which your Excellency, evinced satisfaction over the Indian National Army's advance toward our motherland. On behalf of the Indian people and the Indian National Army. I express my deep gratitude for your Excellency confirmation that Japan is ready and willing to accord us assistance for achievement of the common objective of crushing our common enemies, American and Britain.

"I take this opportunity to express the determination of the Indian National Army to fight on until final victory has been won in close collaboration with the Imperial Japanese Army.

Sübhas Chandra Bosc Head of the Provisional Government of Azad Hind and concurrently War Minister.

1. *Nippon Times*, 28 March 1944.

21

Statement by Capt. Lakshmi Criticising British Slanderous Propaganda against I.N.A.

28 March, 1944

Miss Lakshmi Blasts British Canards Of Impotency of Indian National Army

Miss Swaminathan Lakshmi, Director of the Women's Department of the Rani of Jhansi Regiment, rebuts the slanderous British propaganda in the capability of the Indian national Army in a memorandum entitled. **"The real power of the Indian National Army sent to the Manipur."**

Miss Lakshmi has just returned to Shonan from the Indo-Burmese front and she emphatically shatters the vile British propaganda which plays up to the world that the Indian National Army is a puerile impotent force, drawing this conclusion from the utter lack of fighting spirit and vigor on the part of the Indian troops mustered under arbitrative British coercion.

'It is a matter of boundless rejoicing to us that the Indian National Army in collaboration with the Imprial Japanese Forces should vanquish the opposing British-Indian forces on the Indo-Burmese border and firmly Imprint their foot on the sacred soil of our motherland writes Miss Lakshmi.

"The loss of India through the advance of the Indian National Army will signify that British has been overthrown for all ages to come, she continues. "British on her part is fully aware of this and for this reason will challenge us all the more persistently and stubbarnly.

"However the more objective the British opposition the more determined will be the Indian National Army, spurred on by an unquenchable order to fly the Tri-colour flag of freedom over the whole of India, and to oust the Anglo-Americans to the very last man out of the Indian territory.

1. *Nippon Times*, 29 March 1944.

"The Anglo-Americans may think that the Indian National Army is composed of a conglomeration of prejudiced fanatics, ignoble cowards and incapacltated weaklings, but such is a picture of the Indian troops as depicted under the malicious British Propaganda and scheme disseminated, under the ruthless British policy of oppression coercion, exploitation and deceit. It is a fantasy created by the Anglo-American mind that does not know the Indian National Army of today.

"The Provisional Government of Azad Hind is Indian's own government of independence. It is the hightest authority leading the Indians in their fight for independence against the British and is entrusted with all important role of completely exterminating all British American influence from Indian Government of Azad Hind that has initialed the armed resistance against the British, and the Indian National Army is the fundamental component of the bloody struggle for Indian freedom.

"Moreover. the men have been carefully selected out of the countless volunteers whose souls have been fired with intense love for the motherland and an irrepressible desire to crush the Anglo-Americans. From this alone it can be obviously seen that the men in the Indian Nation Army are diametrically different from the Indian soldiers in the British army.

"Centering around the nucleus of Indian patriots, who have vowed to sacrifice their lives for the attainment of Indian independence, the Indian National Army includes in its rank men who have been liberated from the lethargic bondage of Anglo-American oppression and have been fully reborn as true Asiatics. Therefore these inspired patroits are able to plunge into the enemy positions and courageously graple with the British forces.

"With the fighting spirit at white beat augmented by the marvellous resistance to heat and the wonderful adaptability to training, the Indian National Army commands our wholehearted confidence.

"I firmly believe that the Indian National Army will march into Delhi without fail, and we are sincerely grateful to the men of the imperial Japanese Forces, who have infused the Indian National Army with a vigorous and indomitable fighting spirit.

"During the days of army life under the British, the Indian troops only underwent a very prefunctory training of one or two hours a day but under the leadership of the Japanese Forces, the men throw themselves into hard, vigorous training beginning each day at 9.30 a.m. Truly, the fruit of such efforts must be garnered in the soil of the Indian motherland.

"I would also like to stress the fact that the Runi of Jansi Regiment, too, has advanced to the front lines and are attaining excellent results in the accuracy of bring in the background of the Indian struggle for independence, many women Indian patriots had done their share but it is to be specially noted that the Indian women's army, stripped of all disguise, is valiantily taking an active part in the fight for freedom side by side with the Indian National Army. I am firmly confident that the time will come when I can report to you the numerous brave and courageous deeds of the members of the Rant of Jhasi Regiment."

22

British Assessment of the Strength of the I.N.A.[1]

2 April, 1944

5. Of this new "army" little definite is known. Army H.Q. is in Singapore and the following units have been reported:-

   (a) A Field Force (Gandhi, Nehru and Azad Bdes)

   (b) A Guerilla Regiment.

   (c) Ancillary Units.

   (d) "Crack" Regiment.

   (e) Rani of Jhansi Regiment. (Women's Regt.).

   (f) A Signal Coy.

   (g) An I.N.A. Hospital.

6. The Bahadur (hitherto known as the Special Service Group) and Intelligence Groups, a feature of the pre-Bose I.N.A., have moved into Burma. Reports of strength, training, organization and moral of these units when in Malaya are still conflicting. Units which had finished their training are reported to have left for Burma on 8 Jan 44 by overland and sea routes.

The I.N.A. in Burma.

7. On arrival in Burma the I.N.A. "Advance Party" consisted of 200 picked men from the Gandhi, Nehru, Azad and Field Brigades, and 200 of 'A' coy. of the Bahadur Group. Throughout 1943 little was heard of this body, except that the Bahadur Group representatives were being trained as intelligence agents, had been supplemented by a new ('E') company and that many of them were dispatched to

1. W.O. 203/803, Public Record office, London.

the forward areas on intelligence tasks in Sep. and Oct. 43. on 29 Oct. 43, 'B', 'C', and 'D' companies of the Bahadur Group arrived in Rangoon. This confirms the forecast made in paragraph 8 of W.I.S., Section D, No. 122, 1944. In Dec. 43, Bahadur Group strengths were 700 in Rangoon and 170 in the forward areas.

8. Simultaneously with the arrival of reinforcements for the Bahadur Group, the Intelligence Group of the I.N.A, totalling 350 men, arrived in Rangoon under the command of Capt. (I.N.A. Lt. col.) S.A. Malik, Ist Bahawalpur Infantry. Since then about 70 to 80 have moved up into Arakan and about 80 (two sections) were seen at the end of Jan. in transit to Myitkyina. Three others sections are said to have moved out to an unknown destination. Personnel from this and the Bahadur Group style themselves I.N.A. They are in fact intelligence agents; the Bahadur Group is intended for deep penetration and the Intelligence Group to carry out a role similar to that of our Battalion Intelligence Section, and also to carry out espionage tasks in plain clothes.

9. In addition to the Bahadur Group, the Intelligence Group and elements of the Field Force, unconfirmed reports speak of the arrival in Rangoon of a detachment of artillery and other units of the I.N.A during the latter half of 1943.

Jifs in Arakan

10. The first elements of the Bahadur Group moved up to Arakan in Sep. 43 and others in late October. Captain (I.N.A. Major) Misra, 5/17 Dogra Regiment, who commanded 'A' company of the Bahadur Group in Rangoon, left there in Oct. With a detachment and established his H.Q. in Buthidaung, with Lt. (I.N.A. Capt.) Mehar Das, 3 Lt. A.A. Bty., as his 2nd in command. By 17 Dec. 43 Misra had disposed the Bahadur Group in the Buthidaung and coastal areas. Their duties were chiefly military espionage in forward areas.

11. The Intelligence Group did not arrive in Arakan untill the beginning of Feb., although a captured document states that 73 men of the Group were to come under command of 55 Div. from 15 Jan. They were to operate under the orders of Capt. Misra through an officer of 143 Regiment. The latter was linked with London the Akyab branch of the Hikari Kikan through a small liaison group.

12. An operational order of 20 Jan stated that, in the event of operations,

most of the Hikari Kakan personnel would operate of the Buthidaung-Maungdaw front with one section in the upper regions of the Kaladan. Their tasks were "to collect intelligence necessary to conduct operations and look for deserters from British Indian army and destroy enemy installations."

13. At the beginning of Feb. all Jifs were ordered to concentrate east of the Mayu Range for an operation 'Whose zero hour had been put forward." During the early stages of the Japanese attack they participated in raids, were used as a screen for an out flanking movement, attempted to cause counfusion amongst our troops by shouting in English and Urdu, carried out espionage tasks, and acted as messengers.

14. On 10 Feb. Capt. Misra and Capt. Hottori (O.C. of the Akyab branch of the Kikari Kikan) were joined by '3' section of the Intelligence Group (70 men of the 73f referred to in para 11 above) and 110 men of the Field Force. Personnel of both forces Company of Bahadur Group and about 50 Japanese, this composite force moved to S.E. of Taung Bazar and dug in. From there mixed patrols of Japanese and I,N.A. were sent out.

15. In addition to these purely ex-P.W. bodies of Jifs, agents from the Kanbe Swaraj Training Institute also took part in the operations. In Dec. 43 their H.Q., Known as H.Q. 'J' force, was well forward with a detached H.Q. of the Bahadur Group. Jif strengths in Arakan forward of Akyab in the latter half of Feb. were approximately:—

Bahadur Group	70
Intelligence Group	70
Field Force	110
Kanbe S.T.I. Students	50
Others	110
Total	410

Jifs on other Fronts

16. There are reliable indications that Jifs on other fronts are being reinforced. On the night 2/3 Mar, about 14 miles N.E. of Tiddim, 5 out of a party of 7 Jifs voluntarily surrendered to our troops. They stated that they formed the Intelligence Group of the Nehru Brigade, and that their orders were to report back to a Lt. Col., late of the Bahawalpur

State Forces. This officer is probably Captain (I.N.A., Lt. Col.) S.A. Malik, who as mentioned in para 8 above, is believed to command the Intelligence Group of the I.N.A.

17. From this and other information it seems probable that the Japanese intend using I.N.A. troops in 4 Corps area in a more active role than hitherto. The Hikari Kikan has been paying particular attention to the Manipur plain for some time. A pointer may be the recent Japanese broadcast announcing a new organ for smoother liaison in future between the I.N.A., the Japanese army and the B.T.A. "to strenghen the joint strategic operations of the three allies for frustrating the enemy guerilla attempt to re-capture Burma and to draft important offensive as well as defensive operations."

18. I.N.A. propaganda. Copies of a new I.N.A propaganda leaflet entitled "Enlistment Card" and addressed to Indian Soldiers have been applied up in the forward areas. The leaflet is printed in Engish and Roman Urdu and issued jointly by the commanders of the Japanese and Indian National Armies. Space is left at the bottom for the signature of the prospective recruit. A copy is attached as Appendix 'A'.[2]

6. I.N.A. Awards. Following on the award of Sadar-i-Jang to Captain (Jif Major) Misra (Para 7 sec W.I.S. 1.10.126) 12 other ex-P.W. member of the Bahadur Group have been decorated. The following I.N.A. awards have so far been reported in broadcasts.

Nishi (west) Kikan

7. Previous reports have suggested the existence of a "Nishi" Kikan in Burma. A Chin, recently captured distributing Jif leaflets in the Faman area, was touched to belong to this organization. He wore an arm band bearing a white patch with a red letter "N"- and Japanese characters "Nishi Kikan"

8. He also had in his possession a pass written in Japanese to the effect that the holder was a volunteer guards leaders under the Nishi Kikan, while on the bottom of two of the leaflets in his possession, in Jap writting, he was described as "a propaganda distributor of this organization". The leaflets themselves were cyclo-styled and written in Burmese and Chin. They were addressed to Chins, both military and civilian, which indicates that this Kikan may be engaged particularly in propaganda among the chin tribes.

---

2. Not Printed.

9. Reactions to Jifs. A division which has met armed Jifs cooperating with Japanese troops for the first time, in the area MS 109 Tiddim Road, reports that in spite of the usual deceptive ruses Jifs have met with no success and a number of them have been killed. Forward troops report that the majority wear British type uniform and steel helmets and as a result are difficult to distinguish from our own troops during the hours of semi-darkness. The division comments that identify slips are not a satisfactory answer to the problem of distinguishing friend from foe in these circumstances.

10. Japanese propaganda. Recent batches of propaganda leaflets found in forward areas contain some new types. Of these the most striking is a pictorial leaflet depicting the allied leaders being shattered by Tojo's declaration of independence for the Phillippines, Burma's freedom, "no obstacles to the aspirations of the Indonesians and Japan's willingness to help India in her struggle for independence". The written leaflets contain:-

(a) Declaration of war against the allies by the Provisional Government of India.

(b) An appeal to Indian soldiers to shoot their British officers and help their unarmed brothers and sisters in India, with the consolation that if some are killed their sons and grandson will be proud of their memory.

(c) An appeal to Indians to rise all over India and drive out the British, and

(d) Seven reasons why Indians should not trust the British.

Jifs in Arakan

11. Documents captured in the recent Araken operations provide interesting information on the activities of the Hikari Kikan and I.N.A. "operatives". Intelligence reports concerning strength, composition and movements of our troops and of individual officers were being submitted by Hikari Kikan agents prior to the commencement of operations. Its agents were graded according to three degrees of reliability.

12. 55 Div orders dated 21 Jan, stated that one officer and 73 men of the Intelligence Group of the I.N.A. had been placed under command. As regards the duties of Hikari Kikan personnel, the orders stated 'most of the Akyab-Han personnel will operate on the Buthidaung-

Maungdaw front and one section will operate in the upper reaches of the Kaladan river to collect intelligence necessary to the conduct of operations and look for opportunities to secure deserters from the British Indian army and destroy enemy installations. The O.C. Hikari Kikan, Akyab Branch, was included in the list of intelligence officers to be present at a meeting to be held on 24 Jan intelligence officers to be present at a meeting to be held on 24 Jan.

13. Two messages dated 2 Feb. from this officer to two Japanese controllers of Jifs in the forward areas refer to the suspension of work in the Maungdaw area and the concentration of 'agency personnel" on the left bank of the Mayu. Care and speed are heavily stressed. This obviously has reference to the order to all Jifs to concentrate east of the Mayu Range.

14. An entry dated 2 Feb. in the diary of a Japanese officer envisages the I.N.A. cooperating in attacks scheduled for 3 Feb. by staging a feint attack. This has a possible bearing on a report of Jifs being used as a screen for an out-flanking movement by Japanese troops. An entry dated 8 Feb. in a diary written east of Buthidaung describes the activity of the I.N.A. as "amazing" and on 9 Feb. describes Indian P.W. being forced to surrender and "cooperate with the Hikari Kikan organization and the I.N.A.". An entry dated 11 Feb., in the diary of the officer mentioned above, states that a "Hav. Chief Technician, 10 Signallers, and one intelligence personnel were left behind for use by the Butai." There is no clue as to the indentity or type of signallers but the presence of a "chief technician" indicates the possibility of W/T. In the same diary an entry dated 15 Feb. mentions I.N.A. personnel attached to a Bn. engaged against Indian troops, to be employed in obtaining deserters. An entry dated 26 Feb. states that operatives and tired to be of further use". The writer expresses sympathy for Indian troops and remarks that they are unable to desert "because of the strict watch kept over them by the British". This is obviously the result of letting his own side's propaganda take him in. An entry dated 15 Feb. in this diary mentions the payment of Rs. 60,000/- to I.N.A. operatives. This possibly refers to cash payments to agents infiltrating into India.

23

Proclamation issued after the I.N.A Entry into Indian Territories, Requests the Indian People to Cooperate with the Provisional Government of Azad Hind[1]

4 April, 1944

"Sisters and brothers: under the leadership of the Provisional Government of Azad Hind which was formed on October 21, 1943, at Syonan, (formerly Singapore), by the unanimous will of three million Indians of East Asia, the Indian National Army has crossed the frontier and penetrated deep into Indian territory.

The Provisional Government of Azad Hind, your own Government has only one mission to fulfil and that mission is to expel the Anglo-American armies from the sacred soil of India by armed forces and then to bring about the establishment of the permamnent National Government of Azad Hind in accordance with the will of the Indian people. The Provisional Government of Azad Hind will continue the armed struggle until the Anglo-American forces are annihilated or expelled from Indian.

"While prosecuting the struggle for the complete liberation of India, the Provisional Government of Azad Hind will push on with the work of reconstruction of liberated areas. The Provisional Government of Azad Hind is the only lawful government of the Indian people. The Provisional Government calls upon the Indian people in liberated areas to render all assistance and co-operation to the Indian National Army and to civilian official appointed by the provisional Government.

The Provisional Government guarantees the safety of life and properly of the Indian population in liberated areas, but will inflict severe punishment on those who carry on any activities which might be of help to our Anglo-American enemies or their allies or might disturb the work of reconstruction to be started by the Provisional Government. The Provisional Government calls upon the Indian people to co-operate whole

1. *The Syonan Shimlum*, 6 April, 1944.

heartedly with our Ally, the Nippon army, who is giving unstinted, unconditional assistance in defeating our enemies.

"In the last two years the British have been strongly reinforcing themselves with troops from America, Austria, Chungking, China, and East and West therefore, felt compelled to avail itself of the generous offer of all-out aid made by Nippon, whose armed forces have accorded unparalleled victories over the Anglo-Americans since the beginning of the War of East Asia. The Provisional Government of Azad Hind is supremely confident that the Indian crush the Anglo-Americans and bring about the complete liberation of India.

"The Provisional Government is fully convinced of Nippon's sincerity towards Indian. The Provisional Government is convinced that Nippon has no territorial, political, economic or military ambitions in India. The Provisional Government is convinced Nippon is interested only in destroying the Anglo-American forces in India, which are the enemies not only of India, but of Asia as well. The destruction of Anglo-American imperialism alone will terminate this war and bring peace to the world.

"In accordance with its status as an independent government the Provisional Government of Azad Hind is arranging to issue its own currency in Rupee notes of different denomination. But owing to the rapid development of the war situation culminating in our quick advance into India, it has not been possible to bring into India in time, currency of the Provisional Government. The Circumstance therefore have rendered it necessary for the Provisional Government to borrow from the Nippon Government currency (military rupee notes) already in its possession and to use that currency as a temporary measure. As soon as the Provisional Government's own currency is available, the currency borrowed from the Nippon Government will be gradually withdrawn from circulation.

"Brothers and sisters! Now that our enemies are being driven out of Indian soil, you are becoming once again what you were before-namely free men and women. Rally round your own Government of Azad Hind- and thereby help in preserving and safeguarding your newly-won liberty. Subhas Chandra Bose. Head of State of the Provisional Government of Azad Hind

24

Note by Military Intelligence on the Activities of I.N.A. in Arakan and other Place in Indian Territory

7 April, 1944

I.N.A. Activities

1. **The Bahadur Group**—A Jif, considered reliable, states that the remaining 3 coys of the Bahadur Group (paras 1-10 of Sec.D, W.I.S. No. 122 and subsequent summaries) have moved into the forward areas from Rangoon.

2. **M.T. Company**—The arrival of this unit (Para 1, Sec. D, W.I.S No. 124) in Burma is confirmed. The C.O. was in Mandalay in Jan 44. Details of strengths and vehicles are still unknown.

3. **Reinforcement Group**—This is one of the 4 group (Para 2, sec. D, W.I.S. No. 126) reported to be attached to No. 1 Div. A detachment, strength unknown, has been identified at Kalewa. The function of the Group is reliably reported to be the handling of Indian P.W. with a view to conditions them for enlistment into the I.N.A.

4. **Arakan**—According to a Jif, who states that he is a Havildar of the Intelligence Section, No.2 Bn., Bose Bde., (Para 2, Sec. D, W.I.S. No. 126) No. 1' Bn. of the Bde. was in an area 9 miles SSE of Kaladan on 31 Mar. and intended offensive action against our rear. The platoon of Jifs which attacked a scouts. position on 31 Mar. and the company later reported as engaged in hand to hand fighting With west African troops were probably from the Bde. This identification of a part of the Bde in Arakan is considered relibale in view of previous information that the Bde. had left Malaya for Burma.

---

1. F.No. 601/7378/Historical Section, Ministry of Defence, New Delhi.

5. **Chin Hills**—Unconfirmed reports from Jifs indentify a battalion of I.N.A. in Tiddim and another in the area Haka-falm and along the Falam-Natchaung L of C. These indications of I.N.A. reinforcements are considered reliable.

25

Japanese press on the entry of I.N.A into India[1]

17 April, 1944

The majority of the editorials of the leading newspaper in Tokyo devoted their columns to the progress of war in the Pacific and the great military achievements of the combined Forces of the Japanese and Indian National Armies in India, during the week beginning March 31. These comments on the war progress have been made in special reference to the general East Asia. Other important topics were the intrusion of the Chungking troops into outer Mongolla. The Palestine dispute, the political offensives of Soviet Russia in Europe the situation in Argentina and the British coal mine strike. Comparatively few comments were made on European issues being superseded by the progress of the war in East Asia and further because of the absence of any great changes on the eastern front and other parts of Europe.

Concerning the general situation of the war in the pacific, the *Mainichi*, after dwelling in detail on the latest operations, declared that the existing state of affairs had been fully anticipated. "The enemy may boast of the excellency of their military weapons," the paper continues, "but they are unable to build airplanes that cannot be build air plans that cannot be shot down, nor can they construct ships that are unsinkable. There is no reason why the bases built by the enemy will remain invisible. Moreover. our army and navy defenses are impregnable while the people of our nation have unexcelled fighting spirit that will prevail against any foe."

Turning to the great military accomplishment of the Imperial Japanese and Indian Forces in the Indian compaign, the same journal declared. "We may achieve tomorrow-this will come for it is our furm determination to achieve such war results on all fronts."

The *Asahi* dwelt on the importance of cooperation among the three nations of Japan, China and India and urges their closer collaboration in

1. *Nippon Times*, 19 April, 1944.

order to forestall the invasion of Greater East Asia by the Anglo-Americans. The paper believes that close relations between the three Asiatic nations will be the cornerstone of new Asia and that the recent victory of the combined Japanese and Indian Armies in the Indian campaign the great reprecussions created, thereby in India and the existing strife between Chungking and the United States, indicate that Asia is entering into an era of cooperation among these leading Asiatic nations.

In an editorial entitled "War developments and the Chungking regime," the *Tokyo Shimbun* pointed to the disastrous effects on the Chungking supply routs by the advance of the Japanese and Indian troops into Indian territory. After stating that the latest developments in India pointed to the inevitable downfall of British rule in India the journal continued. "In view of the fact that Chungking's dependence on the Anglo-Americans has been increasing in proportion to the weakling of the anti-Japanese elements it can be said that the downfall of Ching's regime is only a matter of time.

Taking up the latest American offensive on Pulho in the Central Pacific in their ambition to cut the Greater East Asia into two, the same paper declared that attempt was not only completely frustrated by the determined defense of the Imperial Forces, but the American Chungking troops which were to act in concert with the American naval offensive have been rudely shaken by the attacks of the Japanese Army in Burma and that the combined troops of America and Chungking were about to become the "orphans of the Himalyas." The enemies are bound to make still further attempts but each time they will meet the same fate, the paper concluded.

After narrating the latest offensives of the American naval units in the Marshalls, Truk and Saipan in the Central Pacific and the gallant defense put up by the Imperial Forces on land and in air, the *Asahi* said, "The way to our victory cannot be always smooth and easy. The greater our difficulties, the more determined our nation will be to secure final victory for our conviction of ultimate triumph is firm and unshakable le in fact of the most severe trials."

The *Yomrui Hochi* stressed the need of assuming the offensive in the Pacific, after pointing to the latest enemy attacks on the Caroline Group. "In the central as well as in the North Pacific, the enemy may launch attacks upon our nation so that we must be prepared all the time and in fact we have perfected our defense structure against any enemy offensive," the journal asserted. "But what is important is to turn to the offensive from the defensive at the opportune moment for such is the secret of a successful campaign."

The *Tokyo Shimbun* took up the enemy's failure in the Indo Burnese operations and points to the ubiousness of their strategy as the main cause of their complete inibility to meet the attacks of the combined Forces of the Japanese and Indians. The paper also revealed the enemy's plotting against the Chungking regime and the existing friction between them and declared that their present disunity of purpose and views conclusively demonstrate that the enemy's declared object of "advance to Tokyo" was only a hazy dream detached from any real possibility. In another editorial, the same daily touched upon the advance of the combined Japanese and Indian Forces toward Imphal and Bose's second statement and urged the Indian populace to rise against the British to secure their glorious independence because, the paper said the present will be the only opportunity for them to relize their long-cherished aim.

The *Mainichi* compared the progress of the war in East Asia and Europe and concluded that although peculiarities were seen in each, the course of total war was the same for both. The same paper urged the Government to adopt drastic war measures in order to act in advance of any condition due to the progress of the war. The *Yomiuri Hochi* dwelt on the importance in wartime of the native trait of courtesy for the people of Japan stating that it was an object of admiration by Western people and urged the nation to take pride in this racial virtue. Such an editorial as this is in sharp contrast to the enemy press which endorses the inhuman acts committed by their soldiers on the field ofer battle, thereby incurring the enmity of the world.

The *Nippon Sangyo Keizai* warned the people concerning the present strategy of the Untied States naval forces in the inner South Seas, by pointing to the great speed with which the American task forces have been repenting attacks on Japanese possessions in the central Pacific in their island-to-island-strategy.

Warning the peoples of Greater East Asia against the insidious propaganda of the Anglo-Americans regarding the present Indian campaign, the *Asahi* appealed to the Astatic people to trust one another and advance to final victory until the enemy nations are completely crushed in their inordinate ambition to subjugate Asia.

In another editorial, the same journal clarified the nature of the Indian independence movement and the significance of the statement of Subhas Chandra Bose, Head of the Provisional Government of Free India. and concluded with the works, "What is paramount is that the Indians should go ahead with their program of securing independence and of recorstructing their own land. Thus, they can prove to the world that the declared purpose of the Azad Hind Fauj to advance to New Delhi is not a fairy tale," as has been claimed by the enemy. This same statement is characterized by the *Mainichi* as "A historic document of stupendous importance." Pointing to Boss's words that the Provisional Government of Azad Hind is the only lawful government of India. The journal stated that the Provisional Government, by virtue of this statement, has become a full-fledged belligerent government.

26

Military Intelligence Reporting on the I.N.A. Despatch of Agents[1]

19 April, 1944

Bose Brigade

1. The arrival of the Bose Bde. in Burma from Singapore is now confirmed. Al three Bns. arrived in Jan. 44 and were billeted in Mingaladon barracks. At the end of Jan., about 120 of the Bahadur Group were attached to the Bd. of these, 25 were allotted to No.1 Bn which left Mingaladon on 4 Feb., and travelled by train to Prome. From there part of the Bn. marched to the Kaladan area and by 1 April, the whole Bn. was concentrated around Khabaw village (South of Kaladan).

2. According to a Bahadur Group Jif who was attached to Bn. H.Q. the 'plan of operations' for the Bn. was:-

   (a) An initial recce. of our dispositions by Bahadur Group personnel dressed in civilian clothes. The recce. party to return by 2000 hrs. on 31 Mar.

   (b) two companies to take up a defensive position.

   (c) three companies to attack British positions on 1 April This plan was partly carried out.

3. No.1 Bn. moved out to the forward areas according to schedule. The other two Bns. were due to leave Rangoon on 6 Feb., No. 2 for Buthidaung and No. 3 Bn. plus Bde. H.Q. in the Chin Hills is confirmed. According to a former member of the Bn., one coy. moved from Falam to Haka on 1 Apr. and took over garrison duties from the Japanese. Previous information indicated the dispositions of 'a Bn.

1. F.No. 601/7378/H.S.

of I.N.A.' as one coy. in Haka, one in Falam and three along the Falan-Natchaung L. of C. or haka and raiam but no independent operations of Jifs have yet mixed party of Japs, Jifs and locals and killed eight.

4. The location of No. 2 Bn. is still uncertain. If the movement schedule referred to above is accurate (and two Bns. plus Bde. H.Q. are known to have arrived in their present Locations according to plan), No.2 Bn. may be in the Buthidaung-Maungdon area. Other sources have referred to "a Bn." intended for the Mayu front. Recent reports of the activities of Jifs in the Maungdaw area strengthens the possibility of No. 2 Bn. being in that area. On 7 April Japs and Jifs numbering 100 were indentified at point 904 (6 miles S.E.. of Maungdaw). On the night 9/10 April this composite force attacked our positions and inflicted casualties. Reinforcements brought the mixed enemy force up to about 400 on the 11 April Our troops report the presence of increasing numbers of fighting I.N.A. in the front line in this area.

5. The following information comes from a Jif who accompanied No. 1 Bn. from Rangoon to the Kaladan. Bn organization-Bn. H.Q. and five coys, each of three pls., each of three secs. Personnel a 'Sapper" Hav., a Hav. Clerk, two runners, two nursing orderlies' and a "defence platoon." Coy. Comds are 2/Lts; Pl. Comds are Havildars. Two Japanese officers are attached to each Bn. as advisors and interpreters. The Bn. is composed of Sikhs, Jats and Dogras - all ex-P.W. The Bn. possessed no signal equipment, bicycles, or motorcycles, and only one 3-ton ration lorry. Each platoon has a mule cart which is manhandled by 6 men; these carts carry ammunition and officers' kits. There are no stretchers and there is a great shortage of bandages and iodine. Only half the Bn. possess field dressings; the majority of these are the original British issues. Each company has 6 Boyes A/Tk. fifles, 6 Bren L.M. Gs, 6 Vickers M.Gs. and 6 TSM Gs. Each man has a 303 rifle and bayonet and officers wear pistils. The Sapper Hav. at Bn. H.Q. has 6 A/Tk. mines and 6 mines used for blowing bridges. The senior representative of the Bahadur Group has a stock of British handgrenades which he issues to men going forward on duty. Some N.C.Os and men in the Bn. carry grenades. Uniform is the same as that of the Indian army with the exception of special I.N.A. badges. No. 2 and 3 Bns. are said to be similarly organized and equipped.

Strategical Offensive

6. Recent developments show that the enemy; is intensifying his efforts to introduce agents into India. Important agents for deep penetration task are likely to be introduced by submarine or aircraft rather than by the difficult frontier crossing. This intensification of the strategical offensive is co-ordinated with Japanese military operations on the Eastern frontier, probable by Bose himself. Some undetected agents are in the country already, it is certain that other can be expected in the very near future. Upcountry men and Bengalis seem likely to be particularly marked out for this work, and special attention should be paid to the indentification of strangers of these classes who come to notice in suspicious circumstances.

7. Present information suggests a uniformity of plan in respect of the secret parties which the enemy is now sending to India for deep penetration work. They are ordered to collect military economic and political intelligence to conduct propaganda against the Anglo-Americans and in favor of the enemy; to incite subversive elements to commit sabotage; to obtain money and assistance in their work from persons in this country named by Subhas Bose; to operate in pairs and transmit the intelligence they obtain by means of wireless. The invariable means of maintaining contact between different parties, and between the component groups of the same party, appears to be through regular meetings at places selected author prior to loading enemy occupied territory or before the agents separate on arrival.

8. Espionage groups which are already known have been ordered to concentrate on Bengal, Bombay, the U.P. and North India generally, but this should not be regarded as an indication of a lack of interest in South India. The correctness of this view is emphasized by the fact that a party of enemy agents has been recently landed in Ceylon. Little is yet known in regard to intelligence plans and intentions affecting South India and it is therefore necessary for strict precautionary measures to be taken, and for constant vigilance to ensure that security arrangements are maintained at the maximum pitch of efficiency

27

British Counter Measures to Check the Impact of I.N.A. on the Soldiers of Indian Army[1]

15 May, 1944

CONFIDENTIAL
GENERAL HEADQUARTERS (INDIA)
NEW DELHI, MAY 1944

To

All Commanding Officers of Indian Army Units

Instructions of Josh work and Josh Group Organization within Units

1. **"Josh" Vs. "Jif"**—Josh is the strongest and most effective counter propaganda method yet evolved to combat the Japanese 'I' offensive against the morale and loyalty of Indian troops. "Jif" means Japanese inspired fifth column, but it may be taken throughout these instructions to denote any pro-Japanese organization having Indian members "Josh" means "Pep", and it is the morale counter offensive weapon against those dangerous activities.

2. **Rumour as offensive propaganda**—One of the chief weapons of the Japanese 'I' offensive against India has been and still is rumour. Rumour are spread by a variety of means : by radio, by leaflet and by agent. The essence of a rumour useful to the enemy is that however false and tendenaious it is in content, it must contain a quality which makes it likely to be believed. In India the populations largely illiterate and tends to believe starting and plausible stories which spread extremely quickly. And the Japanese have sought to make the maximum use of this type of offensive weapon of psycho logical warfare.

3. **Anti-rumour**—The weapon used so far as Indian troops are, concerned to combat these activities is also the spreading of stories

1. War Office, 203/803. Public Record office, London.

of statement, with this important difference that in the cause they are true. It is of the highest importance that they should be true and that their truth should be implicitly belived in by all who spread them. The Josh Group is told facts, in the form of stories or statements by its leader, and the task of Group members is to disseminate these in the unit by repeating them or otherwise helping in their circulation.

4. **Purpose of Josh Group**—Josh Groups are intended to : (a) build in every Indian soldier the knowledge and firm faith that the Japanese and everyone who represents the Japanese are his own personal enemies; (b) introduce stories of our victories against the Japanese and so turn the conversation round to the topic of why the Japanese are India's enemies and why and how they will be defeated; (c) introduce stories of the bravery of Indian soldiers in action and his comrade-ship-in-arms with his Allies; (d) utilize entertainment, radio, drama, information rooms, picture layouts, etc., to bring home to the sepoy, through every medium that strikes his imagination, the existence of his chief enemy-the Japanese; (e) inoculate the Indian soldier with a sound factual basis of true knowledge so that false rumours and brazen lies spread by Japanese, Jifs and Japanese agents can be easily shown to be such.

5. **Josh organization and mechanics**—It is necessary that all officers in an Indian unit should have received and fully imbibed the basic information contained in the pamphlet "Against Japan".

Officer supervising Josh work in Units—This should be a very, senior officer (either the C.O. or the second in command) working in close conjunction with the Subdar Major.

Josh group Leader—These should work on a Comapany basis and the Josh Group leader of the Company Group ought to be either the Coy. Commander or someone working closely under his direction. Men chosen for the Group should be those in whom the troops have confidence.

All members of Josh Group should know the basic fact of the four talks in Appendix 3 in the pamphlet "Against Japan."[2] They should receive in discussions with the Josh Group leader; this informaion he obtains from material countained in"Josh," the weekly Josh directive. All members should be able to hold their own indiscussions which may arise in the lines about the Japs and the Jifs; their arguments should be reinforced by fact which they have obtained as members of the Josh Group.

2. Not printed.

The Prime essential in Josh work is enthusiasm. This should be felt throughout and should filter down from the officer supervision the work to every member of every Group. In view of this fact in view of the problem of language involved, it is impossible to define the number necessary in a Josh Group, but every Group must give the widest coverage possible for all casts, languages and ranks. A suitable Company Josh Group will contain 3 representative from each platoon of infantry in addition to the Supervision Officer and or Josh Group Leader.

Josh Group Co-ordination-In a battalion, this is the responsibility of the C.O. or second in command close conjunction with the Subedar Major. In a Training centre, co-ordination of Josh Group work through Bn commanders is the responsibility of the Training Centre Commandant (or second in command) and the Subedar Major.

6. **Conclusion**—The responsibility for the success of Josh work within unit lies with the Commanding Officer. If he is fully apprised of the purpose of Josh Groups and fully enthusiastic about it, he can make his enthusiasm felt throughout the Unit. That enthusiasm can be directed towards a most useful training in knowledge of the enemy, a training which goes on after parades are over, in the "Langars," in lines, in the barracks and wherever discussions take place. If Josh work become rigid, it loses freshness and keenness and when it loses these qualities it loses its drive and strength, and a weak spot is made for easy infiltration by Japanese and Jif propaganda.

28

INA Proclamations on Entering India

20 May, 1944

I. The Indian National Army, under the leadership of the Provisional Government of Azad Hind, has now massed in force and advanced into a territory of Eastern India as the spearhead for the creation of Free India.

The Indian National Army with the help and co-operation of the Imperial Nipponese Army, has pushed into Eastern India with the object of crushing the Anglo-American forces, the common enemy of East Asia, of marking India really an India for Indians by liberating her from the shackles of the despotic rule under which she has been groaning for ages; of bringing complete freedom and peace and order to the three hundred and eighty millions of our brothers and sisters in India; and also of driving away the Anglo-American menace from the borders of our neighbours—the Independent Burmese.

Brothers and Sister in India!

Be engaged in your daily work without fear; gather whole-heartedly under your Tricolour Flag of Independence hoisted by the Provisional Governments of Azad Hind; brace yourselves up for winning Complete Independence by retaking our Motherland from the hands of our enemies, Anglo-Americans.

The East Indian Territory into which the Indian National Army has advanced with the powerful aid of the Imperial Nipponese Army, as well as the people thereof, have now been liberated from the bondage of the Anglo-Americans. This territory has become the first free Indian Territory on the Mainland of India under the Provisional Government and will serve as the base for liberating our Motherland, The Imperial Nipponese Army

1. I.N.A. Relief and Enquiry Committee papers, Darya Ganj, New Delhi. The above proclamation was issued by Bose as Supreme Commander of Azad Hind Fauj.

will not establish a military administration but will cooperate with and wholeheartedly help the Provisional Government of Azad Hind in maintaining perfect peace and order.

II. If any person fails to understand the intentions of the Provisional Government of Azad Hind and the Indian National Army, or of our Ally, the Nipponese army, and dares to commit such acts as are itemised hereunder which would hamper the sacred task of emancipating India, he shall be executed or severely punished in accordance with the Criminal Law of the Provisional Government of Azad Hind and the Indian National Army or with the Martial Law of the Nipponese Army, the application of which has been agreed upon between the two allied armies, namely, the Indian National Army and its Ally, the Imperial Nipponese Army.

Punishable Acts

1. Rebellious acts against the Provisional Government of Azad Hind or the Indian National Army, or our Ally, the Nipponese Army.

2. Acts of spying

3. Acts of stealing and taking by force, damaging and destroying war materials which are in the possession of the Provisional Government or belong to our Ally, the Nipponese Army.

4. Acts of damaging or destroying of valuable material resources controlled or utilised by the Provisional Government of Azad Hind or by the Nipponese Army under previous agreement with the Provisional Government.

5. Acts of destroying various installations or equipments for traffic, communication, transportation, broadcasting, etc. which are controlled or utilised by the Provisional Government of Azad Hind and the Indian National Army, or by the Nipponese Army under previous agreement with the Provisional Government; to acts of interference with the employment and utilisation thereof.

6. Violent acts against, intimidation of killing or wounding of, or doing other harmful acts to those who belong to the Provisional Government of Azad Hind and the Indian National Army or our Ally, the Nipponese Army.

7. Acts of spreading enemy propaganda or wild and false rumours, and other acts of distrubing and misleading the minds of the inhabitants.

8. Acts of disturbing the money circulation and economic organisation or of obstructing the production and free interchange of commodities.

9. Any act other than those contained in the above items, that benefits the enemy or is harmful to peace and order and the well-being of the Provisional Government of Azad Hind and the Indian National Army or our Ally, the Nipponese Army.

10. Acts of attempting instigating and abetting those acts contained in the above items.

The trial and punishment of such criminals will entirely be at the discretion of the Provisional Government of Azad Hind except when crime committed are of such a nature as of necessity, owing to wartime emergency, must be dealt with by the Nipponese Army as agreed upon between the two Allied Armies.

III. The Nipponese Army will maintain strict discipline and protect, in the area into which they have advanced, the lives and properties of the Indian masses who do not commit any hostile act; and due respect will be paid to the religious, customs and manners of the Indian people.

It is guaranteed that the Nipponese soldier who may violate these strict injuctions shall be severely punished in accordance with the Martial Law of the Imperial Nipponese Army.

The Indian National Army will maintain strict discipline and protect, in the area into which it has advanced, the lives and properties of the Indian masses who do not commit any hostile act; and due respect will be paid to the religions, customs and manners of our countrymen.

It is guaranteed that any Indian soldier who may violate these strict injuctions shall be severely punished in accordance with the Martial Law of the Indian National Army.

29

Impact on the National Government of China of the Advance of I.N.A. into India

27 May, 1944

In an interview which he granted to the press, immediately after the issue of his historic statement in regard to the breaking through of the indo-Burmese border by the Japanese-Indian forces, Subhas Chandra Bose, head of the Provisional Government of Free India, stressed the far-reaching effects which it would produce on the Chungking regime. He expressed the confidence that the developments of this particular campaign would compel the Chungking leaders to reconsider their attitude seriously.

As Subhas Bose pointed out, the Chungking leaders who, in defiance of the advice of their fellow Asiatics, have been adhering stubbornly to their wrongful course now find themselves in a serious quandary. Reduced to straits military and politically, they are in utter consternation and disappointment.

The very serious nature of the menace to which Chungking is exposed in the new situation is admitted by the enemy camp itself. It was broadcast from Chungking on March 24, for example, that in view of the fact that Assam is not only very important strategically but is on Joseph Stilwell's Indo Chinese air route, the Japanese army would surely attack it relentlessly with the object of severing the supply route to Chungking. The anti-Axis. Headquarters in south-eastern Asia also admitted that in the event of the loss of Imphal, the communication line of Stilwll army operating in the Fukawng Valley would be exposed to a grave menace.

Chungking's great embarrassment and consternationis regarded indifferently by Britain who is responsible for the direction of the border operations. She has already discarded the repeated slogan of the recovery of Burma in favor of that of the defense of India. In his broadcast on 20,

1. *Nippon Times*, 22 May, 1944.

Winston Churchill, the British Prime Minister, simply stated that seeing that Britain had already suffered a staggering blow at the hands of the Japanese army, her best efforts in the theater of war in India and in the Bay of Bengal would be directed to the assistance of the American force so as to realize contact between Chungking and America. This lukewarm statement has naturally served to intensify the discontent of America and Chungking with Britain. Due to the lack of unity in sentiment and policy in the Anglo American-Chungking camp, bad blood is being created between Britain, who is bent on the defense of India, and America, who is eager to secure a speedy contact between Chungking and herself in the belief that delay in aiding exhausted Chungking involves the danger of making a Badoglio of Chungking with the result that the plan to create a second front on the Chinese Continent will fall through. Antagonism is in the meantime growing between Britain and Chungking due to the latter's increasing contempt for the fomer who has betrayed her crass impotence. Futhe, it is noticed that here is a gradual estrangement of feeling between Chungking and America because the latter and her troops in china are ambitious to establish control over Chungking.

Particularly noteworthy is a marked deterloration of feeling between America and Chungking for which the anit-Axis defeat on the Indo Burmese border furnished the occasion. The failure of the Chungking army under General Wet Lihuang on the Nu River to take any positive action when Stillwell's army was threatened with isolation as the result of the advance of the japanese Indian forces across the border caused high discontent among, the Americans with Chungking, and the American press was very bitter in its critucism of Chungking. The *New Republic*, an American weekly, in its recent issue, gave free vent to its sentiment against Chungking. In an aditorial entitled "Confusion, in East Asia," the journal warned Chungking that if it is to continue its present attitude of leaving active registance against Japan in the hands of the Chinese Communist Army, itself doing nothing beyond maintaining the posture of hostillity America and Britain will have to support the Yanan regime instead of the Chungking Administration.

On the other hand, Chungking contends that although friendly relationship between America and itself is maintained on the basis of America's training of Chinese airmen, the presence in China of Brigadier-General Claire Chennault's volunteer air force, the creation of the 14th air force, training by American officers of Chungking troops in India and in China, the supply of materials to Chiang by the Indo-Chinese air route, the formation of the mixed Sino-American air force. Sino-American Cooperative campaign in Burma and America's grant of loans to Chungking. This friendship is only nominal and it does not apply to the Chinese masses. It then proceeds to demand America's faihful fulfilment of all her promises to Chungking. The Ta Kung Pao in its editorial on "Accord between America and Changking." says: "The Chungkng expeditionary army will harbor prejudice against the American army unless Stillwell's declaration finds gerneral application that the officers and ment of the American and Chaing's armies are given the same food and the same conforts and are sharing hardsips. Liaison officers and interpreters are in request inorder to remove discord and antagonism bor of the language difficulty and the sense of rcial superiority on the part of American soidiers who are generally of low educdation."

The sentiment of the Chungking expeditionary army, as pointed out is the Taung Pao, is certainly the sentiment of all in the entire area under the jurisdiction of the Chungking regime also. The reason why the paper Confined its observation to the chungking expeditionary army is presumable that consumed; as it is, with discontent with America, Chungking has to be as mealy mouthed as possible from the necessity of obtaining America's positive aid.

Many episodes that came to light on the Indo-Burmese front bespeak the cruel treatment of which the officers and men of the Chungking army are victims at the hands of Americans. The poor Chungking officers and men are told by the Americans that they are none other than what has been given over in payment of the American arms supplied to Chungking and that they would therefore be shot immediately if they dared to retreat an inch. It is said that a Chungking soldier who was taken prisoner on the Indo-Burmese border declared in a frenzied tone that it was his intention to beat America anti Britain after defeating the Japanese. The officers and men of the Chungking army who are treated so cruelly by American and British officers are witnesses of the triumph entry of the Indian National Army into India. They are also acquainted with the truth about the anti-British movement which is sweeping over India. Nor are they ignorant of the fact that, composed, as it is, of pro-British and opportunist members, the Indian Central Assembly thought fit to reject the budget for the new fiscal year introduced by the government or that the representatives of all circles in India have demanded the reiease of Mahatma Gandhi. Apprehensive of the possible secession of the Chungking army from the Anglo American camp, which they fear would produce very grave effects on the populace under the jurisdietion of the Chungking regime, the Chungking authorities are, as urged by the Ta Kung Pao, asking America to take steps to prevent prejudice against America from being created, out of their desire to maintain collaboration with America. In other words, they are striving to see that the advance of the Japanese-Indian forces into India does not produce grave millitary and political effects.

Whether is the Chungking Administrator drifting? We must try to fathaom the reason why the Chungking army is doing nothing beyond maintaining the posture of hostility against the Japanese, leaving the task of active resistance in the hands of the Communist Army and why the Yunnan army is continuing its strategic attitude of inactivity despite the demand of America. Britain and the Chinese Communist Party for action. It is also important to find out whether it was for cooperative operations with America and Britain, in the true sense of the term, that the Chungking expeditionary army was sent into India.

Chiang Kai-Shek is inwardly distrustful of America and Britain, though he is outwardly maintaining the attitude of reliance on them. He is also secretly resolved on the elimination of the Chinese Communist Party. This double-faced policy is now being exposed by America and Britain as well as by the Chinese Communist Party. It is likely that the Anglo-American Plax and sinister phases with the progress of the war situation in East Asia; while Chungking will be obliged to put an end to its double-faced policy.

30

Special Orders, Regarding Pay, Decorotions of the I.N.A. by Lieut-Colonel I.Z. Kiani Commander No. 10 unit Azad Hind[1]

31 May, 1944.

1. **Rates of pocket money of the Azad Hind Fauj**—To commemorate the victories entry of the Azad Hind Fauj into India, a special monthly

Rank	Present rate in Malaya	Future rate in Malaya	Present rate in Burma	Future rate in Burma
General	400	400	400	400
Lt. General	—	350		375
Major-General		300		330
Colonel	300	270	310	29
Lt. Colonel	220	220	235	235
Major	170	170	185	185
Captain	120	120	135	135
Lietu:	80	90	90	100
2/Lietu:	70	70	80	80
Sub Offr I	60	60	70	70
Sub Offr II	50	50	60	60
Havildar	20	25	24	32
Naik	16	20	19	26
L/Naik	14	18	17	23
Sepoy	18	15	15	20

(A.H.F.O. 144/44)

1. I.N.A. Trial Papers

allowance called the "AZADI ALLOWANCE" will be given to sepoys and N.C. Os. w.e.f. the Ist April, 1944. Along with a slight change will be made in the rate of pocket Money hitherto prescribed for Lieute : and Colonels. The changes introduced are laid down in the table in previous page.

2. **Decoration-recommandations for**—All units forwarding recommendations for any award or decoration shall invariably submit a detailed report about the distinguished services rendered by the individual concerned. These report will be forwarded to H.Qrs., Supreme Command through proper channels. Recommendations in respect of officers and other ranks shall be submitted separately.

Distinguished Services Rendered throughout a Campaign

1. If an individual is recommended for a decoration for distinguished services rendered during the course of operations in a particular sector, a brief summary of the activities of the individual and results achieved shall be submitted.

2. Distinguished services rendered in a particular action-When an individual is recommended for a decoration for distinguished services during a particular action, a detailed report giving date, time, place, act of bravery and results achieved shall be submitted. (A.H.F.O. 118/44)

3. **Promotion-medical Personnel—**

1. Promotion.

(a) Henceforth all Group Commanders can promote Medical personnel upto the rank of Havildar within the war Establishment on recommendations from the senior Medical officer within their own Group.

(b) Information for all such promotions will be forwarded to D.M.S. Rear HQrs. No. 2. Supreme Comd. AHF.

2. E.D. Pay-MEDICAL PERSONNEL.-All Nursing personnel in front line units are entitled to E.D. Pay, provided they are within the war Est: and recommended by the M.O.i/c., units. Units will publish in unit orders and claim such E.D. Pay henceforth.

(A.H.F.O. 144/44)

31

Detailed Scheme for the Administration of Liberated Area by Provisional Government of Azad Hind[1]

15 June, 1944

Chapter 1

For the smooth Administration of a liberated area, Provincial Government (Central Organ) will consist of a Governor, Governor's Secretariat and an Advisory Council.

Organization

1 Governor's Secretariat

(A) Department of Internal Affairs

(I) Police (including Fire Brigade)

(II) Inspection of Local Organizations

(III) Census

(IV) Passports

(V) Air Raid Precautions

(VI) Civil Defence Organization

(VII) Jails

(B) Finance

(i) Revenue

(a) Land Revenue

(b) Income Tax

1. Office of the Strategic Services, Records group 226, U.S. National Archives, Maryland, U.S.A.

- (c) Excise
- (d) Absentee and Enemy property
- (e) Registration
- (f) Customs

(ii) Expenditure

- (a) Budget
- (b) Audit
- (c) Accounts

(iii) Banking

(C) Law

(i) Legislation

(ii) Administration of Justice-

(High, District, Sub-Divisional, Circle and Panchayat Courts)

(D) Public Enlightenment

(i) Internal Propaganda

- (a) Press
- (c) Theatre, Cinema, and
- (d) Literature

(ii) External Propaganda: Areas still under control of the enemy

- (a) Civil
- (b) Army

(iii) Education

(E) Health and Social Welfare

(i) Prevention and Treatment of Diseases

(ii) Relief of destitutes, including Air Raid Victims

(iii) Supply and distribution of medicine

(F) Agriculture and Industries and Labour

(i) Agriculture

(ii) Industries

(iii) Forests

(iv) Supply and distribution of labour and matters relating to the Joint Central Labour Board

(G) Commerce

(i) Production and Collection of Commodities-Food, Clothing etc.

(ii) Distribution (including Rationing)

(iii) Price Control and matter relating to the Joint Central Purchasing Board

(H) Communication and Transport

(i) Posts, Telegraphs, Telephone and Wireless

(ii) Railways, Steamer, Motor Vehicles, Boats, Carts, Cycles,

(iii) Public Works

(I) Roads: Buildings

(ii) Water Supply and Drainage (including irrigation).

(iii) Electricity : Gas

(J) Women's Affairs

(K) Co-operation

(i) Central Purchasing

(ii) Indo-Nippon Co-operation.

Chapter II

Advisory Council—The Governor of the Province or state will constitute an Advisory Council for the Province or State, by nominating 22 members, fifty per cent of whom will be unofficial while the remaining fifty per cent will be officials. The Governor will be ex-officio, President of the Council.

Duties and Functions—The Council will render advice on such matter as are brought before it from time to time. Any member may initiate the discussion of a subject with the previous sanction of the Governor.

The functions of the Council will be purely advisory.

There will be a Secretary to the Advisory Council who will prepare agenda, issue notice of the meetings, etc.

Chapter III

Administration

(a) Organization

1. **Village**—A village will be the smallest administrative Unit.

20 Houses	-	1 Beesghara,
10 Beesgharas	-	1 Mondal (Supervisor).
10 Mondals	-	1Pradhan or Mukhia.
1 Panchayat	-	for every village.

The Pradhan will preside over a Panchayat.

2. **Dasgaon**—(Village Union) Ordinarily 10 Villages will constitute on one Dasgaon. It will have an area of about 10 sq. miles and a populations not exceeding 15 thousand.
3. **Sarkl (Circle)**—5 to 10 Dasgaon will form a Sarkl (Cirlcle)
4. **Mahakume (Sub Division)**—5 to 10 Sarkle (Circles) will form a *Sub Division* or *Mahakuma.*
5. **Zila (District)**—3 to 5 sub Divisions (Mahakumas) will form a district.
6. **Towns** (See Appendix I.)

(b) Duties and Functions

1. **Beesghara**

   (i) Census and Information (Cattle, Poultry, Land, Houses, Education etc.).

   (ii) Birth, Death, Immigration, Emigration.

(iii) Report on Theft, Robbery, and other Crimes, Fire.

(iv) Report on suspicious movements.

(v) Transmit information, instruction and orders of the Government and Local organization to the families for execution.

(vi) Report on prevalence of epidemic diseases and damage to crops.

2. **Mondal (Supervisor)**

(i) Supervision and co-ordination of the work of Beesgharas.

(ii) Transmitting to higher authorities of information received from Beesgharas.

(iii) Transmit information, instruction, orders of the Government and local organizations to the Beesgharas for necessary action.

3. **Pradhan or Mukhia**

(i) Representative of the Government in the area for executive work.

(ii) Will preside over Panchayat.

(iii) Will enforce decision of the Panchayat.

(iv) Transmit to higher authorities of information received from Mondals.

(v) Transmit information, instructions, orders of Government to Mondals Panchayat.

4. **Panchayat (Advisory Body to Pradhan)**

Advisory (i) To render advice to the Pradhan or Mondal in matter of purely local significance.

Judicial (ii) Will have powers to try civil and criminal cases.

(a) **Civil**—Money suits not exceeding Rs. 100/- other claims (small) generally not exceeding Rs. 100/-.

Boundary disputes not exceeding Rs. 100/-

(b) **Criminal**—Petty thefts.

Damage to crops whose value does not ......(sic) power of awarding punishments.

Fine not exceeding Rs. 100/- and/or

Compulsory manual labour not exceeding three month and/or Whipping, not exceeding 10 strokes.

(c) Lawyers will not be allowed to appear for cases.

Executive Panchayats will also undertake:-

(i) Construction and maintenance of :

(a) Village roads.

(b) Village buildings.

(c) Village Wells.

(d) Tanks.

(e) Bridges.

(f) Dispensaries.

(g) Primary Schools.

A Panchayat will consist of four members and one Pradhan to be appointed by the Zila Hakim.

In case where there are no suitable men available for the Panchayat, the Mondal or Pradhan will have the powers of the Panchayat court.

The power given to the Panchayat or to the Pradhan or Mondal may be curtailed by Government to meet any emergent conditions.

5. Ilakadar

Each Dasgaon will be incharge of an Ilakadar whose functions and duties will be:

(i) Co-ordinate and supervise the activities of the Mondals and the Panchayats.

(ii) Transmit orders of the Government to the Pradhan and Mondal for necessary action.

(iii) He will transmit information received from the Pradhan, Mondals, etc., to the higher authorities for such action as they may deem necessary.

(iv) He will refer to higher authorities any case or suit which may come to his notice in which he thinks that there has been a failure of justice dealt with by the Panchayat.

6. Sarkl Hakim (Circle Officer)

(i) Representative of the Government in charge of his area.

(ii) Responsible to the Government for the efficient and economic administration of the Sarkl.

(iii) Tour round his area to see and report how far peace and order prevails, conditions of Crops and economic condition generally: prevalence of any epidemic disease.

(iv) Report suspicious movements.

(v) Transmit to higher authorities of information received from Ilakadars.

(vi) Transmit information, instructions, orders of the Government and Local organizations to the Pradhan or Mondals.

(vii) Insepct and report if necessary on the activities of the different departments of Government functioning within his area, such as police, Public Enlightenment, Health and Social Welfare, Agriculture.

(viii) Will have power to try civil and criminal cases.

(a) **Civil:**

Money suits-value not exceeding Rs. 500

Rent suits-value not exceeding Rs. 50.

(b) **Criminal:**

Grievous Hurt.

Loss or damage to property, up to the value of Rs. 2,000.00

Riot.

Wrongful confinement.

Criminal intimidation.

Power of enquiry, arrest and detention in custody.

Danger to public safety and Welfare.

(c) Power of awarding punishments:

Fine :	Rs. 2000	and/or
Imprisonment	2 Years	and/or
Whipping	20 stokes	and/or

Confiscation of Commodities in Black Market up to Value Rs. 1,000/-.

(d) As a rule trials in Sarkl Courts will be summary,

(e) Lawyers will not be allowed to appear for cases.

7. **Mahakuma Hakim (Sub Divisional Officer)**

(i) Representative of the Government in his area.

(ii) Responsible to the Government for the efficient and economic administration of the Sub Division.

(iii) Officer-in-Charge of Government treasury.

(iv) Transmit to higher authorities of information received from Sarkl Hakim.

(v) Transmit information, instruction, orders, of the Government and local organization to the Sarkl Officer.

(vi) Responsible for the execution of Government orders and instruction.

(vii) Tour round his area to see and report how far peace and order prevails, conditions of the crops and economic condition generally of the people.

(viii) Supervise and co-ordinate the activities of Sarkl officers.

(ix) Submit monthly reports to the District officer and in case of emergency immediately.

(x) Inspect and report if necessary on the activities of the different departments of government functioning within his area, such as Education, Health and Social Welfare, Public Enlightenment, Police, Agriculture & c.

(xi) Report to the District officer immediately any outbreak of epidemics, suspicious movements which may jeopardize either Indo-Japanese. relationship or prosecution of the War of Liberation.

(xii) Carry out relief measures when sanctioned by Government.

(xiii) Enforce orders and instruction of Government or higher authorities.

(xiv) Will have the powers to try both Civil and Criminal Cases.

(a) Civil—Value up to Rs. 500

(b) Criminal—Same plus

Power of Inquiry, arrest and detention.

Rape

Abduction

Kidnapping

Mischief by fire and explosive

Danger to Public safety and welfare

(c) Powers of awarding punishment:

Fine-Up to four thousand	and/or
Imprisonment 3 years	and/or
Simple and Rigorous.	
Whipping: 30 strokes	and/or
Confiscation of Commodities in Black Market	unlimited

The Governor may notify if necessary that certain types of cases have a right of appeal in the Mahakuma Hakim's Court from the Court of Sarkl Officers.

8. Zile Hakim (District Officer)

(i) Representative of the Government in the District.

(ii) Responsible to Government for the efficient and economic administration of the District.

(ili) Enforce orders and instructions of the Provincial Government.

(iv) Transmit to Provisionial Government of information received from Mahakuma.

(v) Transmit information, instruction, orders of Government and local organization to the Mahakuma.

(vi) He will have authority to inspect the activities of the various departments of the Government functioning in the District (e.g. Police, Public Enlightenment, Health and Social Welfare & c.)

(vii) Report any outbreak of epidemic diseases.

(viii) Report on suspicious Movements.

(ix) co-ordinate activities of the different Sub Divisional Officers.

(x) Investigate reports submitted to him and take necessary action or forward to Government for orders.

(xi) Responsible for the appointment, transfer or dismissal of Mukhias or Pradhan, Mondal and Beegharas.

(xii) He will perform any special duties such as Recruitment for the Armed Forces, mobilization of national resources and such other matters as the Government may entrust him with.

(xiv) Will have power to try civil and criminal cases

(a) Civil —Value unlimited

(b) Criminal—All types of cases.

(c) Power of awarding punishment:

Fine	Upto 20,000 Rupess	and/or
Imprisonment	10 Years	and/or
Whipping	50 strokes	and/or
Forfeiture of Property of and kind		unlimited.

Capital punishment : Death (Subject to confirmation of the High Court).

(xv) Will have power of Inquiry, arrest and detention in custody.

(xvi) Will hear final appeal of cases tried in the Mahakuma officer's Court where the punishment awarded amounts to over 75 per cent or the claim is less than 75 per cent.

9. Provincial Government or state-A number of Districts will comprise a Province, in the liberated area. The number of the Districts will depend upon the extent of the territory liberated.

Government of the Province or State

Each Province or State will be administrated by a Governor.

Duties and Functions

(i) Representative of the Provisional Government of Azad Hind.

(ii) Responsible for the efficient and economic administration of his area.

(iii) Responsible for the the promulgation of any orders and instructions received from the Azad Hind Government for his Province.

(iv) Responsible for the general welfare of the people in his Province.

(v) Responsible for the protection of life and properly of the people in Province.

(vi) All the secretaries will be responsible to the Governor for the efficient working of their respective departments.

(vii) The Governor will exercise supervision and control over the day to day working of the Departments.

(viii) The Governor is invested with powers of appointment, dismissal and transfer of all important officer of the Government and he can delegate this power for appointing, dismissing, transferring, etc. in respect of other officers to any other responsible officer by notification from time to time.

(ix) Responsible for co-ordinating the activities of the different Head of Departments of Government functioning within his province, or state.

The Provincial Government or state will have on its own initiative or reference the residuary powers to Enquirer, reduce, commute, increase or reprieve any sentence passed by any Court without assigning any reasons.

The Provincial Government or state may issue an order for the release of any person under confinement or arrest.

Chapter IV

DEPARTMENTAL ORGANIZATION

(a)	*Department of Internal Affairs*		—Secretary
	(i)	Police-Insp. Gen. Police Census.	—Assistant Secretary
	(ii)	Passport, Inspection of Local Organization.	—Assistant Secretary
	(iii)	Air Raid Precautions. Civil Defence Organization	—Assistant Secretary
	(iv)	Jails-Insp. Gen. of Prisons	—Assistant Secretary
(b)	*Finance*		
	(i)	Revenue	—Secretary
		Land Revenue	—Assistant Secretary
		Income-Tax commissioner Absentee & Enemy Property	—Assistant Secretary
		Registraion & Excise	—Assistant Secretary
	(ii)	Expenditure	
		Budget—2 Asstt. Secretary Audit—Auditor General Accounts—Accountant General	—Deputy Secretary
		Banking	—Assistant Secretary

(c) *Law* —Secretary

Legislation —Assistant Secretary

Administration of Justice- High, District, Sub-Divisional Circle & Panchayat Courts —Assistant Secretary

High Court

(i) It will be the Highest Court in the Province. It will have two or more Judges.

(ii) Power of awarding punishment. :

Forfeiture of Property of any kind	Unlimited and/or
Fine	Unlimited and/or
Imprisonment	Life and/or
Whipping	50 strokes
Capital punishment	Death

(iii) Hearing Appeals from District Courts where the punishment awarded amount to over 75 per cent or the claim allowed is less than 75 per cent.

(d) *Public Enlightment*

Internal Propaganda-Press and Publicity other than Press,Theatre, Cinema, Literature. External Propaganda Civil and Army. —Assistant Secretary

Education-Director of Public instruction. —Assistant Secretary

(e) *Health and Social Welfare*

Prevention and Treatment of Disease.
Relief of Destitutes including Air Raid Victims.
Supply and Distribution Welfare of Medicines

Director of Health and Social Welfare

Assistant Secretary
Assistant Secretary
Assistant Secretary

(f)	*Agriculture, Industries, Labour*	—Secretary
	Agriculture-Director of Agriculture Industray-Director of Industries	—Assistant Secretary
	Forests-Chief Conservator Supply and Distribution: Labour Matter relating to the Joint Cent. Lab. Board.	—Assistant Secretary
(g)	*Commerce*	
	Production and Collection of Commodities-Director of Commerce. Price Control—and matters relating to the Joint cent. Pur. Board.	—Assistant Secretary
	Distribution (including Rationing)	—Asstt Secretary
(h)	*Communication and Transports*	—Secretary
	Posts and Telegraphs, Telephone, Wireless-Director of posts and Telegraphs,	—Asstt Secretary
	Railways, Steamer, Motor Vehicles, Boats, Carts, Cycles- Director of Transport	—Asstt Secretary
(i)	*Public Works*	—Secretary
	Roads, Building, (Chief Engineer)	—Asstt Secretary
	Water Supply and Drainage (inclu- ding Irrigation) Chief Engineer. Electricity and Gas	—Asstt Secretary
(j)	*Women's Affairs*	—Secretary —Assistant Secreatry
(k)	*Co-operation.* Indo Nippon Co-operation.	—Secretary —Assistant Secreatry

Note—Necessary Technical, Ministerial and Menial Staff will be employed as and when required.

Chapter V

Relation between departments and provincial administrative organization

(i) The Administrative Organization (e.g. District officer, sub-Divisional officer & c) will have inherent rights of inspection of a general nature, over the activities of the respective departmental officers (e.g. Officers of the Health & Social welfare Department, Police, Agriculture, & v.) of the Provincial Government functioning within the respective area of each administrator.

(ii) They will bring to the notice of the department concerned any matter that may have come to their notice for necessary action.

(iii) Each Department will be responsible for the technical administration of the personnel of their respective department and the maintenance of discipline and efficiency of work.

Chapter VI

Relation between provincial Government and Local bodies (District Board, Local Board, Municipality, & c)

(i) The Local Bodies will not be elected bodies for the present but the member will be nominated by the Government.

(ii) The duties and function of the Local Bodies will be assigned from time to time by notification by the Governor.

(iii) The Provincial Government will enunciate fundamental policies and communicate them to the Local Bodies such as District Boards, Municipalities, etc.

(iv) The Provincial Government will have the residuary power of direction and instruction, and where necessary, of execution of its orders in the territory of the Local Bodies.

(v) The Local Bodies will enforce all ordinances and regulations promulgated by the Provincial Government.

(vi) The Local Bodies may ask for the help of the Provincial Government in any matter considered essential.

Chapter VII

Relationship between Provincial Government and the Provisional Government of Azad Hind.

(i) The Provisional Government will appoint the Governor of each Province or State. The Governor will be responsible to the

Provisional Government of Azad Hind for the efficient administration of his territory.

(ii) The Provisional Government can delegate any of its power to the governor.

(iii) In the first occasion, the Secretaries will be appointed by the Provisional Government of Azad Hind. Thereafter, when vacancies occur, the governor of a province will appoint, subject to the approval of the Provisional Government of Azad Hind. But the Provisional Government may not accept the proposal and may appoint another man.

(iv) The Provisional Government will enunciate the fundamental policies and will communicate the same to the Provincial Government for execution.

(v) The Provincial Government will enforce all ordinances and regulations promulgated by the Provincial Government of Azad Hind.

(vi) The Provincial Government will have the residuary power of directions and instruction and in extreme cases of execution of any of its orders in the territory of the Provincial Government when the latter has failed in the execution of orders.

(vii) The Provincial Government may ask for the help of the Provincial Government in any matter which is considered essential.

Note:—The present constitution may be modified or abrogated when necessary by the Provincial Government or the Governor when duly authorized by the Provincial Government.

Chapter VIII

General Policies and Measures of the Provincial Government of Azad Hind.

(i) To give general direction to the Provincial Government.

(ii) To use the liberated territory for organizing the next stage of the campaign.

(iii) To give necessary help to the Azad Hind Fauj and the Imperial Japanese Army in the matter of defense and future campaign.

(iv) Formation of Provinces (see Appendix III).

Chapter IX

Policies and Measures of the Provisional Government of Azad Hind for self sufficiency.

It is very necessary that self-sufficiency with regard to the requirements of the inhabitants, Azad Hind Fauj and Nippon Army should be achieved as early as possible. But it can only be done by full co-operation between the Provincial Government and the Nippon Army. In this connection three items are of Primary importance:

What the Provincial Government can do.	What is expected of the Nippon Army.
1. Food Ariticles	
(a) Commander, Ration and allot all articles of necessity.	(a) Importation of Food supply for six months recruitments, Rice, salt, sugar, Atta-Dal-Tea.
(b) Organize, encourage and provide facilities for local production as much as possible.	(b) Importation of seed cuttings for growing food crops lacally-paddy, maize, wheat, dal, tapioca, Sweet Potatoes.
(c) Recruit Kisans and Agri-cultural Experts.	
2. Medical supplies	
(a) Recruit Doctors, Dres-sers, Nurses.	(a) Quinine Tablets and Ampoules
(b) Collect and purchase Medi cines Durgs and Dressing and Anti-septics.	Anti-Cholera) Anti-Typhoid) Vaccines Lymph Vaccines
3. Clothing	
(a) Collect and Purchase Burma Khaddar (i.e. Hand Made cloth).	
4. Recruitment of Labour	

5. The quantities required should be as much as can be obtained, because as time goes on, the British are likely to destroy more and more as

they go on retreating and consequently our requirements will also be increasing. It is likely that we may be required to provide for a population of 10 millions within the next few months plus those of the Nippon Army and of the Azad Hind Fauj. And after that, we may have to provide for a population of over 70 Millions. So we should go on collection as much as is possible.

Chapter X

Policies and Measures for the Maintenance of Currency.

In order to maintain the value of currency we will have to adopt preventive as well as curative methods. The preventive method will have to be applied first; these tend to prevent inflation of currency. But later, when inflation of currency does appear, we will have to adopt additional measures which have a deflating effect by taking off from the market surplus currency, that is currency which is not covered by Goods and services and which is really the cause of inflation. The more effectively the preventive methods are applied the lesser would be the necessity to apply the curative (deflative) methods. The following measures are proposed to be applied:

(a) *Preventive Methods to be Applied Immediately*

(i) To control the amount of currency out in circulation, Provisional Government must be informed of the amount of new currency that the Nippon Army is bringing into the country, as well as the amount of old currencies left in the country-in Banks, Treasuries, etc.

(ii) Price Control.

(iii) Control of consumption of essential commodities and food.

(iv) Elimination of Departmental competition in purchasing materials by establishing joint central purchasing Board.

(v) Strict rationing of food and commodities.

(vi) Stern suppression of Black Market.

(vii) Prohibit the export of gold.

(viii) Prohibit private sale or transfer of gold.

(ix) Control of sale and purchase of all commodities necessary for war.

(b) Curative Methods to be adopted. Later if necessary

(i) special taxing of immovable property.

(ii) Levying of a graded tax on incomes over a certain level.

(iii) Levying a tax on amusements, narcotics, tobacco, alcoholic drinks and motor vehicles.

(iv) Organization of State Lotteries.

Chapter XI

Policies and measures of the Provisional Government of Azad Hind for controlling commodities and the restriction of Consumption

(i)	Seizing and scaling of the Commodities.	By Department of Commerce.
(ii)	Dealers, Merchants and manufacturers to be asked to declare their stocks of articles of (a) Rice, Flour, Salt, Sugar, Maize, Dal, Molasses. (b) Cloth, of all kind, including Mosquito Netting. (c) Stationery, machinery of all kinds, motor vehicles, and their spare parts. bicycles, and their spare parts, drugs, chemicals, acids, alkalies and other medicines.	By Department of Commerce.
(iii)	Rationing, Food, Cloth and essential materials (Stationery, mechanical Parts, motor vechicles, & c.)	By Department of Commerce.
(iv)	Forbidding transfer, sale and purchase of the above mentioned articles without a special order from the Provincial Government. Purchases to be Permitted only on the ration scale in case of items in (a),	By Department of Commerce.

	(b) and in very restricted quantity of (c) in sub-para (iii) above.	
(v)	Prohibition of Big Parties- not more than 10 persons and once a month and with special permission of the Rationing Board to be established under the Department of Commerce	By Department of Commerce.
(vi)	Severe Punishment for Blace Marketting-Death Sentence.	Police-Prosecution or Reference by Department of Commerce.
(vii)	No Japanese Firms to go in the country at this stage.	

Chapter XII

Administrative organization for Managing Labour controlling and distributing Commodities, Police work and Civil Defence Work.

(a) Management of Labour

(i)	Collection of Information	Beesghara
(ii)	Change of profession from Non-Essential to essential services (War Material)	Police Thana
(iii)	Supply No forcible recruitment of farm labour No separate recruitment of labor by any party	Joint Labour Board
(v)	Compulsory employment of labor	All unemployed males -18 to 40 year-fi necessary

(b) Controlling and Distribution of Commodities

(i) Seizure and Sealing of the Commodities in the premises of Merchants, Dealers and Manufacturers.

(ii) Declaration of stock by Merchants, Dealers and Manufacturers compiled in the presence of Department Inspectors.

(iii)	Census	Beesgharas.

(iv)	Census Family Ration Cards	Police Thana
(v)	Order to merchants, dealers, manufacturers, forbidding the transfer, sale or purchase of the notified commodities without a permit.	by Department of Commerce.
(vi)	Order publishing the price and scale of ration of each commodity which an adult of child is entitled per week, month, half year, or year as the case may be.	By Department of Commerce.
(vii)	Order to merchants, dealers manufacturers, to sell, or purchase, at the controlled price only or to sell only sanctioned scale and only on the production of the family census ration card where entries must be made in accordance with the articles sold.	By Department of Commerce

(c) **Police Work**

Inspector General of Police

Deputy Inspector General of Police — Provincial Secretariat

A.I.G.P. (Intelligence) — A.I.G.P. — A.I.G.P. (Armed Police)

Criminal Special D.S.P. — ZILA

Dy. Supdt.

I.P.

S.I.P. Thana

A.S.I.

Pradhan — Head Constable & Constable

Mondal

Beesghara

(d) Civil Defence Work—This will be organized on a voluntary basis under the leadership of Mondals and Pradhans in villges and towns. Instruction and guidance will be given by the Police and Military Authorities. People will undergo regular physical and spiritual training and military drill. It will supervised by the Mahakuma and Zila Hakim.

(e) Air Raid Precautions—This will be organized also on a voluntary basis. Doctors, Dressers, Warden, Watchers, etc., will be recruited, organized and trained under suitable leadership. Instruction and guidance will be given by the Police and military Authorities. It will be supervised by the Mahakuma and Zila Hakim.

Chapter XIII

Help wanted from Nippon Army in the matter of :

(i) Imports.

(ii) Whole-hearted co-operational Nippon Army:

- (a) In the case of rationing
- (b) Price Control
- (c) Suppressing the Black Market
- (d) Control their own M.P.
- (e) Protection of women
- (f) Control of sale and purchases of all commodities necessary for war.

Appendix 1

Towns

30 Families	1 Beesgara
10 Beesgharas	1 Mondal
10 Mondals	1 Mukhia or Pradhan
10 Mukhias or Pradhans	1 Ilakadar

The ILAKADAR will submit information received from the Pradhans to the Inspector of Police and will transmit to theMukhias orders of the government.

In a town a number of I lakas will constitute to form a Ward and a number of wards will constitute to form a District.

Relation between the town organization proposed above, and a Municipal organization will settled later on but tentatively a proposal is put forward that the Pradhans will form a town council which will be an advisory body for assisting the Mayor of the town who will be appointed by the Provincial Government.

In those places where elected Municipalities exist and are functioning well, the Provincial Government will consider the question of continuing the system.

The Mayor will have executive functions. He will be not only the Head of the Town but will be the Executive head of the town also.

Appendix II

Scale of Rations

This can only be fixed when the whole stock available can be ascertained plus the quantity that can be imported. Even then it may have to be changed if the circumstances demand. Tentatively:

(a) For those doing Hard Manual Labour:

	Man	Woman			
Rice or	10	8	Seer	(Kilo)	Per month
Maize	9	8	"		"
Salt	1/3	1/3	"		"
Sugar	3/4	1/2	"		"
Cooking oil	1	5/8	"		"

(b) For Others:

	Man	Woman	Child		M.or. F.
Rice or	6	5	3	Seer	Kili/p.m.
Maize	5.5	4.5	2	"	"
Salt	1/4	1/4	1/5	"	"
Sugar	1/2	1/2	1/4	"	"
Coɔking Oil	3/4	1/2	1/4	"	"

Appendix III

Formation of Provinces

1. Any area that is liberated from the British rule and comes under the Provisional Government will be declared a Province or State as the case may be.

2. In case another area is liberated which is not contiguous to the first liberated territory and where a separate administration is necessary on account of the emergencies of the situation, the second liberated territory will also be declared a Province.

3. With the progress of the campaign when two liberated areas are joined up, the Provisional Government will consider the question whether the administration of the two territories should be combined under an unified administration.

4. Subject to the above, the Provisional Government will adhere as far as possible to the existing boundaries of the Provinces and States in India.

32

P.K. Sahgal to M.Z. Kiani Praising the Achievements of I.N.A.[1]

16 June, 1944

Sadar Dafter, Ala Kaman, Azad Hind Fauj.
(Head Quarters, Supreme Command, I.N.A.)

D.O. No. 16/2/18/ MS.

Dear Colonel,

Your report, dated the 15th of May, together with your points for Netaji were received here on the 4th June. A copy of your telegram asking for lorries, horses, sugar and oil, etc., was also received on the same day.

Major N.N. Khosla together with Rear H.Qrs. had already left. I hope the M.T. with the Rear H. Qrs would be able to relieve the transport situation to some extent. We are doing our best to buy some horses, but unfortunately most of the good horses have already raised an A.T. Platoon from among the old 3rd Cavalry personnel and as soon as we have bought 20 horses, arrangements shall be made to send them on to you.

Four thousand ground sheets have already been sent with your Rear H.Qrs. No. 2, Engineer Coy., No. 2 Hospital, No. 1 MPT. Coy. and No. 1 Mortar Coy. have already left for the front. No. 1 M-T. Coy. and No. 2 Eng. Coy. shall come under command of No. 1 Div. after they arrive in Mandalay. Although I have not been able to get the Hikari Kikan to state in absolutely concrete terms, they have given me to understand that No. 1 M.T. Coy. shall be employed to carry out the duties for no. 1 Div.

We tried to get a wagon to send some soap, gur, oil and mess tins to you but unfortunately were not successful. However, a wagon has been promised us next week when No. 4 Engineer Coy., shall leave here.

At present communications between our H. Qrs. and the front line units are most inadequate. We have started a weekly courier service

1. I.N.A. Trial Papers.

between Rangoon and Mandalay and form there the H.Qrs. in Maymyo are trying to make arrangements for D.R.L.S. to the front with the Hikari Kikan. The original objection was that our cipher was too simple, however, we produced other modified forms of our cipher which came up to their standard, but they wish to make another code based on the Nippon Army Code, for us. Even after that the question of equipment and Trinidad personnel shall still remain and we may have to fall back on using the Nippon Units to ascend our messages, In that case a code consisting of numerals alone may solve the script problems. I am at present trying to find some solution to this problem and if you can help me by some suggestions, I shall feel most grateful.

Every one hear has been most thrilled to read about the bold actions of the Init No. 24 from 24th Aprill to 6th may 1944. I shall feel very grateful if you will please convey my heartiest congratulations to Col. I.J. Kiani, Pritam Singh and the others who took part in it.

Staff Officers of the Mori Head Quarter from time to time, inform us of the very good work being done by the units under your command and the other day we were told by a senior officer of Mori H.Qrs. who has recently returned from the front line that he had met you in the front line and that all the neighbouring units spoke very highly of your brilliant leadership and the wonderful work being done by the units under your command. It is indeed a matter of pride for us all that the vanguard of the I.N.A. is creating traditions which the following units shall don well follow.

Please give very best regards to Major Hassan and other officers.

With best regards.

'Jai Hind'

Yours sincerely,

(Sd.) P.K. SAHGAL.

33

Bose to Karuppiah Encouraging him to Complete his Training in Tokyo[1]

18 June, 1944

Arzi Hukumate Azad Hind

(The Provisional Government of Free India.)

Sri N.Karuppiah.,
Tokyo.

Jai Hind.

I am extremely happy to receive your letter and to know that you are getting on very well with your studies. It gives be very great pleasure indeed to know that you are determined, to derive the maximum benefit from your stay in Nippon, and to return to free India as worthy Sons of our Motherland. You ahve gone to Nippon to undergo training which will enable you to become full-fledge soldiers who will defend Indian's Independence with the last drop of their blood. Mean while, the heroism and half-sacrifice with which officers and men of the Azad Hind Fauj are fighting on the battle fields of Arakan, Kaladan, Imphal and Kohima should serve as a shining example to you to follow all your life.

Though you are yet in your teens, you have left your homes and parents and brothers and sisters and you have travelled thousands of miles to far-off Nippon and will stay there for some yours. Though physically you are thousands or miles away from me, you are always in my thoughts.

There was much that I wanted to tell you when I addressed you in Syonan. But the thought of parting form you so overpowered we that I could hardly speak. I wanted to go back to Syonan again in March to see

1. Azad Hind Center, Kaula Lumpur. Number of Young person were sent to Tokyo for military Training. They were known as Tokyo Cadets. Sri N. Karuppiah was one of them.

you off-but I could not, owing to the military operations then going on at the Indian-Burma frontier. I future, I shall be moving further and furter from you and may not, therefore, be able to write to you. But do write to me, my dear boy, whenever you have a chance of writing. Wherever my be, I shall always think of you and pray for your success.

I hope you will continue singing the National Anthem every day during your stay in Nippon. And pray every morning and night that you may become a worthy son of Mother India.

Jai hind

34

Bose Asking Lognandan to Send a Detailed Report on the Administration of Andamans[1]

21 June, 1944

Jai Hind,

1. I was glad to receive your letter or 15th march and the 2nd April. I also received two reports through the Hikari- kikan-one on the 22nd and the other on the 15th June.

2. I am gratified to learn from different sources that you have been carrying on your duties with ability and tact. I am, however, not satisfied at the progress made in actually transferring the administration. For this, I do not blame you.

3. I am anxious to know how you have been keeping in health, because I was informed that when you left Port Blair, you were in poor health. I hope you are taking all impossible care any our healthy.

4. Please let me know by wire, if necessary if you need one money.

5. I wonder if you have in organizing a unit of the there.

6. I understanding that your are the chairman of the Civilized Administration Council of the Andaman and Nicobar Islands. I understand, further, that this Council is an Advisory Body. Is that correct.

7. Along with your letter of the 15the March I received a group photograph taken after your arrival in Port Blair.

8. I am sorry that we have not attended to your needs from this end-but we shall do so in future. Since you left Malaya, events have been moving at a break neck speed and we have all been plunged in work.

1. I.N.A. Trial Papers.

9. I note that in your first letter you wanted cutlery and crockery and also medicine. It we can arrange or the transport through the wavy, we shall send you the articles.

10. I entirely agree with you that without police powers you cannot have prestige in he eyes of the people.

11. You may tell the authorities that I dissatisfied at the progress made in the transference of the administration.

12. You must be aware that our Army is now fighting on Indian soil in Manipur and in Kohima sector (Assam). On the whole, our troops have done very well and have learned the appreciation the Nippon Army. Co. Chatterji is the Governor designate of the liberated Territory.

13. We have started a new organization called the Azad Hind Dal. It is a semi military organization consisting of civilians and administrations who will be going to India in the wake of our victorious armies.

14. I am now in Rangoon on a short visit from the front. I also paid a flying visit to woman and have just returned from there. I shall soon be moving forward again.

Hope this will find you all well. Cordial greeting to all.

Jai Hind

Signed

Subhas Chandra Bose.

35

Bose's Statement on the Reponsibilities of the Provisional Government of Azad Hind[1]

3 July, 1944

"Our activities hitherto have been confined substantially to East Asia but the situation is considerably changed now. Those areas of India which have been liberated have given rise to the problems of administration and reconstruction.

The military operations now progressing with such brilliant results have also created new problems, namely, how are these military operations to be carried farther into India and how is the Indian revolution within India to be completed.

"One year since the present struggle for the liberation of our mother country it has become necessary now to survey the past and make plans for the future.

"As a result, we have three fields of activity. The first is East Asia, which is still to be our political and strategic base. The second is the liberated territory, the problems with which we are confronted there being mainly those of administration and reconstruction and proportions for future development. The third is the rest of India now under enemy occupation. The revolution of India must be completed. For that our troops must penetrate into that territory.

"Until very recently the activities of the Provisional Government of Azad Hind had been virtually restricted to East Asia, but now that the situation has undergone a change it would be necessary to reorganize the Government and expand its activities. In other words, the Provisional Government will have to expand its three spheres of activities, namely. East Asia, the liberated zones and the enemy occupied territories. For this purpose, it will be necessary for the Government to dispose State ministers

1. *Nippon Times*, 5 July, 1944

and Advis with clear responsibility to the respective spheres. The first squad will supervise various activities in East Asia, the second one in the liberated zones while the third one will engage in its duties in the enemy occupied territories. The first squad now active in East Asia is called the east Asiatic Committee of the Cabinet, the second squad now engaged in activities in the liberated zones the Liberated Area Committee of the Cabinet, and the third squad the Wartime Committee of the Cabinet.

"The mobilization of manpower, finance and material in East Asia must be enforced more and more vigorously in the future. For this end a new administrative department should be established or the existing administrative organ expanded to meet the need. The present financial affairs department will be enlarged and its scope of activity greatly expend.

"The new administrative body under the name of 'Mobilization Department' will call for and mobilize the personnel necessary for the activities of each of such bodies as the Indian National Army, the Rant of Jhansi Regiment, the department in charge of reconstruction of the liberated areas and the affairs of the Indian Independence League.

"The recently established Supply Department will also be expend.

"Although there will be no changes in the fields of activies of the various existing organs or of those to be established, in the future the greater part of matters of importance will be entrusted to the three departments of finance, mobilization and supply.

"The East Asia Committee will be composed of a regular East Asia Minister and an Adviser, who will supervise activities in East Asia.

"There are plans ready for the administration of liberated areas and for reconstruction work therein. These will be enforced at a proper time. The personnel needed by the department dealing with reconstruction in the liberated areas has already been sent to the regions where it is required. The member of the department already are at work within India and near the border.

"The Liberated Area Committee is composed of ministers and advisers who have been selected to work in liberated areas and ministers and advisers who are on missions in various regions.

"Lastly, the Wartime Committee is made up of ministers and advisers who are qualified to deal from an expert standpoint with matters connected with military operation, propaganda, revolutionary movements, and re-examination of the existing system of administration.

"The three committees mentioned above will constitute the Cabinet, a step intended to enable it to meet the needs of the existing situation.

The Provisional Government will give every assistance to the committees. As a measure intended to help it in doing this it will be arranged for the work of the committees to be concentrated where they are functioning. The committees will be made to work so as to facilitate the achievement of the first object of the Provisional Government which is the independence of India.

36

Bose's reply to British Propaganda Against I.N.A.[1]

5 July, 1944

The formation of the Azad Hind Fauj has been a source of extreme worry and anxiety to our enemies. They tried to ignore its existence for a time, but when the news could no longer be suppressed, their organ-the anti-India Radio at Delhi-started propaganda to the effect that Indian prisoners-of-war, under Japanese control, had been coerced into joining the army. The propaganda could not, however, endure long, because the news began to infiltrate into India that large number of Indian civilians from all parts of East Asia were joining the Azad Hind Fauj. The experts of the anti-India Radio had therefore to alter their tactics. They then started fresh propaganda to the effect that Indian prisoners-of-war had refused to join the Azad Hind Fauj and that, thereupon, Indian civilians were being forced into joining that army. It did not probably strike the wiseacres at Delhi that if it was impossible to coerce prisoners-of-war into joining the army, it was even more impossible to coerce free civilians into becoming soldiers...

Anybody who has a grain of common sense will realize that though a mercenary army can be organized by coercion, a Volunteer Army can never be so organized. You can perhaps force a man to shoulder a riffle, but you can never force him to give his life for a cause which is not his own.

At an early stage our enemies used to say that the Azad Hind Fauj was not army-that it was a mere propaganda stunt-and that it would never fight. Latter on, the anti-India Radio at Delhi began to shout that the Azad Hind Fauj had not crossed the frontier of India. Now that frontier has been crossed and the battle for India's freedom is being waged on Indian soil, enemy propagandists have taken recourse to a last desperate trick. They are now inventing fictitious dated supposed to have been given out by us

1. *Greater Asia*, 8 July, 1944.

for our entry into Delhi and are abusing us for not rechange our destination according to schedule...

I have already told you that the Azad Hind Fauj is composed not only of men but also of women...

Friends, the Azad Hind Fauj is an army which is not only composed of Indian, but it has also been trained by Indian. That army is today fighting under Indian officers.

The Azad Hind Fauj is the military organ of the Provisional Government of Azad Hind. The Provisional Government and its Army are the servants of the Indian nation. Their task is to fight and liberate India. When that liberation is achieved, it will be for the Indian people to determine the form of Government that they desire. The Provisional Government will then make room for a permanent Government in Free India, which will be set up in accordance with the will of the Indian people. For that glorious day we are now toiling, sweating and fighting.

37

Heroic Deeds of the I.N.A.[1]

5 July, 1944

On the occasion of the first anniversary of the assumption by Subhas Chandra Bose of the Leadership of the Indian Independence Movement in East Asia, a mammoth parade was held yesterday morning with a large number of crack reinforcement forces of the Azad Hind Fauj participating.

In the Parade. a battalion of the Indian National Army marched past in review while Netaji Bose, Commander-in-Chief of the Azad Hind Fauj. saluted with profound confidence in his army of liberation. On the parade stand were high ranking Japanese Army officers and Renzo Sawada, Japanese Ambassador to Burma, as well as Major-General Thakin Aung Sun, Burmese Minister of Defense.

Following the parade Netaji, speaking to the officers and men of the Indian National Army from the platform which was decorated with the national flag of Azad Hind declared that crossing the frontier of India has brought about unique inspiration to the Indian National Army whose unflinching optimism and burning fighting spirit will lead the army into the very heart of India.

"No sacrifice, no hardship and no suffering." the Netaji said, "are too great for the Indians fighting for the liberation of their motherland." and asked his officers and men to throw in every ounce of energy into the struggle, for he declared that, "this war is for us a life and death struggle, and no matter what suffering and sacrifices are involved we are convinced of our final victory."

In the course of his speech, Mr Bose announced the awarding of the medal "Vir-Hind". to Lieutenant Pira Singh for his singular bravery. The Netaji commended the Lieutenant in his address, saying, "This office, who is an example to the members of Azad Hind Fauj, has won our

1. *Nippon Times*, 7 July 1944.

admiration by exhibiting a high standard of patriotism, courage and devotion to duly throughout the campaign in the Arakan area."

Lieutenant Singh distinguished himself in ecounters with the British forces during the Arakan fighting in Feburary this year in the course of which he was injured by a trench-motor and deprived of the use of both legs. When he appeared before the dails, carried by his comrades in an armchair, to receive his award a deep silence enveloped the entire parade ground. The Netaji warmly shook his hand and pinned the medal on his chest.

The ceremonial Parade was brought to a close by the singing of the national anthem. The parade ground was then cleared off for a mock battle which was staged by troops of the Rani of Jhansi Regiment which for the past year has received intense training for combat in modern warfare.

38

In a Broadcast Message to Mahatma Gandhi, Bose Tried to Convince him about the Need for Armed Struggle and Foreign help for India's Freedom[1]

6 July, 1944

Mahatmaji,

Now that your health has somewhat improved, and you are able to attend to public business to some extent, I am taking the liberty of addressing a few words to you with a view to acquainting you with the plans and the activities of patriotic Indians ouside India. Before I do so, I would like to inform you of the feelings of deep anxiety which Indians throughout the world had for several days, after your sudden release from custody on grounds of ill health. After the sad demise of Srimati Kasturbaiji in British custody, it was but natural for your countrymen to be alarmed over the state of your health. It has, however, pleased Providence to restore you to comparative health, so that 388 millions of your countrymen may still have the benefit of your guidance and advice. I should next like to say something about the attitude of your countrymen outside India towards yourself. What I shall say in this connection, is the bare truth and nothing but the truth.

There are Indians outside India, as also at home, who are convinced that Indian Independence will be won only through the historic method of struggle. These men and women honestly feel that the British Government will never surrender to persuasion or moral pressure or non-violent resistance. Nevertheless, for Indians outside India, difference in method are like domestic differences. Ever since you sponsored the Independence Resolution at the Lahore Congress in December 1929, all members of the Indian National Congress have had one common goal before them. For Indians outside India, you are the creator of the present awakening in our country. In all their propaganda before the world, they give you that

1. *Greater Asia*, 7 and 18 July, 1944.

position and the respect that due to that position. For the world public, We Indian Nationalists are all one having but one goal, ond desire and one endeavor in life.

In all the countries free from British influence that I have visited since I left India in 1941, you are held in the highest esteem, as no other Indian political leader has been, during the last century. Each nation has its own internal politics and its own attitude towards political problems. But that cannot affect a Nation's appreciation of a man who has served his people so well and has bravely fought a first-class modern power all his life. In fact, your worth and your achievements are appreciated a thousand times more in those countries that are opposed to the British Empire that in those countries that pretend to be the friends of Freedom and Democracy. The high esteem in which you are held by patriotic Indians outside India and by foreign friends of India's Freedom, was increased a hundred-fold when you bravely sponsored the "Quit India" Resolution in August, 1942.

From my experience of the British Government while I was inside India-from the secret information that I leave gathered about Britain's policy while outside India-and from what I have seen regarding Britain's aims and intentions throughout the world. I am and honestly convinced that the British Government will never recognize India's demand for Independence. Britain's one effort today is to exploit India to the fullest degree, in her territory to her enemies and another part to her friends. Even if the Allies could somehow win the war, it will be the United States of America, and not Britain that will be the top dog in future and it will mean that Britain will become a protege of the U.S.A. In such a situation the British will try to make good their present losses by exploiting India more ruthlessly than ever before. In order to do that, plans have been already thatched in London for crushing the nationalist movement in India once for all. It is because I know of these plans from secret but reliable sources that I feel it my duty to bring it to your notice.

It would be a fatal mistake on our part to make a distinction between the British Government and the British people. No doubt there is a small group of idealists in Britain-as in U.S.A.-who would like to see India free. These idealists, who are treated by their own people as cranks, form a microscopic minority. So far as India is concerned for all practical purposes, the British Government and the British people mean one and the same thing. Regarding the war aims of the U.S.A. I may say that the ruling clique at Washington is now dreaming of world domination. This ruling clique and its intellectual exponents talk openly of the "American Centurey", that is, that in the present century the U.S.A. will dominate the world. In this ruling clique, there are extremists who go so far as to call Britain the 49th State of the U.S.A.

There is no Indian, whether at home or abroad, who would not be happy if India's freedom could be won through the method that you have advocated all your life and without shedding human blood. But things being what they are, I am convinced that if we do desire freedom we must be prepared to wade through blood.

If circumstances had made it possible for us to organize an armed struggle inside India, through our own efforts and resources, that would have been the best course for us. But, Mahatmaji, you know Indian conditions perhaps better than anybody else. So far as I am concerned after twenty years experience of public service in India, I came to the conclusion that it was impossible to organize an armed resistance in the country, without some help from outside-help from our countrymen abroad, as well as from some foreign power or powers. Prior to the outbreak of the present war, it was exceedingly difficult to get help from a foreign power, or even from Indians abroad. But the outbreak of the present war threw open the possibility of obtaining aid-both political and military-from the enemies of the British Empire. Before I could expect any help from them, however, I had first to find out what their attitude was towards India's demand for freedom. British propagandists, for a number of years, had been telling the world that the Axis Powers were the enemies of Freedom and, therefore, of India's freedom. Was that a fact? I asked myself. Consequently, I had to leave India in order to find out the truth myself and as the whether the Axis Powers would be prepared to give us help and assistance in our right for freedom.

Before I finally made up my mind to leave home and home land, I had to decide whether it was right for me to take help from abroad. I had previously studied the history of revolutions all over the world, in order to discover the methods which had enabled other nations to obtain freedom. But I had not found a single instance in which an enslaved people had won freedom without foreign help of some sort. In 1940, I read my history once again and once again I came to the conclusion that history did not furnish a single instance where freedom had been won without help of some sort from abroad. As for the moral question as to whether it was right to take help, I told myself that in public, as in private life, one can always take help as a loan and rapay that loan later on. Moreover, if a powerful Empire, like British Empire, could go round the world with the begging bowl, what objection could there be to an enslaved and disarmed people like ourselves taking help as a loan from abroad. I can assure you, Mahatmaji that before I finally decided to set out on a hazardous mission, I spent days, weeks and months in carefully considering the pros and cons of the case. After having served my people so long, to the best of my ability, I could have not desired to be a traitor, or to give anyone a justification for calling me a traitor.

It was the easiest thing for me to remain at home and go on working as I had worked so long. It was also an easy thing for me to remain in an Indian prison while the War lasted. Personally, I had nothing to lose by doing so. Thanks to the generosity and to the affection of my countrymen, I had obtained the highest Honour which it was possible for any public worker in India to achieve. I had also built up a party consisting of staunch and loyal colleagues who had implicit confidence in me. By going abroad on a perilous quest, I was risking-not only my life and my whole future career-but what was more, the future of my party. If I had the slighest hope that without action from abroad we could win freedom, I would never have left India during a crisis. If I had any hope that within our lifetime we would get another chance -another golden opportunity-for wining freedom, as during the present war, I doubt if I would have set out from home. But I was convinced of two things, firstly that such a golden opportunity would not come within another century-and secondly, that without action from abroad, we would not be able to win freedom, merely through our own efforts at home. That is why I resolved to take the plunge.

Providence has been kind to me. In spite of manifold difficulties, all my plans have succeeded so far. After I got out of India, my first endeavour was to organise my countrymen, where I had happened to meet them. I am glad to say that everywhere I found them to be wide awake and anxious to do everything possible for winning freedom for India. I then approached the Governments that were at war with our enemy, in order to find out what their attitude was towards India. I found out that contrary to what British propaganda had been telling us for a number of years—the Axis Powers were now openly the friends of India's freedom. I also discovered that they were prepared to give such help as we desired, and as was within their own power.

I know the propaganda that our enemy has been carrying on against me. But I am sure that my countrymen, who know me so well will never be taken in. One who has stood for national self-respect and honour all his life and has suffered considerably in vindicating it, would be the last person in this world to give in to any other foreign power. Moreover, I have nothing to gain personally at the hands of a foreign power. Having received the highest honour possible for an Indian at the hands of my own countrymen, what is there for me to receive from a foreign power. Only that man can be a puppet who has either no sense of honour and self-respect or desires to build up a position for himself through the influence of others.

Not even my worst enemy can dare to say that I am capable of selling national honour and self-respect. And not even my worst enemy can dare to assert that I was a nobody in my own country and that I needed foreign help to secure a position for myself. In leaving India, I had to risk everything that I had including my life. But I had to take that risk because only by doing so could I help the achievement of India's freedom.

There remains but one question for me to answer with regard to the Axis Powers. Can it be possible that I have been deceived by them?

I believe it will be universally admitted that the cleverest and the most cunning politicians are to be found amongst Britishers. One who has worked with and fought British politicians all his life, cannot be deceived by any other politicians in the world. If British politicians have failed to coax or coerce me no other politician can succeed in doing so. And if the British Government, at whose hands I have suffered long imprisonment, persecution and physical assault, has been unable to demoralise me, no other power can hope to do so.

Moreover as you personally are aware, I have been a close student of international affairs. I have had personal contacts with international figures before the outbreak of this war. I am therefore no novice who could be duped by a shrewd and cunning politician. Last but not least, before forming an opinion about the attitude of the Axis Powers I established close personal contact with important leaders and personalities in the Axis countries who are responsible for their national affairs.

Consequently, I make bold to say that my countrymen can have the fullest confidence in my judgment of the international affairs. My countrymen abroad will testify to the fact that since I left India. I have never done anything could compromise in the least, either the honour or the self-respect or the interests of my country. On the contrary, whatever I have done has been for the benefit of my nation, for enhancing India's prestige before the world and for advancing the cause of India's freedom.

Mahatmaji, since the beginning of the War in East Asia our enemies have been carrying on a raging and tearing campaign against Japan. I shall, therefore, say something about Japan—particularly because at the present moment I am working in the closest co-operation with the Government, Army and people of Japan.

There was a time when Japan had an alliance with our enemy. I did not come to Japan so long as there was an Anglo-Japanese alliance. I did not come to Japan, so long as normal diplomatic relations obtained between the two countries. It was only after Japan took what I consider to be the most momentous step in her history—namely, declaration of war on Britain and America—that I decided to visit Japan of my own free will.

Like so many of my countrymen I had read anti-Japanese propaganda material for a number of years. Like so many of my countrymen. I did not understand why Japan went to war with China in 1937. And like so many of my countrymen, my sympathies in 1937 and 1938 were with Chungking. You may remember that as President of the Congress, I was responsible for sending out a medical mission to Chungking in December, 1938. But what I realised that after my visit to Japan and what many people at home do not yet realise, is that since the out-break of the war in East Asia, Japan's attitude towards the world in general, and towards Asiatic nations in particular has been completely revolutionised.

It is a change that has overtaken not merely the Government, but also the people of Japan. A new consciousness—what I may best describe as an Asiatic consciousness—has seized the souls of the people of Japan. That change explains Japan's present attitude towards the Philippines, Burma, and India. That is what explains Japan's new policy in China.

After my visit to Japan and after establishing close contact with the present day leaders of that country I was fully satisfied that Japan's present policy towards Asia was no bluff but was rooted in sincerity.

This is not the first instance in history when an entire nation has been seized with a new consciousness. We have seen instances of it before in France during the French revolution and in Russia during the Bolshevik revolution. After my second visit to Japan in November, 1943, I visited the Philippines, and met Filipino leaders there and saw things for myself. I have also been in Burma for a fairly long time and I have been able to see things with my own eyes, after the declaration of Independence. And I have been to China to find out if Japan's new policy was real or if it was a fake. The latest agreement between Japan and the National Government of China has given the Chinese people practically all that they had been demanding. Japan, under that agreement, has even agreed to withdraw her troops from China on the termination of hostilities.

What then is Chungking-China fighting for? Can one believe that Britain and America are helping Chungking-China out of purely altruistic motives? Will not Britain and America demand their pound of flesh in return for the help that they are now giving to Chungking to make her continue the fight against Japan? I clearly see that Chungking is being mortgaged to Britain and America because of past hatred and antagonism towards Japan.

So long as Japan did not initiate her present policy towards China, there might have been some justification or excuse for the Chinese to seek British and American aid for fighting Japan. But now that an entirely new chapter in Sino-Japanese relations has begun, there is not the slightest excuse for Chungking to continue her meaningless struggle against Japan. That is not good for the Chinese people; it is certainly not good for Asia.

In April, 1942, you said that if you were free to do so you would work for an understanding between China and Japan. That was an utterance of rare statesmanship. It is India's slavery that is at the bottom responsible for the chaos in China. It is because of the British hold over India that Anglo-Americans could bluff Chungking into hoping that sufficient help could be brought to Chungking to enable Chungking to continue the war against Japan. You were absolutely right in thinking, Mahatmaji, that a free India would work for peace between Japan and China. I go so far as to say that the freedom of India will automatically bring about an honourable understanding between Chungking and Japan, by opening the eyes of Chungking to the folly that she is now committing.

Since I came to East Asia and visited China, I have been able to study the Chinese question more deeply. I find that there is a dictatorship ruling in Chungking. I have no objection personally to dictatorship, if it is for a righteous cause. But the dictatorship that rules at Chungking is clearly under foreign American influence. Unfortunately, the Anglo-Americans have been able to deceive the ruling clique at Chungking into thinking that if Japan could be somehow defeated, that China would become the dominant power in Asia. The fact, however, is that if Japan were defeated by any chance, then China would certainly pass under American influence and control. That would be a tragedy for China and for the whole of Asia.

It is through this false hope of becoming the dominant power in Asia, if Japan could be somehow defeated, that the ruling clique at

Chungking has entered into an unholy alliance with the ruling clique at White House and at Whitehall. I know something of the propagandist activities of the Chungking Government in India and of its efforts to play upon the motions of the Indian people and win their sympathy. But I can honestly say that Chungking which has been mortgaged to Wall Street and Lombard Street, does not deserve the sympathy of the Indian people any longer specially after Japan has initiated her new policy towards China.

Mahatmaji, you know better than anybody else how deeply suspicious the Indian people are of mere promises. I would be the last man to be influenced by Nippon if her declarations of policy had been mere promises. But I have seen with my own eyes, how in the midst of a world war Nippon has put through revolutionary changes in countries like the Philippines, Burma and National China. In General Tojo, Nippon has a leader and a Prime Minister, who is true to his word and whose actions are in full conformity with his declarations-and a leader who, in moral stature, towers head and shoulders above contemporary statesmen.

Coming to India, I must say that Nippon has proved her sincerity by her deeds. There was a time when people used to say that Nippon had selfish intentions regarding India. If she had them, why should she recognize the Provisional Government of Free India? Why should she decide to hand over the Andaman and Nicobar Islands to the Provisional Government of Free India ? Why should there now be an Indian Chief Commissioner of the Andaman and Nicobar Islands stationed at Port Blair? Last but not least, why should Nippon unconditionally help the Indian people in East Asia in their struggle for their Independence? There are Indians all over East Asia and they have every opportunity of seeing Nippon at close quarters. Why should three million Indians distributed all over East Asia, adopt a policy of the closest co-operation with Nippon, if they had not been convinced of her bona fules and of here sincerity? You can coerce one man or coax him into doing what you want him to do. But no one can coerce three million Indians distributed all over, East Asia.

If Indians in East Asia had taken help from Nippon without putting forward them own efforts and without making the maximum sacrifice, they would have been guilty of wrong-doing. But, as an Indian, I am happy and proud to be able to say that my countrymen in East Asia are putting forware the maximum effort to mobilize men, money and materials for the struggle for India's freedom. I have had experience at home in collecting funds and materials and in recruiting men for national service for a period of twenty years. In the light of this experience, I can properly assess the worth and value of the sacrifice that our country men in East Asia are now making.

Their effort is magnificent. It is because they are putting forward a magnificent effort themselves and are prepared to make the maximum sacrifice that I see no objection to taking help from Nippon, for such necessary articles as Arms, Ammunition etc., that we ourselves cannot produce.

Mahatmaji, I should now like to say something about the Provisional Government that we have set up here. The Provisional Government of Azad Hind (or Free India) has been recognized by Nippon, Germany and seven other friendly Powers and this has given Indians a new status and a new prestige in the eyes of the whole world. The Provisional Government has, as its one objective, the liberation of India from the British yoke, through an armed struggle. Once our enemies are expelled from India and peace and order is established, the mission of the Provisional Government will be over. It will then be for the Indian people themselves to determine the form of Government that they choose, and also to decide as to who whole take charge of that Government. I can assure you, Mahatmaji, that I and all those who are working with me, regard themselves as the servants of the Indian people. The only reward that we desire for our efforts, for our suffering and for our sacrifice is the freedom of our Motherland. There are many among us who should like to retire from the political field, once India is free. The remainder will be content to take up any position in Free India, however humble it may be. The Spirit that animates all of us today is that it is more honourable to be even a sweeper in Free India, than to have the highest position under British rule. We all know that there are hundreds of thousands of able men and women at home to whom India's destiny should be entrusted, once freedom is achieved

How much help we shall need from Nippon till the last Britisher is expelled from the soil of India, will depend on the amount of cooperation that we shall receive from inside India. Nippon herself does not desire to thrust her assistance upon us. Nippon would be happy if the Indian people could liberate themselves through their own exertions. It is we who have asked for assistance from Nippon after declaring war on Britain and America, because our enemy has been seeking help from other powers. However, I have every hope that the help we shall receive from our countrymen at home will be so great that we shall need the minimum help from Nippon. Nobody would be more happy than ourselves, if by any chance our countrymen at home should succeed in liberating themselves through their own efforts, or if by any chance, the British Government accepts your Quit India Resolution and gives effect to it. We are, however proceeding on the assumption that neither of the above is possible and that an armed struggle is inevitable

Mahatmaji! There is one other matter to which I shall refer before I close and that is about the ultimate outcome of this war. I know very well the kind of propaganda that our enemies have been carrying on in order to create the impression that they are confident of victory. But I hope that my countrymen will not be duped thereby and will not think of compromising with Britain on the issue of independence, under the mistaken notion that the Anglo-Americans will win this war. Having travelled round the world under wartime conditions with my eyes open, having seen the internal weakness of the enemy on the Indo-Burma frontier and inside India, and having taken stock of our own strength and resources, I am absolutely confident of our final victory. I am not so foolish as to minimise, in the least, the strength of the enemy. I know that we have a long and hard struggle in front of us. I am aware that on the soil of India Britain wil fight bravely and fight hard in a desperate attempt to save her Empire. But I know also that however long and hard the struggle may be it can have but one outcome—namely our victory. India's last war of independence has begun. Troops of the Azad Hind Fauj are now fighting bravely on the soil of India and in spite of all difficulty and hardship they are pushing forward, slowly but steadily. This armed struggle will go on, until the last Britisher is thrown out of India and until our Tricolour National Flag proudly floats over the Viceroy's house in New Delhi.

Father of our nation! In this holy war for India's liberation, we ask for your blessings and good wishes.

Jai Hind

39

Bose's Message to I.N.A. Soliders

12 July, 1944

The ceremonial Parade was brought to a close by the singing of the national anthem. The parde ground was then cleared off for a mock battle which was staged by troops of the Rani of Jhansi Regiment which for the past year has received intenise training for combat in modern warfare.

As I study the events of 1857 and think of the atrocities perpetrated by the British after the revolution collapsed,-my blood begins to boil. If we are men, we will certainly see to it that the heroes of 1857 and after, who suffered so much from British terror and brutality, are properly avenged. India demands revenge. The British who split the blood of innocent freedom-loving Indians and tortured them in an inhuman manner—not only during the war, but after it was over—must pay for their crimes. We Indians do not hate the enemy enough. If you want your countrymen to rise to heights of superhuman courage and heroism, you must teach them not only to love their country but also to hate the enemy.

Therefore, I call for blood. It is only the blood of the enemy that can avenge his crimes of the past. But we can take blood, only if we are prepared to give blood. Consequently, your programme for the future is to give blood. The blood of our heroes in this war will wash away our sins of the past. The blood of our heroes will be the price of our liberty. The blood of our heroes—their heroism and their bravery—will secure for the Indian people the revenge that they demand of their British tyrants and oppressors.

1. *Greater Asia*, 12 July, 1944

40

Japanese View of the Provisional Government of Azad Hind and Indian National Army[1]

12 July, 1944

The Japanese Government has decided to despatch a diplomatic envoy to the Provisional Government of free India as a concrete measure of promotiing cooperation and friendly relation. This decision was made by the Japanese Government on the occasion of the recent visit here of Subhas Chandra Bose,s President of the Provisional Government. I shall take this opportunity to review the various events that have occurred since the establishment of the Indian Provisional Government on oct. 1943.on the occasion of an assembly at Shonan of East Asian delegates of the Indian Independence League in East Asia. Prior to this assembly in July the same year Bose went to Shonan to assume leadership of the Indian Independence League and the position of Commander-in-chief of the Indian National Army. At a plenary session of the assembly of the delegates of the Indian Independence League on the afternoon of Oct. 21. Bose proposed the inauguration of a Provisional Government of Free India. His motion was unanimously supported by all the delegates present and the assembly promptly elected Bose as President of the Provisional Government. After Bose had taken the oath as the head of the newly established Government its organization and other important matters were decided by the assembly and the first declaration of the Government was promulgated. Thus the Provisional Government of Free India came into being.

The declaration of the newly inauguarated government in part said "With the approach of the emancipation of our fatherland, the Indians have the task of establishing their own Government and of commanding their last fight under its direction. In view of the fact that the leader are all being imprisoned and our brethren in our native country have been

1. *Nippon Times*, 12 July 1944.

deprived of arms. It is impossible to establish a Provisional Government with in Indian territory, to direct our struggle. Thus the Indian Independence League in East Asia must take up this task with the aid of the patriots within and with out country....The task of the Provisional Government is tó commence a struggle in order to bring about the complete expulsion of Britain and her allies from Indian territory and to guide this struggle. The Provisional Government also has the duty of establishing a free and permanent national government which shall be based on the will and trust of the Indian people. The Provisional Government shall carry out its national affairs with the confidence of the people until a permanent and free Indian Government is established on Indian soil." Thus, did the declaration clarify the combative and transient character of the newly established Provisional Government.

The Provisional Government of Czecho-Slovatia estatblished during the First World War. The Czecho Solvakian National Congress was orgainzed with Dr. Masaryk heading it in the early part of 1916 with its headquarters established at Paris. It appealed to the moral suppart of the world for its aspirations for the establishment of an independent Czecho-Slovakian State. The organization also created a Cecho— Slovakin army which cooperational with the Allied and Entente force on the German and Austrian fronts in summer of 1918, the Allied maltons extended to the Czecho-Slovakian. Czecho-Slovakian Nation Congress, as the supreme organ of the Czech-slovakian people and its army, as a belligerent army on the Allied side. When this National Congress created a Provisional Government at parts at the end of September the same year, and notification of the same was sent to the powers, both France and Italy formally recognized the newly created government. Another independent organ was created in Austria and Hungary and was amalgamated with the Provisional Government later on. On Nov. 14,1918 the National Parliament, convened at Prague, announced the creation of the State of Czeco-Slovakia. Masaryk was elected the first President of this nation and a formal government was then organized.

Immediately after the Japanese Government announcement of its recognition of the Provisional Government of Free India. Bose came to Tokyo on Oct. 31 to convey his gratitude for the cooperation shown his government by the Japanese Government. He attended the Assembly of East Asiatic. Nations which was held in Tokyo on Nov 5 and 6 in the capacity of an observer. At the meeting of the Assembly on the sixth, Dr Ba Maw, Burmese Prime Minister, proposed after the adoption of the Joint Declaration by the Assembly that the Assembly declare itself in favour of giving its wholehearted support to Bose in his attempt to emancipate India together with the Indian National Army as the head of Provisional Government of free India. After the adoption of this motion for support, Mr. Bose rose to thank the Assembly for his unanimous decision on this motion.

Due to this provisional nature of the Indian Government. its organization is simple. It is composed of the Military. Foreign Affairs, Finance Propaganda and Women's Affairs Departments all under the direction of the head of the Government. The direction of Military and Foreign Affairs Departments were concurrently held by the head of the Government. There are several Ministers without Portfolio and several Cabinet Advisers.

The Indian National Army was placed under the Provisional Government and the supreme direction of Bose. The Indian Independence League continued its activities in cooperation with the Government in order to stimulated the Indian National Movement. The Provisional Government was to be located within Burma.

On Oct. 23,1943, the Imperial Japanese Government announced its recognition of the newly created Provisional Government of Free India. The statement of the Japanese. Government is as follows. "Firmly beliving that the newly established Provisional Government of Free Indian with Mr. Subhas Chandra Bose as President makes a great advance towards the complete realization of an independent India which has been the aspiration of the Indians for many year we hereby announce that we shall extend recognition to the Provisional Government of Free India and to accord it all conceivable cooperation for attainment of its objects." The Board of Information also issued a statement regarding the above announcement. On the same day Burma also recognized the Provisional Government. "This was followed by the extension of recognition by Germany on Oct. 28 the Phillipine republic on Oct 29 China and Manchoukuo on Nov. 1 Italy on Nov 2, Thaliand on Nov. 17 and Croatia on Nov. 19.

Viewed from the standpoint of International Law the Provisional Government of Free India resembed the National Congress and its success.

Then, former Prime Minister general Hideki Tojo. the Japanese delegate, made the following announcement in connection with Dr. Ba Maw's motion and the speech of the head of the Provisional Government of Free India. "The imperial Japanese Government has repeatedly announced its intention of giving support to all movements for the temancipation of India from the Anglo-American yoke and for the realization of this aspiration. In view of the fact that the firm goundation of the Provisional Government of free India have been laid down and because of the growing patricle endeavors and unity of purposes on the part of the Indian who are now working towards their National Independence under the Provisional Government. I have the honor of declaring herewith that Japan is prepared to return shortly to the Provisional Government of Free India the Andaman and Nicobar Islands which are now under Japanese occupation as the first step toward the realization of India Independence.

At the time of the advance of the Japanese Force into India in the spring of 1944 the Imperial Headquarters announced on March 23 that our Army together with the Indian National army had entered Indian territory in the middle of March. Further communiques of the Imperial Headquarters on March 31 and April 8 also stated that our army together with the Indian National Army had been engaged in operations.

On the occasion of this advance into India. Bose issued a second statement on April 4 in which he declared that the Indian National Army. under the direction of the provisional Government of Free India which was established at Shonan on Oct. 21, 1943 by 3,000,000 Indians, had penetrated far into Indian territory after crossing the Indian frontier that the Provisional Government is the only legal Government requests the Indian nationals in the liberated areas to extend their cooperation and assistance to the Indian National Army and to all administrative officials appointed by the Provisional Government.

Later on Oct 15th, Prime Minister Tojo referred in his speech at the meeting of the mixed committee based on the Tripartite. Treaty among Japan Germany and Italy to the Indian problem and declared that the Japanese Army together with the Indian National Army, ahd crossed the Indian border and had marched into Indian territory and that the fact that the indian National Army, under the command of Bose, has been fighting the support of Burma and other number states of Greater East Asia. He said that with this, an opportunity for India'emancipation had presented itself and that our objective of freeing the oppressed peoples was about to be realized.

On November 1, Bose arrived in Japan in order to consolidate the close relations existing between the Provisional Government of Free India and Japan, and also to exchange views with the Japanese Government and military leaders. We have already noted, as a result of this, the Japanese Government decide to send a diplomatic envoy to the Provisional Government. Regarding this, the Board of Information issued the following statement of November 26 : "Following conversation, carried out between Subhas Chandra Bose, head of the Provisional Government of Free India, who has been staying in the capital, and the leaders of the Japanese Government, regarding the prosecution of the Greater East Asia War and means for promoting collaboration between the two governments, the Imperial Japanese Government had decided to dispatch a diplomatic envoy to the Provisional Government.

On the same day, Bose issued a statement in which he said, "It is a source of great joy for me to observe that formal diplomatic relations have been established between the Japanese Government and the Provisional Government of Free India and that the Japanese Government has decided to dispatch a diplomatic envoy to our Provisional Government."

This diplomatic envoy is to be installed by viture of Imperial decree Number 64, promulgated in 1917 which provides that, in case of the necessity of dispatching a diplomatic official abroad. In order to execute a special duty, a temporary extra-ordinary Ambassador or Minister may be installed until the execution of such duty may be completed.

41

Message by the Provisional Government of Azad Hind to the New Japanese Government[1]

27 July, 1944

On receipt of information on the formation of a new Cabinet with General Koise as Premier, Netaji Subhas Chandra Bose, Head of the State, Provisional Government of Azad Hind cabled congratulations and felicitations to General Koise and other Ministers of his Cabinet, and assured them of the determination of Indians in East Asia to continue to fight shoulder to shoulder with Nippon until victory is achieved.

His excellency Netaji Subhas Chandra Bose, Head of the State, Provisional Government of Azad Hind and Supreme Commander of the Azad Hind Fauj sent the followning message of felicitations to His Excellency Nainggandaw Adipadi Dr. Baw Maw, Head of State, Independent Burma, on the occasion of the Anniversary of Burmese Independence.

On behalf of freedom loving Indians, the Provisional Government of Free India, the I.N.A. and myself, I wish to offer my warmest congratulations to Your Excellency, to the Government and the people of Independent Burma on the occasion of the Anniversary of Burma's independence.

I wish to take this opportunity to express the heartiest thank of the Provisional Government of Free India, the Indian National Army and of myself to your Excellency to the Government and to the people of Independent Burma for all the valuable help that has been and is being rendered to us in our fight for the Independence of India.

I wish also to assure your Excellency that we, Indians, are irrevocable resolved to fight shoulder to shoulder with Independent Burma and Nippon, under all circumstances until our common enemies are curshed and our common Victory is achieved.

1. INA Trial Papers.

42

Rules of the Indian Independence League, and the Organisation of I.N.A. in Andamans[1]

30 July, 1944

Article 1—This league will be called the Indian Independence League, Andaman Branch and it will have its office at the so-Soncho's Office, Port Blair.

Article 2—This branch will be organised by Indians, residing in the South Andaman, who are fervently willing to attain the independence of India.

Article 3—This branch will maintain contact with the Headquarters of the Indian Independence League at Syonan and its chief objects will be to take measures to popularize the idea of Indian independence among the Indians in Andaman, to co-operate with the local Imperial Japanese Forces and to accelerate the independence of India.

Article 4—This branch will take undermentioned steps to execute the objects of Article 3.

(1) It will positively organise the independence movement.

(2) It will explain the real meaning of the war of Greater East Asia.

(3) It will propagate and spread the idea of Indian independence among the public.

(4) It will give mental and spiritual education to the young and adults (e.g. unity, honesty, equality etc.)

1. I.I.L. Papers. F. No. 45/3

(5) It will give relief and first aid in case of fire and air raid.

(6) It will give relief to the poor and distressed.

(7) It will enlighten the women and children..

Article 5—The undermentioned honorary officials will be appointed for the management of this branch.

President	1
Vice-President	1
Member	20 (about)

Article 6— In a public meeting, 50 candidates who have strong idea of Indian independence and who are gentlemen of judgement and nobility will be elected. Out of these 22 men will be selected and appointed as office bearers by the Minseibucho. The term of their office will be for 1 year but they can be re-elected.

Article 7—Three candidates will be elected for the post of the President from among the offcials, out of which the Minseibucho will select and appoint the President. Three candidates will be elected for the post of the Vice-President from among the officials, out of which the President will select the Vice-President and will appoint him after the approval of the Minseibucho.

Article 8—The President will manage the affairs of the league. The Vice-president will help the President in his work and will act for him in his absence. A meeting will be held once in every month when the President as a chairman will execute all the important matters. A special meeting can be called if the President thinks it necessary.

Article 9—This branch will request the following officers to act as advisors.

Minseibucho and All Kachos from Minseibu.

Assistant Commander-in-chief from Shireibu.

Shibutaicho from Army.

The advisors will give advice when consulted and thus help the President in carrying out his duties (in the management of the branch).

Article 10—The public meeting will be called twice in a year but a special meeting can be called if the President thinks it necessary.

Article 11—The expenses of the branch will be met out of the fees and contributions received from the members. The annual fee will be Rs. 1 only.

Article 12—In order to carry out the objects of articles 3 and 4 successfully the following departments will be organised. In addition to these, an Indian Independence Volunteer Corps will also be organised. The officials of the Branch will be distributed in all these departments and they will work according to the instructions from the President.

(i) General Affairs Department.

(ii) Propaganda Department.

(iii) Relief Department.

(iv) Youth Department.

(v) Women Department

Article 13—Every department will work as defined below:-

(i) General Affairs Department - The cashier will give report on the income and expenses of the branch twice a year in the public meeting.

(ii) Propaganda Department - (a) Spread the idea of Indian independence and the Japanese language.

(b) Real explanation of the East Asia co-prosperity sphere and other propaganda.

(iii) Relief Department - (a) Give relief in case of actual fighting and fina.

(b) Give relief to the poor familes in distress.

(iv) Youth Department - Start movement of the youths and adults.

(v) Females Department - Enlighten the women and children.

Article 14—The organisation of the volunteer corps will be made as follows :-

(i) This corps will be organised from those Indians of South Andaman, who are very enthusiastic about the independence of India and who are able bodied between the ages of 20 and 45.

(ii) At present about 100 men will be selected from the undermentioned villages for enrolment.

A. Abderdeen Town	25
B. „ Village	20
C. Phoenix Bay	10
D. Delaneypore	10
E. Junglighat	15
F. Deane Street	10
G. South Point	10

(iii) The leader of the corps will be selected by the President from the officials and will be appointed after the approval of the Minseibucho. Each group will contain 10 volunteers. Each group will select its own head from the group. Such 3 or 4 groups will make a company. The head of the company will be selected by the heads of the groups mutually. Assistant heads will also be selected. They will officiate for the heads when they are absent.

(iv) The leader will get orders from the President of the League. The other heads will get their orders from their seniors and lead their subordinates.

(v) The corps will receive systematic mass training on fixed days and will mutually cultivate the unity of mind and body and discipline. It will always be prepared for the event.

(vi) Band parties will be organised in the corps

(vii) All the members of the corps will have badges.

(viii) Indian National Flag will be the flag of the volunteer corps.

Supplementary Rules—

1. January to December will be the calendar year for the above rules.
2. The term of the members for the first term will finish in the end of the year 2604.
3. The general affairs department will have the list of the members and corps always ready at the office.
4. The volunteer corps will have the list of the members always ready.
5. The organisation of the branch will be as shown in the table below.

Indian Independence League.

President Advisors.

Loganandan on his Position in the Andamans[1]

31 July, 1944

Your letter of the 21st June was received on the 15th instant.

1. Transference of Departments. "Minseibu" is the Department which is directly responsible for all the care of the Civilian population in Andamans; hence all my work is wholly linked up with this department.

   (i) I am the Adviser to the Head (Minseibucho);

   (ii) Captain Mr. Alvi is in charge of Education and volunteers;

   (iii) 2nd Lieutenant Subha Singh is attached to Finance and Propaganda;

   (iv) 2nd Lieutenant Iqbal is attached to the Police.

   It is hoped that each of us would not miss the opportunities placed at his disposal to make himself useful, and later indispensable. A good deal of mutual good will and cooperation is essential and this shall not be working from our side.

   Taking condition and circumstances as they stand or could be visualised in the near future, I am of opinion that transference of Departments should not be speeded up. Hence the need for further funds would not arise in a hurry.

2. Spying. As indicated in my previous reports handling of this problem is the most important as it adversely affects all our activities here. I have had detailed discussions with the Authorities, and we do hope to succeed in reducing it to the minimum, or not completely controlling it, by intensive propaganda and local executive action.

---

1. F. 601/7510/H.S.

I am pleased to report that the most recent case of June, wherein 37 were arrested (including witnesses) terminated in the release of all, except one who was sentenced to seven years' imprisonment.

This favourable judgement has dispelled the gloom and is bound to cheer up the people to greater war efforts.

3. Unit of INA and Azad Hind Dal. Owing to extreme shortage of labour of all kinds and greater shortage of persons of the fighting fit class raising of a Unit of the I. N. A., is out of the question. This applies equally to A. H. Dal.

The Andaman Administrative Advisory Council.

4. The members of the above council consist of ten Officials and ten non officials of all classes of interests are well represented. It is purely an advisory body with a selfimposed restriction on the freedom or speech, in spite of apparent official encouragement. They can become more useful with increase in their personal liberties.

5. Finance. Expanditure incurred up to the end of July is approximately Rs. 3,000.00. The staff has not drawn any allowance, as it is not required for use locally.

Further Funds for transferred subjected will not be required for some good time.

6. The Monthly Teachers' Conference, the Assembly Meeting and the Provisional Government Day were held as usual.

7. We are proud of the achievements of our Army earning the appreciation of the Nippon Army being in itself an achievement. The Staff and I do feel sincerely that we are left out from the more thrilling excitements of the front line.

8. Our needs are small, and we are sufficiently self contained. There is no longer any need for crockery and cutlry or medicines, as we have salvaged sufficiently for our daily needs.

9. I am writing as a separate notes to the I. I. League headquarter at Syonan to conform to the promise of a more regular despatch of newsprint, which we greatly look forward to.

10. My health has improved quite to my satisfaction. All the staff are keeping fit.

11. With the termination of the monsoon we expect to hear of something really happening up there.

44

Special Order of the Day for the Temporary Postponement of the Operation[1]

14 August, 1944

Comrades of Azad Hind Fauj,

In the middle of March this year, Advanced units of the Azad Hind Fauj, fighting shoulder to shoulder with their valiant allies, the Imperial Nippon Forces, crossed the Indo-Burma border and the fight for India's liberation thereupon commenced on Indian Soil.

The British authorities, by ruthlessly exploiting India for over a century and bringing foreign soldiers to fight their battles for them, had managed to put up a mighty force against us. After crossing the Indo-Burma border, our forces inspired by the righteousness of our cause, encountered these numerically superior and better equipped, but heterogenous and disunited forces of the enemy and defeated them in every battle.

Our units, with their better training and discipline and unshakable determination to do or die on the path of India's freedom, soon established their superiority over the enemy, whose morale deteriorated with each defeat.

Fighting under the most trying conditions, our officers and men displayed such courage and heroism that they have earned the praise of everybody. With their blood and sacrifice, these heroes have established traditions which the future soldiers of free India shall have to uphold.

All preparations had been completed and the stage had been set for the final assault on Imphal, when torrential rains overtook us and to carry Imphal by an assault was rendered a tactical impossibility.

Handicapped by the elements, we were forced to postpone our offensive. After the postponment of the offensive, it was found disadvantageous for our troops to continue to hold the line that we then

1. I.N.A. Trial Papers.

had. For securing a more favourable defensive position, it was considered advisable to withdraw our troops. In accordance with this decision, our troops have withdrawn to a more favourable defensive position. We shall now utilise the period of lull in completing our preparations, so that with the advent of better weather, we may be in a position to resume our offensive.

Having beaten the enemy once in several sectors of the front, our faith in our final victory and in the destruction of the Anglo-American forces of aggresion has increased tenfold. As soon as all our preporations are complete, we shall launch a mighty offensive against enemies once again. With the superior fighting qualities, dauntless courage and unshakable devotion to duty of our officers and men, victory shall surely be ours.

May the souls of those heroes, who have fallen in this campaign inspire us to still nobler deeds of heroism and bravery in the next phase of India's War of Liberation.

JAI HIND.

(Sd.) SUBHAS CHANDRA BOSE
Supreme Commander,
Azad Hind Fauj.
Burma

45

P. K. Sahgal to M. Z. Kiani Promising Re-inforcement[1]

20 August, 1944

I received your report , sent from Yeu, on 13rd August 1944, together with a copy of Col. Shah Nawaz's report (incidentally original of that report has never been received here yesterday) and I immediately took up the reports to Netaji. Yesterday evening Netaji had a conference with Lt. Gen. Ishoda concerning the matter mentioned in your report, I was also present during the discussion. Throughout the conference, although he promised to send telegrams here and there, it was quite apparent that either he (Gen. Ishoda) could or would do little.

Ever since, the Japanese have decided to go on the defensive, I feel a change in their attitude, which I find very difficult to explain, may be you can explain it better than I can. Anyhow, one thing is certain that we can expect little help from Nippon authorities in Rangoon. You will have to tackle Hayachi Butai to solve most of your problems. We even offered to send a steam launch from Rangoon to relieve a Nippon steam launch in the front line, which could be despathched immediately to Yirwam to evacuate the four hundred men of No, A Grla. Regiment. But even that they did not agree to.

We have managed to collect about six lorries, which are being touched up in our workhouse and as soon as they are ready, they shall be sent forward to help solve the transport problem. Another emergency hospital to function in Mandalay has also been organised and as soon as we can get some equipment from the Japanese, it shall be sent there.

Arrangements are also being made to buy enough cloth to give two sets of clothing to all our men coming back and a Boot shop is also being organised to make enough boots for whole of No. 1 Division. Our main difficulty is to get the materials, they are not available at any price. We,

---

1. I.N.A. Trial Papers.

here, are truing to do our best, which is mighty little, to help the people coming back. Fèeling of impotence and frustration for not being able to do anything to lessen the suffering or our comrades is terrible.

Lt. Col. Habib-ur-Rahman has gone to receive the new area where Nos. 1 and 2 Div. are going to be sent, and he is expected back here any day. As soon as he returns I shall try and move up to see if I could be of any help.

Please give my best regards to Inayat, Hassan and Arshad.

46

P. K. Sahgal to M. Z. Kiani Regarding Deployment of I. N. A. and Supply Position[1]

21 August, 1944

Comd. No. 1 Division

Sub:—Situation Report.

Reference your report, dated 13th August 1944 sent from You to rear H. Qrs. No. 1 Div.; and forwarded on to the Supreme Comd. under Rear H. Qrs. No. 1 Div. No. 77/8/44, dated 15th July, and the report submitted by Lt. Col. Shah Nawaz Khan, Comd. No. 1 Div Grla. Regt.

*1. The Supreme Commander took up the matter with the Chief of the Hikari Kikan, who has promised to take the following action in the matter:—

(a) Approach the Mori Head Qrs. to allow No. 2 M. T. Coy I. N. A. to retain their lorries until the evacuation of No. A Div. troops is completed.

(b) Send a telegram to make arrangements to supply rations to 150 men in Mawlik, if these men have not already been withdrawn.

(c) Send a telegram to Hayashi Butai to try and arrange the withdrawal of 250 men from Sittong by boats.

*2. It is not possible to send any boats from here to Tirwan and it also appears that the Yeu River is in floods and transport up-stream is most difficult, however, Chief of Hikari Kikan has promised to take up the matter with proper authorities to arrange for the evacuation of these 400 men of No. 1 Grla. Regt. in Tirawan. If it is not possible to evacuate these men at the present moment, arrangements shall be made to send ration supplies and medicines to them.

1. I. N. Trial Papers . M. Z. Kiani was Commander No. 1 Division I. N. A.

3. The Chief of Hikari Kikan pointed out that by the time reports from No. 1 Div. are received in Rangoon, it is sometimes too late to take any action, therefore, he suggested that Comd. has agreed to this suggestion and wishes Comd. No. 1 Div should stay near the H. Qrs. of Hayashi Army, who may be able to help in solving our problems. The Supreme Comd. has agreed to this suggestion and wishes Comd. No. 1 Div. to establish his H. Qrs. in the vicinity of the H. Qrs. of Hayashi Butai.

(Sd.) P. K. SAHGAL,
Lt. Col.,
for Assistant Chief of Staff.

Copy to :—
H.Qrs. Supreme Command.,
Rear H.Qrs. No. 1 Division.

* I have just been informed that the Hikari Kikan have already taken action on these points.

(Sd.) P. K. SAHGAL
Lt. Col.

47

Bose to Kiani Assuring all Help[1]

29 August, 1944

Colonel M. Z. Kiani,
Commander, No.1 Div.,
AZAD HIND FAUJ.
Jai Hind

Your telegram of the 23rd instant, brought by messenger, reached me on the 27th. I cannot say that my anxiety has been allayed. On the contrary, I am still very anxious about what is going on at Sittaung and at R. H. Tirawan.

Ever since I got your letter (along with that of Lt. Col. Shah Nawaz) from Yeu, we have left no stone unturned at this end. Lt. Colonel Habib-Ur-Rahman, who left for Mandalay on the 26th will tell you something of what we have been trying to do here. But, I am afraid, that what we have been able to do is not much. We have been able to get a few lorries but unfortunately they are not yet quite road-worthy. As soon as they are, they will be sent up to be used between Sagaing and Shewgyin. I hope to be able to get sixs in all, of which only three are now in our possession. Two motor-boats, donated by Indians, are expected tomorrow and we hope to send them up soon, if no difficulties are raised from the Japanese side. Whatever we can spare in the way of Medicine, blankets, mosquito nets, etc., have either been sent up already or will be leaving immediately. A few days ago, two wagon-loads were sent. Today, one and a half wagon loads are leaving. Mr. Paramanand, before he left for Mandalay, was fully instructed by me about purchasing any food supplies available there or anywhere within reach in North Burma.

In your telegram of the 23rd, there is a reference to the need of fresh Officers,. I would have sent up a few without further reference to you. But

1. *Ibid.*

since No. 4 Guerilla Regiment is there, as well as your Rear Headquarters, it may not be necessary to send any Officers from here at present. But if you need any, do not hesitate to ask for them and I shall gladly send as many as could be spared from here. Without any further reference to you, I am arraging to send up as many Doctors as I can from here by reducing the staff here to the very minimum. These Doctors may be used either for the new hospital in the vicinity of Mandalay or they may be sent up to Yeu, Akibono and Kalewa with medical supplies.

Priors to this, I sent Lt. Col. Rai and Lt. Col. Raju with instructions to go up as far as circumstances will permit, and render what help they can on the medical side.

Now I have sent Lt. Col. Habib-ur-Rahman with the same instructions. I hope he will be able to go up as far as Shwegyin.

With regard to front-line needs, the Indian public here is not only sympathetic but generous. Consequently, you can rest assured that whatever is possible to get, will be procured. Since our stock of Blankets had run short, we made a house to house collection and got quite a good response. Now we are trying to make a house to house collection of Tinned Milk. My only regret is that transport is the prime need today and in that we can do little.

Wishing you all the best and with the most cordial greetings.

"JAI HIND"

48

P. K. Sahgal to Hikari Kikan for Deployment of I.N.A.[1]

31 August, 1944.

No. 103/2/11/G.,
Rear "H. Qrs., II. S. C.
A. H. F. Burma

Most Secret
Immediate

To,
H. Qrs.
Hikari Kikan, Rangoon.

Sub:—Movement of troops.

Lt. Col. Takagi of H. Qrs. Hikari Kikan gave the following advance information to Lt. Col. P. K. Sahgal of Rear H. Qrs. No. 2 Supreme Command, A. H. F. on 30th August 1944:—

The H. Qrs. of the Mori Army are going to issue orders to the following effect in the near future:—

The following units of the I. N. A. at present under the command of the Hayashi Army shall revert to the command of H. Qrs.

Supreme Command, A. H. F.:—

(a) No. 1 Division less 1st Bn. of 1 Grla Regt.

(b) No. 2 Engineering Coy.

(c) No. 3 Engineering Coy.

(d) No. 1 M. T. Coy.

(e) No. 11 M. T. Coy.

(f) No. 2 Hospital

(g) No. 1 Medical Staging Section.

---

1. *Ibid.*

2. These units shall revert to the command of H. Qrs. Supreme Command, I. N. A. on the day of their arrival in Mandalay.

3. The future location of I. N. A. troops shall be as under:—

   (a) No. 2 Div. Will move to the Pakaku area.

   (b) Two Regiments from No. 1 Div will be in Myingyan area.

   (c) Remainder of No. 1 Division units will be in Pyinmena area.

4. Supply points for these units will be at Myingyan, Pakakku and Pyinmena.

5. The Provision of medicines and building of barracks in these areas shall be the responsibility of the Nippon Garrison Commander of Mandalay.

6. No. 2 Hospital, Menywa, as soon as situation permits, will start evacuating its patients and when all the patients have been evacuated the Hospital will leave that area and move to a place to be selected by the H. Qrs., Supreme Command, A. H. F.

7. Wherever the accommodation is not available new barracks shall be built. The H. Qrs., Mori Army takes the responsibilities of supplying the necessary materials and funds, but the construction work shall have to be carried out under the direction of Engineers of the I. N. A.

With reference to the above information, it is requested that when the final and executive orders are issued by the Mori Army, administrative details should also be worked out and special instructions issued on the subject at the same time.

It is considered most necessary that information on the following points should be included in the administrative instructions:—

(i) The method of sending supplies from the Nippon supply points to I. N. A. Units.

(ii) The amount of material that shall be provided at each place for building of barracks.

(iii) The amount of money that shall be placed at the disposal of I. N. A. for carrying out these construction works.

(iv) When will the Nos. 1, 2 and 4 Eng. Coy. of I. N. A. be available to be sent to the areas where the construction work has to be carried out.

(v) What other facilities for this construction work may be expected from the Nippon side.

(vi) What shall be the means of communication between H. Qrs. Supreme Command, I. N. A. and No. I and II Divisions of the I. N. A.

(viii) What shall be the means of communication between the troops of No. 1 Div. situated in Pyinmena area, and other troops in Myingyan area.

(Sd.) P.K. SAHGAL
Lt. Col.,
Asstt. Chief of Staff.

49

Bose to Kiani Assuring him Necessary Medical Supplies for the Wounded I. N. A. Soldiers[1]

3 September, 1944

Col. M. Z. Kiani,
Commander
No. 1 Division,
A. H. F.
Jai Hind,

Your telegram of the 7th July from Chamol, No. 078, and your telegram of the 17th July No. 082 reached me by post on the 31st August. The actual telegrams never reached me. Your telegram of the 26th August, No. 22, also reached me on the 31st August.

You have probably misunderstood my intention regarding the loacation of your Headquarters. You are the best judge as to where your Headquarters should be located for the time being. I wrote to you about remaining near the Hayashi Headquarters because in the discussions with the Hikari Kikan Headquarters here we thought that since we could do little at this end, perhaps you could do more up by remaining close to the Hayashi Headquarters. Please do not have any hesitation in establishing your Headquarters wherever you find it most suitable and beneficial to the formations under your command.

Your telegrams have been immediately attended to in the case of matters which depend on the Hikari Kikan, or on Hayashi Command or Mori command — though we have done our best to move them I cannot tell you what resutls will actually follow. In those matters which rest with us, we are doing our very best. Necessary supplies., including medical supplies, have been sent up and will continue to be sent up in future, so far as our resources permit. After reducing the medical staff here to the

---

1. *Ibid.*

minimum we are sending up some more Doctors. Two lorries are in stock and if and when they are made road worthy, they too will be sent at once. We hope to be able to send up two motor-boats, but I can not tell you when they will actually reach their destination. These efforts namely in the matter of supplies and transport- will continue in full swing. I hope at Tirawan is great. I am equally anxious about conditions at Sittaung. The ony relief I have is that judging from enemy news broadcasts, enemy troops are still five miles from Sittaung. I hope this will give time for our men to evacuate.

As soon as you have news about Sittaung, and Tirawan, please send me a messenger.

The lorries that we are sending today and hope to send in future are meant for front line needs. But if you find transport arragements between Ye-u and Shwegyin are perfectly satisfactory, you may divert them, to other stretches of the road. So far as these lorries are concerned, I wanted Lt. Col. Habib-Ur-Rahman to take them upto Akibobno and beyond if necessary. Consequently, if he is still in Mandalay, when the lorries reach there, it would be desirable to ask him as to how he would like to use them. I have told Lt. Col. Habib-ur-Rahman to go up as far as possible - even beyond Kalewa.

Lt. Col. Sahgal is writing to you on other points I hope that your health will now steadily improve. Please convey my most cordial greetings to the Regiments Commanders and Officers and men who are within your reach.

With the most cordial greetings,

"JAI HIND".

50

Indian Minorities in South And East Asia. The Background of the Indian Independence Movement (Extract)[1]

8 September, 1944

Table of Contents

1. The above survey report was prepared by the office of Strategic Services U.S. Government Record Group 226 U.S. National Archives, Maryland USA.

C. Indian Organizations

D. Early History of the Indian Independence League in Thailand and its Founders

III. Indians in Malaya

A. Population Statistics

B. Principal Occupations

C. Indian Associations

D. Indians under British Administration in Malaya

IV. Indians in Indochina

V. Indians in Netherlands East Indies

IV. Indians in China

A. Population Statistics

B. Indians in China and Indian Nationalism

C. Indian Organizations

VI. Indians in Japan

A. Indian Population of Japan

B. Indian Revolutionaries of Japan

1. Maulvi Mohammed Barkatulla

2. Hariharnath Thulal Atal

3. Raja Mahendra Pratap

4. Rashbehari Bose

5. Anand Mohan Sahay

C. Indian Organizations in Japan

VII. Indian National Congress and Indians overseas

Summary

The Indian Independence Leagues in South-East Asia, as far as manpower is concerned, have in several areas a large population upon which to draw for membership. Indians are most numerous in Burma and

Malaya, where they form a considerable proportion of the laboring class. There is also a fairly large group in the N.E.I. In Thailand and Indochina the Indians are a rather small, compact merchant community with the laboring class a relatively insignificant minority in the Indian group. The Indians in China are settled chiefly in Hongkong and Shanghai. Their number is small and for the most part they are former members of the police force or army who remained in China when their term of service was completed. The Indian population of Japan consisted of a small group of merchants settled in the principal cities. There were in addition a number of students and a few exiled Indian patriots

In all of these areas Indian males greatly outnumber the females, and a large proportion of them are between the ages of 15 and 35. Although the population of Indians born in the country of enumeration is increasing, Indians in all countries of South— East Asia are largely immigrants who return after a period to the country of their birth. In 1931 for example, four-fifths of the Indian population of Malaya has been born outside the country, the figure for Burma in the same year was 62 per cent. A certain index to the immigrant nature of the population, and its temporary character, is the sex ratio.

There is no indication that the majority of those Indians took any interest in Indian political problems. In Burma, before its separation from India, there was a provincial committee of the Indian National Congress. It is probable that members were drawn from the professional, educated classes among the Indians of Rangoon, and that the laborers who formed the bulk of the population had no part in the organization. On the whole, Indian organizations in Burma and Malaya had as their objective the economic and social advancement of Indians in those countries. In Thailand and Indochina, Indian societies were probably business associations or social clubs. Certainly in Thailand and perhaps in Indochina as well there were a few Indians who where interested in the Indian struggle for freedom but they seem to have made little headway among their fellow countrymen.

The situation in China seems to have been somewhat different. The Indians formed a small, compact group largely belonging to the Sikh community. A revolutionary movement, dating from the years of the last war, fed by resentment against the British and influenced by Chinese nationalist activities, in present-day Indian nationalism with its creed of nonviolence and civil-disobedience, but in the older terrorism which long ago ceased to play a part in Indian politics. In recent years, however, the activities of the Indians in Shanghai have been increasingly inspired by the Indian National Congress.

Japan has a smaller Indian population than any other country in East Asia. Nevertheless the presence in Japan of a small group of Indian revolutionaries and the fact that they have received encouragement and support from the Japanese has made Japan the center of Indian nationalist activities in eastern Asia. Several associations were devoted to the cause of Indian Independence and the degree of organization for this purpose surpassed anything achieved or attempted in other countries of Eastern Asia.

It seems clear that the Indian Independence Leagues have not been built up on the basis of pre-existing nationalist organisations in South-East Asia. Nor is it likely that there was any widespread demand on the part of Indians in this area that the war be made the occasion of obtaining India's freedom, although a few Indians in Japan, such as Rashbehari Bose, probably regard the present war as the opportunity missed in 1914-18.

The Independence Leagues are, then, the creation of the Japanese. These is very little reliable information regarding the degree to which the Japanese have been successful in enlisting the support of Indians in this movement. There were doubtless in each country a few Indians ready to respond to appeals to their patriotism. It is likely that Japanese anti-British propaganda would prove effective especially in Burma and Malaya; and "Asia for the Asiatics" is an old and attractive slogan throughout the area. Pro-Japanese sentiments dating from the Russo-Japanese war provided a basis upon which to erect Japanese aid, of national status for India. There is no reason to believe that politically intelligent Indians in the area would have had many qualms about accepting much aid, and if Japan's ultimate inentions were ever called into question, it is probable that few Indians would have been found to prefer British to Japanese domination. Furthermore, in the early years of the war Japan appeared to have established herself firmly in south Eastern Asia. Britain's defeat in Indian must have seemed to those Indians who were informed as to the course to events, a matter of months merely. Expediency demanded that they cooperate with the Japanese. It is probable also that the Japanese resorted to coercion when persuasion failed. It has been reported, for instance, that the Indian merchants in Bangkok were forced, by threat of boycott, to provide funds for the League, and there have been statements to the effect that prisoners of war volunteered for service in the Independence Army to escape torture at the hands of their captors.

A notice in the *Shanghai Times*, 22 January 1944, states "In order to make a complete official list, all Indian nationals who have not yet registered with the Indian Independence League are urgently requested to register before the end of the month, otherwise much inconvenience may arise to the defaulters." It would seem that the Indians of Shanghai have not been in a hurry to join the League and the mention of "inconvenience" suggests that enrollment is not altogether a voluntary matter.

The appearance of Subhas Bose on the scene gave a great impetus to the movement. A former Congress President with a large following in India, an able leader, widely considered to be a sincere patriot, he would have had little difficulty in persuading even the hesitant that an opportunity was at hand to drive the British from India. Generally speaking, it may be concluded that the Japanese have successful in mobilizing Indian opinion in their favor.

Indian Minorities in South and East Asia: The Background of the Indian Independence Movement

Introduction

In all countries of South and East Asia now occupied or controlled by the Japanese the Indian residents have organized Independence Leagues, the purpose of which is to free India, with the aid of the Japanese, from British domination. These Leagues were established under Japanese, from British domination. These Leagues were established under Japanese sponsorship in the early days of the war, and by June 1942, when representatives met for a conference at Bangkok, a large membership was claimed for each country. Increased activity followed the arrival of Subhas Bose a year later. Chief in importance was the formation of the Independence Army, composed of Indian volunteers.

In order to assess the potentialities of this movement, it is essential to have available the facts concerning the Indian populations of these areas: vital statistics; social and economic position; the degree to which Indians were organized before the war, and for what purpose; contacts with nationalist and other groups in India; attitudes towards Japan. The following account of Indians in South and East Asia attempts, insofar as possible, to provide the facts.

I. Indians in Burma

A. Population Statistics

Politically a part of India until 1937, Burma had a large Indian population. According to the most recent estimate available, Indians in

Burma numbered 1,017,825. The 1941 figure would be somewhat higher. Since roughly 400,000 Indians escaped from Burma at the time of the Japanese invasion, the present Indian population is probably between six and eight hundred thousand.

1. Geographic Distribution. The following account of the distribution of the Indians in Burma is taken form the 1931 census. At that time 93 per cent of the total number of Indians were concentrated in the delta, coast and center subdivisions. Forty-two per cent lived in Rangoon and Akyab district. In Rangoon, Indians formed 53 per cent of the population and in Akyab district, 33 per cent. In northern Burma the number of Indians was small except for Myitkyina district where there were 17,000; a larger number of these were Gurkhas who had settled there, and in addition there was a considerable number of Indians among the military police.

2. Racial Affiliation. The following table classifies Indian by race.

Race	*Number of persons*	*Number per thousand persons*
Bengali	65,211	64
Chittagonian	252,152	248
Hindustani	174,967	172
Tamil	149,888	147
Telugu	159,759	157
Oriya	62,585	61
Others	153,263	151

"Others" include 39,532 Gurkhas and 28,289 Punjabis.

The largest single group is the Chittagonian, of which 74 per cent were located in Akyab district. Over 50 per cent of the Indian population were from North India. Tamils and Telugus together constituted less than 33 per cent.

3. Birthplace. The majority of Indians in Burma are immigrants to the country. In 1931, 62 per cent of the total number of Indians in Burma has been born outside the country. However, the district of Akyab presents a striking contrast to conditions elsewhere in Burma: in that district only 21 per cent had been born outside Burma. There is also a considerable difference in the percentages for males and for females. For Burma as a whole 72 per cent of the males had been born outside Burma, while only 36 per cent of the Indian females were foreign born. Here again Akyab is not typical of Burma as a whole: 30 per cent of the males, and 7 per cent of the females were born outside Burma.

It is interesting to contrast the racial classification of Indian immigrants with that of the Indian population of Burma as a whole.

Race	*Persons*
Bengali	39,809
Chittagonian	83,511
Hindustani	125,054
Oriya	57,906
Tamil	84,327
Telugu	131,727
Others	107,757

It will be noted while the largest single group of Indians in Burma is composed of Chittagonians, the Telugus form the largest single group among Indian immigrants to Burma,

4. Sex and Age Grouping. The sex ratio for Indians in Burma in typical of an immigrant population. In 1931 there were 387 females per thousand males. For the Indian immigrant group considered separately the sex ratio was 191. The various racial groups among the immigrants differ considerably in this respect. The Tamils had the highest sex ratio with 43 females per 100 males; the figure for the Telugus was 21; for Bengalis 13; for Oriyas 3.

The age distribution per 10,000 Indians indicated in the following table. The district of Akyab is omitted in the calculations since "figures for the whole province would be representative neither of the Akyab district nor of the remainder of the province.

	Whole Province less Akyab district	
Age Group	*Males*	*Female*
0-5	565	1,732
5-10	535	1,292
10-15	576	1,086
15-20	1,023	1,030
20-30	3,051	2,227
30-40	2,389	1,363
40 and over	1,861	1,269

5. Religious Groups. The following table ciassifies Indians by religion.

	Actual Population			
Religion	*Persons*	*Males*	*Females*	*Per 1,000 Persons*
Hindu	565,609	425,389	140,220	556
Muslim	396,594	271,514	125,080	390

Religion	*Persons*	*Males*	*Females*	*Per 1,000 Persons*
Buddhist	12,600	9,778	2,822	12
Christian	30,135	18,015	12,120	30
Sikh	10,896	7,882	3,014	11
Others	1,991	1,333	658	2

It is important to note that over half the Indian population is Hindu by religion. Muslims form the only other large group. Another fact of some importance is the large number of female Muslims compared to the proportion of females to males in the other religious groups. It appears that this is largely due to the inclusion of Akyab district in the enumeration; in this district, where many of the Indian Muslims are permanent residents, the sex ration is 787, while it is only 246 for the rest of the country. The overall figures for Muslim female given in the table above are therefore misleading: with the exception of Akyab district the proportion among Indian Muslim is one female to every four males, while among Indian Hindus, there is one female per 3 males.

6. Occupation. The following table shows the chief occupations of Indian in Burma.

Occupations	*Indians Born in Burma*	*Indian Born Outside Burma*
Exploitation of animals and vegetation	67,366	108,842
Exploitation of minerals	402	14,350
Industry	7,178	97,489
Transport	5,510	96,020
Trade	9,151	87,060
Public Force	617	13,378
Public Administration	1,012	12,810
Professions and Liberal Arts	1,593	8,825
Persons living on their income	283	1,546
Domestic Service	2,339	21,687

The table given below brings out more clearly the difference with respect to occupation between Indians born in Burma and those born outside. The distribution by occupation of 1,000 workers is indicated.

Occupations	*Indians Born in Burma*	*Indian Born Outside Burma*
Production of raw materials	486	249
Preparation and supply of material substances	374	578

Public Administration and Liberal Arts	55	75
Miscellaneous	86	98

It is possible to make a rough classification of racial groups by occupation. Bengalis as a rule are employed in government service or work in a clerical capacity, while some are shopkeepers or traders; in addition a number of Bengalis are mechanics. The Chittagionians are engaged in small craft traffic and furnish labour for ship and launch crew; many of this group works in mills and dockyards. The Tamils are usually engaged in agriculture or work in the rice mills, but middle class members of this group are employed in various clerical activities. A small but very important minority among the Tamils are the Chettyars, the moneylenders and the principal financing agency in the country. Telugus for the most part work in mills and factories, though many are rickshaw pullers, porters and carries. Hindustanis from the United Provinces serve as watchmen and messengers, and many are petty vendors. The Oriyas work on railroads and in the Public Works Department on road construction; some are engaged in mills and dockyards. Gurkhas are generally cultivators, though some are to be found in domestic service. Punjabis work largely in railway and motor workshops, dockyards and foundries as mechanics and overseers.

7. Summary. The Indian population in Burma is largely an immigrant group composed chiefly of people from the southern and northeastern part of India. The Indians are for the most part concentrated in southern and central Burma, and nearly one half of them were in Akyab and Rangoon. Both the age grouping , which shows a majority between the age grouping, which shows a majority between the ages of 15 and 40, and the sex ratio, with a great preponderance of males, are typical of an immigrant group. Over half of the Indians are Hindus, and Muslims whom are largely located in Akyab district, are next in respect to numbers of immigrants are engaged in administrative and professional activities.

B. Relations between Burmans and Indians

A fact of outstanding importance in considering the position of Indians is Burma is the hostility of the Burmans towards the Indian immigrants and residents in the country. This hostility has an economic base and has been intensified since 1930 due largely to the economic depression and to the fact that rising Burman nationalism has tended to make capital of economic grievances and the exploitation of Burman resources by foreign elements. This hostility was never veiled and in 1938 severe riots broke out in which Indian lives and property suffered at the hands of the Burmans. The Riot Inquiry Committee in discussing the causes of the disturbances drew attention to the fact that while in 1930 Indian Chettiars occupied area in the thirteen principal rice-growing districts of Lower Burma, in 1937 they had acquired possession of 25percent. This did not take into account the areas over which the Chettiars held mortgages. The city of Rangoon and its business was to a large extent in Indian hands. Indian owners and landlord paid over 55 percent of the total taxes of the city, and all large private bazaars were Indian-owned. The depression resulted in a drain on the resources of the poorer class of Burmans who were forced to turn to industrial where Indians were already established, and this led to additional dissatisfaction.

Another grievance against the Indians was the problem created by intermarriage between Burman woman and Indian men. Objections on the part of Burmans to such marriages were based "sometimes on the ground of their race purity of the Burmese nation, sometimes on the fear that mixed marriage may tend to remove a portion of the population from Burmese nationality and from the national religion and sometimes on the ground that it results in material hardship." Under Burmese law a widow fares better than either Muslim or Hindu law. The question of the Burmans woman's status was also involved; since laws pertaining to marriage differed, a Buddhist Burman woman might consider herself a married women under Buddhist law, but would bot be so considered under either Hindu or Muslim law.

Burmese nationalism has made an issue of the position of Indians in Burma since 1916. When the separation of Burma from Indian came up for discussion in 1932-33 " the whole question of Indian in Burma was thrown into the political arena, attention became focussed upon it, and the whole question... received a prominence and a reality which is never before assumed and possibly does not deserve...... It was continuously represented as a menace to Burma's national life and even to the Buddhist religion."

Indians in Burma, and this applies to those domiciled in the country rather than to the shifting immigrant population, were conscious of being a racial minority and jealous of their status as a separate political group. Indians had formed a separate electorate as early as 1922, and at the Round Table Conference in London in 1931-32 the Indian delegates demanded that separate electorates be continued to safeguard their interests. This insistence and the separate electorate in the present constitution were contrary to Burman desires.

C. Indian Organization. It is probably a safe assumption that members of the labouring classes had few definite opinions regarding political affairs in India. The majority of the educated Indians in Burma appears to have sympathized with the aims of the Indian National Congress. With few exception the Indian owned and edited newspapers were pro-Congress Committee, the members of which were nearly all Indians, and delegates regularly attended the annual conference of the Congress. After the separation of Burma, the provincial committee was abolished and in its place the Burma Committee was set up to work for the freedom of Burma. This committee continued to elect members to the All India Congress Committee and in 1939 two Indians and one Burman, All from Rangoon, Were elected.

Other Indian organization including the All Burman Muslim league, and the Burmans Provincial Hindu Sabha, founded in 1930. It is not known whether or not these were branches of National organizations in India; the All Burman Muslim League appears to have has some connection with the All India Muslim league, but probably was not directly affiliated with it. The Young Chulia Muslim League was an organization of Tamil Muslim from Madras. Another organization was the All Burma South Indian Association. Most of the groups appear to have been concerned mainly with the advancement of Indians in Burma, and the improvement of their social and economic status.

II. Indians in Thailand

A. Population Statistics

It is impossible to state accurately the number of Indians living in Thailand. According to the 1931 Census of Thailand, Indians and Malays together numbered 379,618. Since 272,484 of these were located in Pattani circle, an area adjoining Malaya, presumably the great majority of the total number are Malays. Dr. Lanka Sundaram, who spent some time investigating the condition of Indians in Thailand, estimated that there were 100,000 in the country. His figure included Burmese Indians and Karens not even if allowance is made for a possible total of 50,000 Karens this figure seems high. A brief account of Indians in Thailand in the *Indian Review* gives 10,000 as the total Indian population. The Indian Year Book for 1940-41 states that thereare appoximately 5,000 Indians in Thailand and the some figure is given in the Indians Abroad Directory by S.A. Waiz. Some figures from the *Statistical Year Book of the Kingdom of Siam* may bee considered as evidence favoring acceptance of the last estimate as more nearly correct. The number of Indians arriving at the Port of Bangkok from 1918 to 1933 are listed in table 18. The figures vary from 708 in 1919-20 to 293 in 1919-32; generally from 300 to 500 Indians per year entered Thailand during this period. Table 19 lists departure from Bangkok during the same period. The number of Indian leaving Thailand by the port of Bangkok varied from 250 in 1927-28 to 600 in 1925-26. Table 20 lists arrivals of aliens at A Bangkok, and presumably included persons arriving overland, probably from Malaya, as well as by sea. In 1931-32 the number of Indian arrivals was 1,333; in 1932-33, 1,195. These figures do not support an estimate of 100,000 Indians resident in Thailand. Five thousand may probably be considered a reasonable minimum, with 10,000 as the outside limit.

Little can be said concerning the place of origin of these Indians. Virginia Thompson states that two-thirds of the Indian merchants were Tamils from south Indian, while the other third were speakers of Hindustani. It is evident from her account that there were also some Sikhs. Mukerjee mentions "a fair number of South Indians" and "a few Muhammadan agriculturists from eastern Bengal" who entered Thailand by way of Burma.

Of 1,333 Indians arriving in Bangkok during the year 1931-32, 894 were married males, 284 were unmarried, adult males. There were only 49 married females, and 17 unmarried females over 15 years of age. The largest number of Indian males (410) were between the ages of 25-35; 775 were between the ages of 15 and 25.There were only 19 males aged 65 and over, and children under 7 years numbered only 44. Although these data refer to only a section of the Indian population, they suggest that the average Indian immigrant is a male, that he comes to Thailand at the age of 25; and it is possible to infer from the scarcity of women and children among the immigrants that the average Indians resident of Thailand is a transient who regards India as his home and expects to return after a few years. It should be noted, however, that two Thai informants, Dang Tilaka and Tularaksa stated in conversation that Indians in Thailand regard themselves as Thai rather than as Indians and have become permanent residents of the country. It seems probable that this observation refers chiefly to second generation Indians.

B. Economic Status

The majority of the Indians in Thailand are merchants. A few, probably Sikhs, are employed in the Bangkok police force; other serve as watchmen and messenger boys. The yearbook for the Kingdom of Siam lists the occupations of 1,178 male Indians aged 15 or over who arrived in Thailand during 1931-32:

General laborers	8
Professional	57
Commercial	583
Agricultural, etc	2
Personal and Domestic	371
Theatrical, etc	7
Others	150

Some, at least, of the Indians are well to do. A.E. Nana and Bhagwan Singh are said to be among the largest landowners in Thailand. The Sikh community in 1933 spent Tcs. 80,000 ($35,200) to build a temple in Bangkok.

C. Indian Organizations

There were two Indian organizations in Thailand. The Indian Association of Siam was founded in 1930 and A.E. Nana [became its life president with Hira Lall as secretary, Baboo Chhangur Singh was president of the second organization, the Hindu Dharma Sabha (Hindu Religious Society). There was also the Thai-Indian Cultural Lodge, founded by Swami Satyananda Puri, to foster cultural relations between Thailand and India. It is doubtful whether there were any political organizations as such among the Indians prior to 1941. Messrs. Tilaka and Tularaksa have expressed the opinion that attempts to establish organizations of this type would have been discouraged and that furthermore Indians as a whole were not vitally interested in political developments in their homeland. As followers of Gandhi, Indians sympathized with the Indian National Congress, but there seems to have been no local branch of the Congress in Thailand.

D. Early History of the Indian Independence League in Thailand and its Founders

Many, if not most of the Indians probably regarded the Japanese invasion with some apprehension. Indians and other Asiatic subjects of Great Britain in Thailand were assured by the Japanese that they had nothing to fear. Nevertheless, on 14 and 15 December 1941, about 50 Indians, "including some principal agitators," tried to escape and were arrested. The Bangkok Times in a notice of this affair stated that "in view of the fact that the establishment of an Indian association is being planned to collaborate with the Japanese Army force and because some Indians are enthusiastically cooperating with the Japanese Army force, those who were arrested were especially liberated under the guarantee of the founders of the association." The notice concludes with a warning that no mercy will be granted in the future.

There were undoubtedly a few individuals in the community who were ardent nationalists with a record of participation in subversive activities in India. The end of 1941 found them eager to take the lead in organizing their countrymen behind the Japanese program. One of these was Giani Pritam Singh, who had been in Thailand since 1933. He was born in Lyallpur district in the Punjab, of a "respectable" Sikh family, and educated at a Sikh missionary college. During the years from 1920-23 he participated in the Akali movement, during the course of which Akali Sikhs came into conflict with the Government of India over questions of religious reform. When in 1930 the government fired upon the Red Shirts, a nationalist group in the North West Frontier Province, Giani Pritam Singh, together with 300 other Akalis, went to Peshawar to protest against the government's action. He was arrested in Gujarat and jailed for a year and a half. It has been stated that while in prison he came into contact with Indian nationalist leaders. In April 1933 he was invited by the Singh Sabha, a Sikh religious organization, to go to Bangkok as a "lecturer," and as far as is known he did not return to Indian.

Another Indian revolutionary in Thailand when Japan entered the war was Amar Singh. During the last war he engaged in seditious activities in India and seems to have been involved in one of the various plots to obtain Indian's freedom with German aid. The *Bangkok Times* states that "he is the person who acquired 1000,0000 rifles from Germany during the last great war." In 1917 or 1918 he was imprisoned and sent to the Andamans. After his release in 1940 he went to Thailand where he joined forces with Giani Pritam Singh. Together they started an anti-British movement in which they are said to have received help from the Japanese government. These two men probably formed the nucleus of what later became known as the Independent League of India. It is doubtful if there was any organization, properly speaking, before the end of 1941. A note in the Bangkok Times for 12 February 1942, says that the Independent League, of which Giani Pritam Singh was the leader, "though it had its origin before [the declaration of war by Japan] did not do any work openly." It is further stated that Giani Pritam Singh "had some to an understanding with the Japanese Government concerning the Independence of India." The entry of Japan in the war found these men anxious to play a more active role. On

9 December 1941, the Bangkok Times carried an advertisement signed by A Representative of the Independent League of India: "Attention all Indian residents in Thailand. All patriotic Indians who wish to serve their Motherland India are, requested to enlist their respective names at 1840 (Green House) Saphan Maha Megh." Two days later the same newspaper contained an appeal to Indians to look to Japan to free India. This was signed by "Giani Pritam Singh," very probably a garble for Giani Pritam Singh.

A third Indian who achieved considerable prominence in the early days of the war with Japan was Swami Satyananda Puri. Profulla Kumar Sen, as he was named, was born in 1902 in Bengal. He was educated at Calcutta University where he obtained the degree of M.A. During his student days he was a member of Anushilan Samiti, a society for the promotion of culture and training, which, however, functioned chiefly as an organization "to arouse public opinion against the Government by circulating seditious literature, popularizing revolutionary songs, and organizing secret associations." His connections with this group landed him in jail. While still a young man he became a follower of Tagore and Gandhi. He decided to become a sannyasi (holy man), and having made over his entire property to the National Congress, wandered about in India for four years and spent another three years meditating in the Himalayas. He was afterwards appointed Professor of Oriental Philosophy at Calcutta University and held this post for two years, during which time he founded the Society of Oriental Culture. In 1932 Tagore was requested by the Royal Family of Thailand to send an Indian as unofficial cultural ambassador to Thailand. Tagore selected Swami Satyananda. While in Thailand, the Swami wrote several books on Indian history, philosophy, etc., as well as a biography of Gandhi in the Thai language. There is no indication that he had any dealings with the Japanese prior to December 1941 nor does he seem to have been associated with Amar Singh and Giani Pritam Singh. On 22 December 1941, Swami Satyanada gave notice in the *Bangkok Times* of a meeting to inaugurate an Indian National Council for the Freedom of India. The council was formed several days later and the Swami became its president with Debnath Das as secretary.

For some time the two groups, the Independent League of India and the National Council for the Freedom of India, continued as separate organizations. The first appears to have been the more active. Some of its members, including S. Kishan Singh, Babu Sudarshan Aouja, and Bhagwan

Singh went to Malaya in December 1941, to do propaganda work among the soldiers of the British Indian army. They apparently met with a certain amount of success, but an article in the *Bangkok Times* comments that some of the soldiers "it seemed, had lost their sense of reason and stayed where they were." Giani Pritam Singh went to Malaya shortly after its fall and was instrumental in founding branches of the League in that country.

Towards the end of March 1942, Swami Satyananda Puri and Giani Pritam Singh were killed en route by air to Japan. In May 1942 the Indian National Council and the Independent League merged; the union is reported to have been brought about by Colonel Gill, "a very senior officer," formerly of the army in Malaya. Debnath Das became general secretary and Amar Singh was made a patron.

Such information as is available indicates a general lack of enthusiasm on the part of the Indian community for this Japanese-sponsored organization. It is said that the merchants of Thailand are forced by threat of boycott to become members of the League and to contribute to its funds. Many of them apparently are becoming Thai citizens in order to avoid this pressure.

III. Indians in Malaya

A. Population Statistics

Indian emigration to Malaya in modern times dates from beginning of the nineteenth century. Today Indians form over 12 per cent of the total population of the country 754,849. Detailed information relating to the Indian population, however, is taken from the 1931 Census of British Malaya when the total number of Indians was 624,0009. The following table shows the distribution of Indians in the political subdivisions of Malaya:

Singapore	51,019
Penang	58,020
Malacca	23,238
Straits Settlements	132,277
Perak	159,152
Selangor	155,924
Negri Sembilan	50,100
Pahang	14,820
Federated Malay States	379,996

Johore	51,038
Kehad	50,824
Perlis	966
Kelantan	6,752
Trengganu	1,371
Brunei	377
Unlocated	408

Following is the Indian population of the principal towns.

	Total Population	*Indian Population*
Singapore	445,719	51,019
Kuala Lumpur	111,738	25,342
Alor Star	11,596	2,746
Penang	149,408	58,020
Taiping	31,881	7,726
Seremban	21,650	4,087
Johore Bahru	21,777	3,220
Ipoh	53,183	12,301

About five-sixths of the total Indian population are Tamils from South India. The Following is a tabulation according to sectional groups of the Indians in Malaya;.

Tamil	514,959
Telugu	32,541
Malayali	35,125
Punjabi, etc.	31,001
United Provinces	1,898
Bengal, etc.	1,833
Burmese	1,160
Bombay, etc.	1,388
Bihar and Orissa	219
Nepal	490
Other and unidentified	3,395

As regards religion, the great majority are Hindus, as might be expected considering the great preponderance of Tamils in the population. The Mohammedans are also chiefly from southern India, especially the Malabar coast, but in addition there is a number of Pathans, Punjabis, and natives of Bombay and Bengal in the Muslim group. The following table lists Indians by religion.

	British Malaya	*Straits Settlements*	*F.M.S.*
Hindus	509,202	93,793	322,272
Mohammedans	56,506	24,797	20,184
Sikhs	18,180	4,326	12,117
Christians	36,614	8,507	23,787
Buddists	1,204	398	562
Others	2,303	456	973

The following table showing age distribution per 1,000 Indians indicates clearly the immigrant nature of the population.

Age	Male	Female
0-10	136	279
10-20	124	178
20-30	312	290
30-40	275	162
40-50	138	78
Over 55	15	13

As in almost all countries where Indian immigrants are found, the number of males is greatly in excess of the number of females. In 1931 there were 421,0028 males and 2002,981 females. The several racial groups, however, show wide variation in the sex ratio. Among the Tamils there were 514 females per 1,000 males; for the Telugu, the figure was 717; for the Malayali, 2009; for the Punjabi, 263.

In British Malaya as a whole, about one-fifth of the Indian population is Malaya born. It has been reliably estimated that the "average duration of the southern Indian's continuous stay in Malaya is under three years." As the following figures show, there is little variation between different areas with regard to the number of Indians born in Malaya and those born elsewhere.

	Indian born in Malaya		*Indian Born elsewhere*	
	Number	*Percent of total Indian population*	*Number*	*Percent of total Indian population*
Straits settlements	30,236	23	101,974	77
F.M.S.	84,036	22	295,903	78
	131,505	21	491,919	79

It should be noted that between 1921 and 1931 the percentage of Indians born in Malaya greatly increased. For British Malaya as a whole in 1921 only 12.4 per cent of the total population was born in Malaya, while 87.6 per cent were born elsewhere. Presumbly this tendancy has continued and the 1931 figures therefore cannot be considered typical of conditions today. Lennor A. Mills, writing in 1942, remarked that Indian labor in Malaya is now in a transitional stage. "Formerly the labourer migrated to Mayala for two or three years and then returned to India with his earnings. Today the majority still return to their villages, but increasingly they come back to Malaya, often accompanied by relatives and friends, and even more important, wives... During the past decade the number who have been in Malaya and regard it and not India as their home has been growing...On a few on the older plantations the majority of the labourers have been born on the estate."

B. Principal Occupations

In British Malaya (exclusive of Brunei) 189,998 Indians including men and women, were engaged in the cultivation of rubber. Of these 101 were estate owners, managers, and assistants. The 42,650 Indians employed in commerce included proprietors and managers of businesses, salesmen, shop assistants, peddlers, moneylenders, etc. Most of the 25,595 Indians occupied in transport and communication were railway laborers, drivers of vehicles, bullock cart owner and drivers; in the Straits Settlements a large number worked as dock laborers, boatmen and lightermen. Only in the Federated Malaya States was there a large number of Indians in the mining industry. The total number was 6,189 and over half of these were in Perak. Laborers general and indeterminate, numbered 61,237; 3,712 were in the police force, most of these in the Straits Settlements and Federated Malay States. In the unfederated states the total number of Indians in the police was 266. With the exception of four commissioned officers and inspectors among the Indian police, all were in the ranks; these four were in Singapore municipality. Of the 920 Indians in the army, 736 were in the Federated Malay States, with 94 in the Straits Settlements and 70 in Johore. One in Singapore and six in the Federated Malay States were commissioned officers.

Broadly speaking sectional groups are associated with occupational divisions. Thus the Tamils, Telugus, and Malayalis are for the most part engaged in the cultivation of rubber. The Punjabis are found mainly in and near the large towns. A considerable proportion "are accounted for the Police Forces, they are also extensively employed as watchmen... and frequently combine money-lending with this and other pursuits. In suburban and rural areas, they are characteristically associated with stock farming and bullock cart driving." Natives of Bombay are usually shopkeepers, and the Bengalis, who are few in number, are also engaged in occupations other than agriculture.

In summary, the Indian population of Malaya consisted chiefly of Tamils from South India who were occupied on plantations or engaged in menial labor of various types. The length of their stay in Malaya was short and their ties were with the homeland, where for the most part their families remained and to which they returned. There were no trade unions, and opportunities of developing a spirit of independence and cooperation were slight. Situated on isolated plantations, these Indians were almost completely under the control of the employers and cut off from the outside world. A small number of Indians were located in the towns and engaged in business or professional activities. For the most part these were northerners who apparently had little contact with Chinese in Malaya, who, rich or poor, have a feeling of kinship with each other. "Among the Indians this is far from being the case: the Tamils and other south Indians are a despised proletariat who have virtually no bond joining them to their alleged brethren from other parts of India who have done better for themselves in Malaya."

C. Indian Associations

In almost every town in Malaya there were Indian associations, and delegates chosen from these men once a year to hold the All-Malayan National Congress. This annual conference was founded in 1927 by Mr. S. Veerasamy, one of the most prominent Indians in the country who in 1931 represented the Indian community in the Federal Council. In 1936 a Central Indian Association was founded in Kuala Lumpur. Its objects were "(a) to promote and safeguard the political social and economic interest of the Indians in Malaya; (b) to represent, express and give effect to Indian public opinion; (c) to consider all questions affecting the interests of the whole or any section of the community; and (e) to do all such things as may be conducive to the furtherance of the above mentioned objects or any of them." How far any of these associations were representative of the Indian masses is not know. Probably the membership was drawn almost entirely from the urban population.

However, these organizations proved to be useful nuclei for the present Indian Independence Leagues, and several of the Indians who were prominent in the old associations are today actively aiding the Japanese. It should not be assumed from this fact that the Indians in Malaya were, previous to the Japanese invasion, primarily or actively interested in the Indian struggle for independence. With regard to the masses of the Indian population it is doubtful if they took any interest in political affairs, either of India or Malaya. It has been said that the Hindu merchants of Singapore were mostly loyal to the Indian National Congress and when Jawaharlal Nehru visited Malaya in 1937, he was very enthuseastically received. There appears, however, to have been very little contact with the Congress group in India. As is indicated by the program cited above, the Indians in Malaya were more concerned with advancing their political and economic position in the country of their adoption than n working for the independence of India.

D. Indians under British Administration in Malaya

Indians believe that they have serious grievances in regard to their treatment by the British in Malaya. Numerically they have a strong claim to consideration, and the prosperity of the country undoubtedly owes much to their labor. Indian criticized the Government of Malaya for failure to safeguard the economic interests of the Indian laborer. Wages have been low and the means of livelihood uncertain for the past decade. During 1931-32 when the rubber industry suffered from the general depression, large number of Indians were thrown out of work; wages were reduced by 20 per cent from the 1928 figure of 50% per day. According to proposals made by the Government of India, 73,000 Indians were repatriated free of cost and all recruitment of labor in India was brought to an end. As conditions improved, assisted immigration was resumed in 1934 at the request of the Malayan Government. Wages remained low until 1936, when,, acting on the advice of a deputation from India, the Malayan government restored half of the cut imposed in 1930. Finally in 1937 wages raised to the former level of 50% per day for men and 40% for women. When the rubber industry again deteriorated in 1938 the wages of Indian workers were once more reduced, but with the advent of war and the increase in the price of rubber, wages were fixed at 50% per day, the cost of living however, had greatly increased and the laborer did not profit from the war in any material way.

Indians declare that facilities for education of their children have been unsatisfactory. In Penang, Malacca, and Singapore, there was not a single Government Tamil school, in spite of large numbers of Tamil government employees in these places.

In regard to public services and representation in public bodies, Indians believe that their status was not commensurate with their importance. Indians were not permitted to enter the Malaya Civil Service, and they had no municipal or political franchise. There was one non-official Indian member nominated to the Federal Council and another on the Straits Settlements Legislative Council.

IV. Indians in Indochina

It is impossible to state the exact number of Indians living in Indochina; 6,000 is probably a fair estimate. About half of these are from French colonies in India, and for the most part they have established themselves in Cochinchina, though there are about 350 in Cambodia. The natives of British India are nearly all Muslims from the northern provinces. There is also a fairly large group of Chettyars from South India and a few Parsis form Bombay engage in import trade.

Indians from French India are for the most part minor government employees, postmen, policemen, assistant registrars, customs or excise clerks. The Muslims from British India are shopkeepers and pawnbrokers, cashiers and watchmen. The Chettyars, or moneylenders, most of whom are located in Cochinchina, where in 1937, there were 120 Chetti firms, from the wealthiest group among the Indians. They own a considerable amount of land and engage extensively in trade. In Cochinchina alone, Chettyars own one-fourth of the total rice-growing area. In 1933, their business methods and the hold they had acquired over the agriculture of the country aroused wide-spread antagonism. As a result of the depression, the Chetti system of short-term loans resulted in great hardship particularly for the agriculturists. Five Chetti bankers were expelled from Indochina on "the alleged ground that they created political disturbances in the country. " Later on the order of expulsion was cancelled but French authorities by establishing long term credit offices have considerably undermined the position of the Chettyars, and in the first eight months of 1933 about 65 per cent of the Chetti capital was removed to Burma, Malaya, and India. It seems probable that the Chettyars who remain form a dissatisfied group, hostile to continued French domination in Indochina.

V. Indians in N.E.I.

In the Netherlands East Indies there were, according to the 1920 census, 27,684 Indians. Of these 12,654 were born in the area; 15,030 were born abroad, presumably for the most part in India, though it is possible that emigrants from Malaya were a numerous group. The men outnumber the women by about two to one. The Indians located in Java and Sumatra number 25,638, the greater proportion of these being in Java. In Bali and Western Lombok there is "a handful of Indians," and a few more in Dutch Borneo.

Speaking of the Indians generally, the Handbook for the Dutch East Indies says," The majority are Mohammedans and come from the coastal districts of Coromandel and Malabar. Many are found in the plantation areas of Deli as coolies, car drivers, cattlemen, etc., owing to their fine physique, these so-called Klings.... Are engaged as night-watchmen on the plantations. In Java they are mostly smaller shop-keepers. They are conspicuous owing to their height, heavy growth of beards and large turbans." This reference to their height and growth of breads suggests that there is a Sikh element in the Indian population.

VI. Indian in China

The principal Indian colonies in China are in Shanghai and Hongkong. Indians in Hongkong numbered 4,475. These included the troops which formed part of the garrison, the Sikh contingent of the police, and a few merchants and clerks. According to the 1921 census of Hongkong, about 85 percent of the adult male Indians were employed as police or watchmen, or in various government departments. Most of the Indians were Punjabis or native of the North West Frontier Province. In 1930 there were 1,842 Indian living in Shanghai. "Practically all of these Indians were brought to Shanghai originally as policemen..... but after completing their term of enlistment, many remained here to engage in business or professional activities," For the most part the Indians of Shanghai are Sikhs.

B. Indians in China and Indian Nationalism

Indians in China have taken an active interest in Indian political affairs for many years. Before the last war, in both Hongkong and Shanghai there were Ghadr (revolution) societies, affiliated with similar organizations on the west coast of the Unites State and elsewhere, which conspired for the overthrow of the British government in India. A number of Indians in Hongkong and Shanghai were involved in the Komogata Maru affair in 1914 in order to test Canadian immigration law which made it practically impossible for Indian immigrations in Canada to be joined by their wives and children, and also to "embarrass the British government by compelling it either to interfere with Canada's immigration policy or to suffer a further loss of popularity in India. A Japanese vessel, the Komogata Maru, was chartered by Sikh name Gurudutt Singh, a man prominent in the Far East.

The ship sailed from Hongkong to Canada with 351 Sikhs and 21 Punjabi Muslims recruited at Honkong, Shanghai, Moji and Yokohama. The Great Majority of the passengers were not permitted to land in Canada. During the return trip war broken out and for various reasons the passengers were not allowed to land at the part of embarkation but were taken to Budge Budge in Bengal. These men formed the nucleus of the agitation in the Punjab which lasted during the war and for several yeas after. Other conspirators arrived shortly after the Komogatu Maru, and these also were for the most part Sikhs from America, Japan, Manila and Shanghai, who had been in touch with German agents en route to India. The disturbances in the Punjab which these men helped to further were for a time directed by Rashbehari Bose.

From 1920 to 1940 Indian political development in China was influenced by two separate organizations, the Indian National Congress and the Chinese Kumointang Party. Reliance on methods of terrorism was modified by the Congress policy of passive resistance, and the growing strength of the Congress in Indian encouraged increased activity among the Indians in China. At the same time the development of nationalism in China proved an inspiration to the Indian group. To a certain extent the Communists also played a part, but their influence on the Indians in China does not appear to have been very great at any time, and was probably much less after the break occurred between Chiang Kai Shek and the Chinese Communists.

C. Indian Organizations

In 1927 some Chinese members of the Kuomintang, some Korenans, a few Filipinos, some Japanese "proletarians" and a number of Indians formed the Eastern Oppressed Peoples' Association. The organization was formed originally when the radical section of the Kuomintang was in power, and its headquarters were in Hankow. Later on these were moved to Nanking, and the organizatin remained under the protection of the Kuominatang party. It has been said that Jawaharlal Nehru sponsored the establishment of the Eastern Oppressed Peoples' Association. It is possible that the idea was conceived at the Brussels Congress of Oppressed Nationalities at which Nehru was present, and in which the leftist members of the Kuomintang played an active part.

The Indian section of the Eastern Oppressed Peoples' Association in Nanking published for some years a bi-weekly called Ghadr Dhandora (Declaration of Revolution).

In line with the sympathy expressed by the All India Congress Committee for China in her struggle for freedom, and the Committee's condemnation in 1927 of the action of the Government of India in sending Indian troops to China engaged in propaganda among the Indian troops stationed at Shanghai. These troops on their way to China, had been subjected to propaganda to the effect that Indian temples in China were being destroyed, women violated, etc. "But they were met, almost at the dock, by certain men of their own nationality, who were working for the cause of Indian freedom among the large groups of Indian freedom among the large groups of Indian police and watchmen already in Shanghai.....The reaction of the troops when they discovered the untruth of the stories which had been circulated among them was great." As a result, these troops had to be sent back to Hongkong. Later two battalions, Punjabis who spoke a different dialects from that of the Indian nationalist workers in Shanghai arrived, but these too were infected with sympathy for the Chinese cause. Expenses of the Indian organization are alleged to have been paid by donation from Chinese friends and members of the Kuomintang. On the whole, the Indians in Shanghai were too poor to contribute large sums to the movement, though they gave what they could afford.

It has been stated that there were two groups of Indian agitators in Shanghai at this time. One group believed in "the passive resistance policy of Mahatma Gandhi, their leader," while the second group consisted of Communists "working for the complete overthrow of British rule in India and its members are fanatical believers in the most radical measures." Gujjan Singh, Daswanda Singh, and Gainda Singh were members of this Communist group. An Indian, M.N. Roy, was in China at this time as a delegate of the Communist International. It is not known, however, whether or not he played any active role in the Indian organization; certainly during this period he was more concerned with developments in China than in India.

Harchan Singh, an Indian nationalist of Shanghai and a member of the Eastern Oppressed Peoples' Association, who had taken part in the propagandist activities referred to above, was murdered in 1929. Shortly before his death he had compiled a list of Indians in Shanghai who were alleged to be in the employ of the British Indian Secret Service. Five Indians also members of the Eastern Oppressed Peoples' Association were charged with his murder. These were Norang Singh, Sadu Singh, Mewa Singh, and Karm Singh. They were acquitted of the charge of murder but shortly after rearrested on charges of sedition, and were given jail sentences to also Sikhs, Ishar Singh, Indar Singh, Hakim Singh, Asha Singh, and Narain Singh were arrested on charges of sedition. They were accused of reading aloud in a Sikh temple in Chapei nationalist papers received from India. This temple had been closed in 1927 by the British authorities "on the grounds that the premises were being used for Bolshevik propaganda," but it was reopened in 1928. The seditionists in question were sentenced to prison with hard labor and later deported.

In 1930, while civil disobedience was in progress in India there were a number of other arrests on charges of sedition among the Indians of China. The Indian Youth League of China issued several manifestos condemning British rule and calling upon all Indians to fight for a free Asia. In June 1930 the British police raided the League headquarters and made two arrests. In July of the same year Zapuran Singh distributed pamphlets printed in English and Chinese and published by the E.O.P.A. He was sentenced to two months hard labor and deportation.

The Indian Youth League which had its headquarters in Chapei had "some kind of agreement with the Kuomintang and Brueau of Public Safety," which enabled it to hold meetings and carry on political activity. The leaders were young working men who were literate and intelligent. They kept in touch with events in Indian and informed their countrymen in Shanghai by means of leaflets, magazines and pamphlets as well as public meetings. Chanan Singh and Kartar Singh, leading members of the League, and Surjan Singh were arrested in December 1930. All were tried for sedition, and two of the men were sentenced to imprisonment and deportation.

The instances cited above are probably only a few of many such cases of friction between the Indians and the British in China. They are, between the Indians and the British in China. They are, however, indicative of the degree to which the Indians were organized and of the enthusiasm felt there for the cause of nationalism of India.

VII. Indians in Japan

According to the Japan Year Book for 1938-39 there were 874 Indians resident in Japan. Of these, 670 were males. For the most part the Indian group consisted of businessmen and students, located chiefly in the large cities, Tokyo, Kobe, Yokohama, with a few in Osaka.

B. Indian Revolutionaries of Japan

Japan has for many years been a refuge for Indian patriots of various hues. After the Ruksso-Japanese war, Indians generally regarded Japan with admiration and respect, and to a great extent looked to Japan as the leader of Asia. At the same time certain groups in Japan pursued the policy of actively encouraging revolutionary tendencies in Asiatic countries, especially those under European domination.

The story of the Indian nationalist movement in Japan is a summary of the life histories of a small number of Indian revolutionaries who used their contacts with the Japanese to ends. In the background of this Indian movement stands Mitsuru Toyama, the power behind almost all the Japanese patriotic societies. It is not to be doubted that Toyama conspired with these Indians, extended to them his patronage and protection, and used them for his own ends.

1. Maulvi Mohammed Barkatulla: Maulvi Mohammed Barkatulla was one of the earliest Indian revolutionaries with contacts in Japan. He was born in Bhopal in 1868 and educated in Bombay and London. He became a strong advocate of Pan-Islamism and extremely anti-British. In 1909 has was appointed to the chair of Hindustani in Tokyo Foreign Language School, and while in Japan he founded a paper called *Islamic Fraternity*, which he edited for some years. In 1911 he traveled for a time in Europe, visiting Cairo, Constantinople, St. Petersburg and Paris, where he came into contact with Krishnaverma, one of the best known Indian exiles of the period. On his return to Japan "the tone of his paper became so anti-British that it was suppressed by the Japanese Government in 1912. Early in 1914 he was deprived of his appointment in Tokio....." From Japan, Barkatulla went to the United States. There he joined forces with Har Dayal who had, a few year previously, founded the Ghadr (revolution) Party among Indian immigrants settled on the West Coast. In March 1914 Har Daya was arrested by the United State Government and was about to be deported as an undesirable lien when he, together w2ith Barkatulla, fled to Switzerland. The outbreak of the war found these two in Germany. In Berlin, Har Dayal and Barkatulla, with Chatthopadyaya and Pillai, well-known Indian seditionists, directed the activities of the Indian Revolutionary Society, and conspired with the aid of Germany to overthrow the British Government in India. In 1915 Barkatulla and Raja Mahendra Pratap went to Kabul, where they formed the Provisional Indian Government. During the war this "government" "continued to encourage seditious agitation in Indian and hostile action by the frontier tribes...... After the war it threw all its influence into promoting the rebellious outbreaks in India in April 1919."

In 1927 Barkatulla represented the Hindustan Ghadr Party at the Brussels Congress against Imperialism, and later in the same year he died in San Francisco.

2. Hariharnath Thulal Atal: Hariharnath Thulal Atal was another Indian who went to Japan in the early days of the twentieth century. Like Barkatulla he held the chair of Hindustani in Tokyo Forging Language School. In 1914 the Department of Education, according to report, wanted to renew his contract, but the British authorities would not permit it. Atal stayed on in Japan but the British began to "harass him in every way," and finally in 1921 he committed suicide.

A memorial ceremony, arranged by Rashbehari Bose, was held in Tokyo, 14 June 1931, in honor of Barkatulla, Atal and Vikramratne. The last of these three lived in Tokyo for a few year where he worked with Bose "for the cause of Indian freedom." He died in Ceylon in 1928.

3. Raja Mahendra Pratap: One of the most interesting, and certainly the most picturesque of all the Indian in Japan is Raja Mahendra Pratap, a native of the United Provinces and formerly a wealthy landowner. Whether or not he played any part in the seditious movements of the period in Indian is uncertain. He is said to have founded Braindaban National University, of which he became President , and to have been the owner of a newspaper Narmalsewak. At the outbreak of the war in 1914, he went to Europe and came under the influence of Har Dayal. Through him, Pratap had an interview with the Kaiser, who "impressed with a megalomania akin to his own," sent Pratap with Barkatulla to Kabul. He became a citizen of Afghanistan and continued to live there for some years.

In 1925 Pratap, accompanied by Daswanda Singh, a student at California University started out for Tibet and Nepal to see whether they "could do any service to India from these countries." " Indian friends in California probably members of the Ghadar organization, collected money to pay the expenses of the trip. A member of the Kuomintang party went along as interpreter and Mr. Charan Singh seems to have been a member of the group. To the various Chinese generals Pratap met along the way, he presented a copy of his book, *The Religion of Love.* Shortly after this, in 1926, he went to Japan, but for some reason he was not permitted to remain there. It has been suggested that the British authorities objected to his presence in Japan, and he returned to Afghanistan. He had, according to his own account," no political ambition for the time being."

About 1930 he was sent by the Government of Afghanistan on an economic "mission" to America and on his way home, he stopped in

Japan. From there he went to Vladivostok where he was informed by the Soviet authorities that he could not proceed further. On his return to Japan, he learned that the Afghan government did not want him in the country for the time being; Pratap declared himself at a loss to explain this. He seems to have gone to Peiping shortly after this, where he published a monthly called *World Federation,* and busied himself collecting $1,000 for a building to serve as a permanent office for *World Federation.* Early in 1933 he returned to Japan. The *Voice of India*, organ of the Indian Nationalist group in Japan, published a statement by Pratap who signed himself, The Servant of Mankind, and announced that he had temporarily closed his Peiping office. He started that if Japan would realize that the British Empire was working for Japan's destruction, Japan could come to dominate Asia. When the Pan-Asiatic Congress was held in Dairen in 1934, Pratap attended it. He proceeded to Canton where he tried to organize an Oppressed Oriental Races Emancipation Society, but he was arrested by the Canton government authorities and deported to Shanghai. He was again arrested in Shanghai, but "friends" secured his release. The *China Weekly Review* reported that " It is understood that the Afghanistan leader is in Shanghai on some mission on behalf of the Japanese." According to the *Japan Weekly Chronicle*, Pratap spent his time addressing the Sikh police. On his return to Japan Pratap set out the visit Siam. In 1935 he again visited the United States. It was said that his reception was rather cold and that he found the "atmosphere not suitable for his message."

Pratap has never been one of the most influential Indians in Japan. As far as is known he has never held office in any of the numerous Indian organizations, and he seems never to have worked in close collaboration with Rashbehari Bose. Ideas or World Federation and Pan-Asianiam have been obviously more appealing to him that the narrow cause of Indian freedom. He is not at present an important figure, and is said to be regarded as a crank by his fellow Indians, although a few of the Indian students in Japan have become his disciples. A recent report suggests that Pratap has not been able to reconcile Japanese imperialism with his ideas of world federation. It has been started that he refused, "though pressed hard to do so," to attend the Japanese sponsored Bangkok Conference in June 1942.

4. Rashbehari Bose: The most prominent Indian in Japan today is Rashbehari Bose. He was born in Bengal in 1886 and educated in Calcutta. For a time he was employed as a clerk in the Forest Research Institute, but while still a young man he became involved in the Indian revolutionary movement, in which Bengalis played so large a part. In 1912-15 he directed terrorist activities in the Punjab, but when a number of the ringleaders were arrested, Bose fled to Japan. The Japanese Government ordered him to be deported, but he was protected by Mitsuru Toyama, and to avoid further trouble he took out Japanese citizenship papers. He married the daughter of a Japanese who kept a restaurant and eventually succeeded to the business.

The Japanese who's who for 1937 lists him as a journalist, lecturer, author and correspondent of Indian newspapers. This account is probably somewhat flattering. His reputation as a journalist rests chiefly upon the fact that from time to tome he has written articles for several newspapers, among them the *Calcutta forward.* He claims authorship of several books in Japanese on the Indian nationalist movement, but it is doubtful whether he has written them himself.

Bose is said to be politically honest and scrupulous, and sincere in his efforts to win freedom for Indian. According to reports he is equally convinced that this can be obtained with Japanese aid. Asked in 1933 why he did not return to India, he replied that he would come at the head of armed forces which would enter India by way of Assam. He is said to have Communist leanings and to have had contacts with the Soviet Embassy in Tokyo.

5. Anand Mohan Sahay: Anand Mohan Sahay is one of the few Indian in Japan who were ever closely connected with the Indian National Congress. He was born in 1898, the son of a landlord in Bhagalpore in the province of Bihar, and was educated at Patna University, where he studied medicine. When the Congress urged students to boycott government institutions, he have up his work at the University and joined the independence movement. He worked actively with the Bihar Provincial Congress Committee. In 1923 he set out for America via Japan, to study medicine, but decided to settle in Japan to "work of the promotion of Indo-Japanese friendship and dissemination of correct information regarding India in Japan.

Since that time he has remained in Japan. According to his biography in the Japanese *Who's Who* for 1937 he is journalist, writer, educator, teacher and lecturer on India, Japan, Asia, and international problems. He was also for some time professor at Kobe Foreign Language School. Sahay is said to be completely...... and insincere in political matters. One informant (name withheld) believes he could be bought by anyone prepared to pay the price of securing his support. The same source accuses him of extorting funds from Indian merchants to support himself and his various enterprises. Sahay and Bose are extremely jealous of one another and continually at logger-heads. Sahay is probably the cleverer of the two men.

C. Indian organization in Japan

One of the earliest Indian organizations in Japan was the Indo-Japanese Association, founded in Tokyo about 1905 by the Rev. Dharmapala and Mr. Sakurai. Viscount Nagaoka was the first president and was succeeded by Marquis Okuma. Valentine Chirol, writing in 1910, started that this society had "no connection with politics and the Indians claim that it is run for the benefit of the Japanese rather that for theirs. Those who have joined it in the hope of using it as a base for anti-British operations have certainly got very little for their pains. They occasionally write papers for the very few socialist papers of Japan, but their effective contribution to the cause is of trifling account." By 1937 this organization had no Indian members, and during theprevious decades its main activity was the development of economic relations between Indian and Japan.

The Indian National Congress Committee of Japan was organized in 1928, with its headquarter in Kobe. A.M. Sahay was on of the leaders of the Committee and retained control over it. D.P. Mahabubani of Kobe was a delegate at the annual session of the Indian National Congress in 1928. The Committee has for some years published the *Voice of India*, with A.M. Sahay as editor. Originally the paper was published in English as a monthly, but was later printed in Japanese and English and usually appeared every fortnight. Congress activities in India were well covered, and considerable space was given to the activities of the committee in Japan. In 1931 the committee opened the Indian Lodge to accommodate Indian students studying in Japan.

It probably is incorrect to assume that the committee had any close connection with the Indian National Congress. Sahay claimed that it was recognized by the parent organization in 1929, but according to report, Kripalani, the General Secretary of the Indian Congress wrote to Shay denying that this was the case, and pointing out the fact that it was contrary to Congress policy to establish or recognize branches outside of India.

Other Indian organizations include the Indian National Association founded about 1930 with branches in Yokohama, Kobe and probably elsewhere; and the Japan-Indian Society of Kanasai, established about the same time. In 1931 Rashbehari Bose organized the Indian Independence League, which had as its objects "the attainment of Independence League, which had as its object "the attainment of Independence for India by all possible means. Bose became the first president, and P.S. Deshpande secretary of the League. The League functioned as a rival organization to

Sahay's Japanese Congress Committee. The Indo-Japanese Young Peoples, Association was formed about 1934-35 "the encourage the study of Indian and Japanese problems. The Gandhi Society of Tokyo, a small and poorly organized group, seems to have been chiefly interested in economic relations between India and Japan. It is said to have been ideologically opposed to Gandhi and scornful of the doctrine of non-violence.

There were in addition to these, various Indian social and business organizations, such as the Indian Social Society, and the Indian Merchants Association.

VIII. Indian National Congress and Indians Overseas

The general attitude of the Indian National Congress to Indians abroad is best summed up in a resolution passed by the Congress at its annual session in 1936. "The Congress sends greetings to our fellow-countrymen overseas and its assurances of sympathy and help in their distressful condition and in the continuing deterioration in their status in the territories in which they have settled. The Congress is ready and willing to take all action within its power to ameliorate their condition, but desires to point out that a radical ameliorate in their status must ultimately depend on the attainment by India of Independence and the power effectively protect her nationals abroad. Except for numerous resolutions, dating from the early days of the Congress, which did little more than express sympathy with the plight of Indians overseas, interest on the part of Congress in their problems has been slight. This is especially true of Indians in South-East Asia. Gandhi's early connections with South Africa, where Indians are settled in large numbers, has tended to focus attention on that area, while Indians is South-East Asia,, expect in times of crisis such as the riots in Burma or the severe economic depression in Malaya, have been more or less ignored.

The Indian National Congress has never to any extent developed contacts with Indians abroad for political purposes. The Congress Working Committee in 1936 passed a resolution advocating the establishment of a foreign department "with a view to creating and maintaining contacts with Indians overseas and with international labor and other organizations abroad with whom cooperation is possible and with international labor and other organizations abroad with whom cooperation is possible and is likely to help in the cause of Indian freedom". This department, however, was not very active and beyond issuing a circular to Indians overseas inviting them to keep in touch with the Congress, and printing a short pamphlet on Indians abroad, did very little to fulfills its expressed function. The unofficial visit of Jawaharlal Nehru to Burma and Malaya in 1937 probably served to arouse the interest of Indians in these countries in the National Congress, but there seems to have been no attempt to follow this up with propaganda or definite programs. Sometime before 1940 the Congress opened a department of Indians overseas, and published a pamphlet entitled "Our Countrymen Abroad." This was chiefly to inform the Indian people regarding conditions of Indians overseas, and to awake interest in their problems. Perhaps, had the war not intervened, more active contacts with Indians overseas would have been instituted.

51

Indians Urged to Push Anti-British Movement by Netaji

14. October, 1944

Somewhere in Burma, October 14—In a statement on the present situation in India regarding the breakdown of the Gandhi-Jinnah talks, Netaji Subhas Chandra Bose, Head of the Provisional Government of Azad Hind on Wednesday, exhorted his compatriots inside India to intensify the civil disobedience movement. The statement follows "A few days ago, news was flashed all over the world that the Gandhi-Jinnah talks had broken down Indians everything heaved a sigh of relief, No nationalist could have adopted an attitude of approval or even of equality toward the talks that were based on the proposal to divide India into a number of states. The proposal had become still more obnoxious because it appeared that these states would all be under British domination and because there was no possibility that the Muslim League would ever cooperate with the Indian National Congress in fighitng the British Government.

I had said clearly in a previous statement on the subject that in view of the pro-British attitude of the leaders of the Muslim League, any agreement arrived at by Mahatama Gandhi and Mohammed Ali Jinnah President at the Muslim League could not put any pressure on the British Government—either in extracting more political reforms in my opinion the Gandhi Jinnah talks, even if they had led to an agreement would not have helped the attainment of Indian independence or even a compromise between the Congress and the British since the policy of the British Government under Prime Minister Churchill is strongly opposed to granting any political concessions whatsover to the Indian people.

By now it should be clear even to a child that the British Government which is based on brutal force will surrender only to brutal force. That is

1. I.N.A. Trial Papers.

why the ındians in East Asia have taken up arms for the liberation of their motherland, and what they demand is not compromise with the British Government but the total expulsion of the British from India.

The problem that now faces our countrymen inside India is what they should do now, the situation is similar to that of May in 1942. The patriots in India should intensify the civil disobedience movement but without going in for sabotage activity. Sabotage acitivities should in the future synchronise with our military operations and they should be started only when we are inside India and give the signal.

If for any reason the Civil disobedience movement cannot be intensified immediately a passive opposition to the British Government should continue and all possible preparations should not be misled by bumptious propaganda of our enemies into thinking that the Anglo-Americans are going to win the war.

Every war must have its ups and downs—particularly a world war of the present magnitude. During the first phase of this war, the Axis Powers had sweeping victories on every front, in the second phase our enemies started a counter-offensive and had some success. That phase is now coming to close. The turning point of the war is fast approaching when the initiative will pass out of the hands of our enemies and our friends and allies will take the offensive once again.

We Indians in East Asia are busy preparing ourselves for the next offensives and the day is not far off when the British retreat from Delhi will begin. During the seven months of fighting all along the Indo-Burma frontier and inside India, we have been able to take the measure of our enemies. Having beaten the enemy in several sectors while we are on the offensive our confidence in final victory has increased a hundred fold. We know that the fight will have one result, namely the expulsion of the enemy from Indian soil and establishment of a free and united India.

52

Azad Hind Fauj Orders by Lieut. Colonel Aziz Ahmad Khan regarding the formation of War Council.

BURMA *30 October, 1944*

Appointments–Officers:

444. During the absence of the Supreme Commander, A. H. F., from H Q No. 11 Unit, Lieut, Col. Aziz Ahmad Khan will deal with all routine add urgent matters, which would ordinarily have been dealt with by the Supreme Commander.

Lt. Col. Aziz Ahmad Khan will, during this period, exercise the powers of the Chief of Staff.

War Council:

445. Since the establishment of the Provisional Government of Azad Hind on the 21st October 1943, a year of intensive activity has elapsed. In the meantime, the war has reached a stage when the initiative is going to pass from the hands of our enemies to those of our friends and of our Allies. To prepare for the coming offensive, it is absolutely necessary to make an all out effort at Total Mobilisation and to further intensify and co-ordinate all our activities connected with our war-preparations. In order to achieve this objective, a special organ of the Provisional Government of Azad Hind has to be set up. The War Council of the Provisional Government has, thereofre, been formed. The War Council which is the Supreme organ of the Provisional Government for directing and controlling the war effort and the war preparations of the Government will have the following duties:

1. I.N.A. Trial Papers.

1. To further intensify the war activities that will be found necessary for the war effort and for war preparations.

2. To initiate any new activites that will be found necessary for the war effort and for war preparations.

3. To co-ordinate all these activities with a view to producing the maximum result, namely, to launch the offensive that will bring about the speed and complete otherthrow of our enemies—

The following is the composition of the War Council:—

1. Colonel	J. K. Bhonsla
2. Colonel	M. Z. Kiani
3. Lt. Col.	Ehsan Qadir
4. Lt. Col.	Aziz Ahmad Khan
5. Lt. Col.	Habib-ur- Rahman
6. Lt. Col.	Gulzara Singh
7. Shri	N. Raghavan
8. Sri	S.A. Ayar.
9. Sri	Parmanand
10. Col.	A.C. Chatterjee
11. Sri	A. Yellapa.

Appendix I

Intercepted Radio Broadcast on the Activities of I. N. A. and Provisional Government of Azad Hind 1943-44[1]

In concert with the historic Greater East Asia proclamation of Premier Tojo in the Imperial Diet on the fall of Singapore, the Indian Independence leader, Mr. Rash Behari Bose and 800 other Indian residents of Japan gathered at ... Hotel in Tokyo and issued an important statement in connection with the Indian Independence Movement, strongly urging the Indian nation to rise to the establishment of India for the Indians and India for the Asiatics. These people issued and signed this manifesto: "We Indian nationals have fought for the past fifty years against British aggression with the object of making India for Indians and India for Asia. Despite thousands of personal sacrified, our efforts so far have failed because we have had no armed support. The present war of GEA has given us a goldern opportunity for realizing our century old objective. Fellow countrymen of India, take advantage of this...... support and liquidate all of India's past quarrels with Britain. In accordance with the spirit of Buddah and Islam rise up to greet the truth and doctrine of Mahatama Gandhi." *Tokyo, English, 2.12.42*

Shigoru Hata stated "Representing this rally, wires relative to the preceding resolution will be sent to the following headquarters throughout the GEA : the Moanchukuo Genral Society, the North China Hsin Min Society, the Mongolia Far East cooperative Society, the Nanking Asia Development Fedaration and the Indian Independence Movement Office at Bangkok and others. The contents of these wires will be read to you through my representatives. At the Rally for the Rescue of India, we have resolved to give all-out support to India in her work for independence. The complete destruction of our common enemy America and Britain, has been pledged." *Tokyo, Japanese 8.27.43*

1. This report was prepared by the office of the Strategic Service, U.S. government. O.S.S. Record Group. 226. copy obtained from Diet Library, Tokyo.

Tokyo Kabuki Theatre became the scene of India Rescue People's Rally and the following resolution "Britain took a cruel measure to bring pressure on Indian people by disregarding Gandhi's attempt. Tojo promised Philippenes independence and he also promised the fullest support to India." The resolution was wired to appropriate organs.

Tokyo, Japanese 2.27.43

A capacity crowd of 5,000 attended the All-India National Meeting held in Tokyo Saturday at the Kabuki Theatre under the joint sponsorship of National Service Association, Nippon Asia Development League and the Asahi, Mainachi and Yamuri Haki newspapers. It was held in a most favourable atmosphere with popular sentiments running high in sympathy with Mahatma Gandhi. In addition, the decision reached Friday by the Japanese Government that Indians who cooperate with Japan will be accorded treatment similar to that given to the Indian nationals was met with deep satisfaction. The resolution and declaration passed were cabled to the Cencordia Association of Manchukuo, the Hain Min. Society of North China, the Chinese Council of the East Asiatic League in Nanking, the Indian Independence League in various localities in the Southern Regions, Kiwao Okamura, Vice Chief of the Tokyo Board of Information, spoke on Gandhi, as did also Nitaro Nagal, Chief of the Asia Developement Bureau of the National Service Association. *Tokyo, English, 2.23.43*

To celebrate establishment of the Provisional Government of Azad Hind, 45 representative Indian residents in Tokyo, Yokohama, Kobe, Osaka and other leading lives of Japan held a "Rice India" meeting..... Rash Behari Bose, Supreme Advisor of the Provisional Government of Free India, who recently returned from Snoyan resorted on progress of the Independence movement there. *Tokyo, English, 10.25.43*

Japan Indian Independence League

The Indian Independence Legue had four branches in Japan but since there was not good connection between them, a territorial committee was established and a first meeting held. The representatives from each branch will form a Council and their first meeting will be at Tokyo, May 2. Heretofere they have worked independently. *Tokyo, Japanese, 5.3.43*

Representatives of the Tokyo, Yokohama, Osaka and Kobe Branches of the Indian Independence Legue decided to establish a central committee for Japan which will organize and guide the work of the branches and will further strengthen the freedom movement. The committee consists of 8 members, 2 from each branch and their work is distributed among three sections and officers is charge have been appointed. These are Department of Publicity and Information, Department of Planning and Department of Welfare. *Tokyo, Hindustani 8.3.43*

The central office of the Indian Independence Legue in Japan has named the Nippon...... committee has removed to its permanent site at No. 5 (Kaminchi Akasakahu). The opening ceremonies will be held at the new premises on Jan 12, whom the Acting Chief of the new office will be formally inaugurated. This office will represent in Japan the headquarters of the Indian Independence Legue in East Asia, which is now at Shonan. The office will guide and central all the activities of the new branches in Japan while carrying on the Indian Independence Movement under the command of the Supreme Leader, Subhas Chandra Bose.

Tokyo, English 12.39.43

Immediately upon receipt of the tragic news of the demise of Mrs. Kasturbai Gandhi in the British prison at Poona, the Indian Independence League in Japan called a meeting yesterday of Indians in Nippon at its central officers to mourn her lost, with members of the League in Tokyo and representatives from the Yokohama, Osaka and Kobo Branches also participating . The meeting was held in the presence of Rash Behari Bose, supreme Advisor to the Provisional Government of Azad Hind.

Tokyo, English, 2.24.44

Local Indian residents will assemble at Honaji Temple here Wednesday afternoon to hold a prayer meeting in memory of the Late Kasturbai Gandhi who died Feb. 22 while imprisoned by the British at Poona. It is learned the function is planned in accordance with instructions from Subhas Chandra Bose, head of the Provisional Government of Free India and Commander of the Indian Independence Army, to the Indian Independence Legue in Japan. *Tokyo, English, 2.25.44*

Tokyo Branch

Rama Murti, spokesman of the Tokyo Branch of the Indian Independence Legue expressed gratitude over exemption of the Indians from the rule for control of enemy property of the casot-freezing order.

Tokyo, English, 2.27.43

The members of the Tokyo Branch of the Indian Independence League held a rally at the Sanno Hotel Monday to express their joy at the assumption of the presidency of the League by Mr. Subhas Chandra Bose. The members expressed their heartfelt gratitude to Mr. Rash Behari Bose outgoing president for his invaluable services to the cause as the father of the Indian Independence Legue of East Asia. They sent a cable to Mr. Subhas Chandra Bose pledging that..... and devotion to him.

Tokyo, English, 7.6.43

The Tokyo Branch of the Indian Independence League hold a meeting Tokyo on Dec. 2...... in regard to the transfer of the two islands of Andaman and Nicobar to the Free India Provisional Government by Japan. The Indian Independence Legue Council in Japan decided to have its headquarters in Tokyo and establish branches in Yokohama and Osaka for the purpose of .....

Tokyo, Japanese, 12.2.43

Kobe Branch

Taking advantage of the GEA war which will liberate the one billion people of East Asia, 67 Indian living in the region of Osaka and Kobe this afternoon held a meeting at Kobe, at which the Kobe Branch of the Indian Independence Association was disbanded and merged with the New India Indian League. It was decided to establish local branches of this League at Kobe and Osaka..... and headed by..... Subhas Chandra Bose of Tokyo. It was decided to work for the Independence of India.

Tokyo, Japanese, 2.23.42

As a representative of the Indian people residing in Japan, the Kobe Branch head (Tahan) of the Indian Independence League attended the formation ceremonies of the Indian Independence Army of the Free India Provisional Government.

Tokyo, Japanese, 11.20.43

Yokohama Branch

Celebrating the seventy-third brithday of Mahatma Gandhi, more than 300 Japanese and Indian friends and supporters Friday gathered at the Indian Club at Yokohama. The celebration was hold under the auspicious of the Japanese headquarters of the Indian Independence League.

Tokyo, English, 10.2.42

The Yokohama Branch of the Indian Independence League held its general meeting at the India club on Monday and unanimously elected the following officers President. (Digovio Sagani), Honorary Secretary, (Shilapi Colazani).......

Tokyo English, 10.14.42

A solemn ceremony commemorating the first anniversary of the outbreak of the current war was observed today in Yokohama by the Indian President, including President (Cordona) of the Indian Independence League. Mr. (Mahtani) of the Indian Merchants Association of Yokohama, Professor (Kimlon), the Indian representative from Tokyo. The program started with saluting the Rising Sun flag and the Indian Independence Flag. *Tokyo, English, 12.8.42*

Deep concern is being shown by Indian residents in Japan over Gandhi's hunger strike. Indian residents in Yokohama held a 24 hours fast upon receipt of the news that he challanged Britain with a gallant gesture. Indians in Tokyo and Kobe are expected to observe similar fasts in manifestation of their all-out sympathy with Gandhi's move. Professor Nichi Kimurn of..... the University in Tokyo will broadcast to Indian leaders from Radio Tokyo tonight. *Tokyo, English 2.17.43*

P.V. Sadani, President of the Yokohama Branch of the Indian Independence League, and his party are hurrying to Shonan to join the Indian Independence Army under the command of Subhas Chandra Bose. *Tokyo, Japanese, 7.27.43*

Japanese Cooperation

"Victory is ours"—The days of British tyranny over Indians have now passed, declared Rama Murti, Chairman of the Indian Independence League in Japan, in hailing the Imperial Headquarters' announcement of the destruction of the main force of the British 7th division on the Burma-India border..... Murti revealed that Netaji S.C. Bose several days ago cabled a message to the Indian residents here, saying "Victory is ours, since we are fighting in cooperation with the strong Japanese army." He also disclosed that the Indian residents of Tokyo on February 2 contributed a half million yen toward the Indian Independence Army war fund, while many young Indians, formerly residents of Tokyo, already have joined Bose's army. *Tokyo, English, 3.1.44*

Indian Nationals not Enemies. The Board of Information announced that hereafter Indians who will cooperate with Japan's prosecution of the war will after March 1, not be treated as enemy nationals in Japan and the Southern regions. *Tokyo, Japanese, 2.26.43*

Contributions

Burma: The Provisional Government of Azad Hind had disclosed the reciept of a contribution of 1,000 yen to India's Freedom War Chest, as well as a message of encourgement from Masanori Isoda, who represented 8,000 villagers of Otaki village. Saitamu Perfecture, Japan. In the message addressed to Netaji Subhas Chandra Bose, Isoda writes," You seized the great opportunity of the GEA war and, collaborating with the Imperial Japanese Army in smashing the wild ambitions of the Anglo-Americans to continue hegemony in East Asia, you now are striving to drive the

Anglo-Americans out of your country and the Indian !ndependence Army under your leadership now is fighting on the Indian mainland. It is now time for the 400,000,000 people to rise up and.... with the Indian Independence Army. We pray God that He will give you sufficient strength to fight out the war until you achieve independence, surrounting the many hardships that will come your way. We are sending you the sum of 1,000 yen, which is the contribution of 8,000 villagers of Otaki village, who will be pleased if You Excellency would use it for your conduct of the war."

Tokyo, English, 8.10.41

Leaders

Subhas Chandra Bose

Chandra Bose, the leader of the Indian Independence League who has been in Germany recently arrived in Tokyo and on June 14 conferred with Tojo. He also was present at the Diet........ The significance of his visit to Japan is great. Premier Tojo in every Diet address has related in regard to Indian Independence that the Empire has firm faith for support and will wipe out Britain and America from India. *Tokyo, Japanese, 5.18.43*

The recent visit to Japan of Chandra Bose is bringing forth numerous comments among the German people. "In his recent addressed, Premier Tojo has reiterated that Japan is prepared to give every assistance to India in order to extricate India from the yoke of England..... Mr. Bose has travelled at ease from India to Germany and then from Germany to Japan. This points out to the people of India that the Anglo-Saxons are not the rulers of the world any longer and this psychological effect is unfathomable.... It is clear as day that the independence movement of India will rapidly become stronger. There is no room for doubt that India will gain true freedom under the leadership of such a patriot as Bose." The editorial of a German foreign agency stated the above. *Tokyo, Japanese 6.19.43*

Chandra Bose will deliver a lecture entitled, "The People of my Motherland," under the auspices of the Imperial Rule Assistance Political Society and will ask for the understanding and cooperation of the political world of Japan in connection with the movement for the liberation of India.

Tokyo, Japanese, 5.19.43

Subhas Chandra Bose, before the newspaper men in Tokyo, declared, "I am standing before you in the heart of Nippon instead of sitting idle in a prison house in India, which is symbolic of the new movement that is now sweeping over my country.... Indian outside India should make every effort to help Indians inside India and fully cooperate with each other for the attainment of independence. What Indians inside India cannot do must be done by Indians outside India." *Tokyo, English, 6.19.43*

The Borliner (Machtausgabo) commented as follows : When the visit to Japan of Chandra Bose and the appointment of Wavell as Viceroy of India were announced, the Indian Independence movement was in progress now under very favourable conditions. Bose has arrived in Japan and together with several million Indian countrymen who have already been serving in the independence movement in the Greater East Asia Co-Prosperity Sphere will be able to carry on a more native independence movement." *Tokyo, Japanese 6.20.43*

Berlin : On Saturday a message of greeting was sent by Reich Foreign Minister Joachim von Ribbentrop to Subhas Chandra Bose who recently arrived in Tokyo. The message reads as follows: "I convey my cordial greetings on the occasion of your arrival is East Asia. I thank you for your parting telegram sent to the Fuhrer, wherein you stress your solidarity with Germany in fighting against a common enemy. We trust you will be successful in your future fight for the liberty of the Indian people." *Tokyo, English, 6.20.43*

A welcome meeting was held in Tokyo by Indian residents in Tokyo and Yokohama in honor of Mr. Subhas Chandra Bose (sic), leader of the Indian Independence League in East Asia. Mr. Bose has retruned to Tokyo from his tour of encouraging all the Indians in the Greater East Asia Co-Prosperty Sphere..... his arrival in Tokyo of Mr. Subhas Chandra Bose, another leader of the Independence movement. The meeting was held in a very cheerful atmosphere expressing desire for...... and also win their home country from Britain Shockles. *Tokyo, English, 6.22.43*

In order to ask for the understanding and cooperation of all circles in our political world, also as regards Indian Independence, Subhas Chandra Bose, the Indian Independence Leader who is now in Japan, visited Headquarters of the Imperial Rule Assistance Political Society on June 23... He stated "The disobedience movement of older Gandhi has achieved no satisfactory results substantially up to the present. Moreover, Gandhi's objective of compromising with Britain and of acquiring autonomy is not the way to bring about ture independence..... Complete independence for India can only be realized by carrying on strike by force of arms, taking advantage of the outbroke of war..... I firmly believe that Indian Independence will surely succeed through the cooperation and aid of the Japanese Government and people." *Tokyo, English, 6.23.43*

Upon arrival at Haneda airport, Subhas Chandra Bose was warmly welcomed by prominent Japanese officials, including Foreign Minister Mamoru Shigomitsu, GEA Affairs Minister Aoki, and President of the Board of Information Eiji Amau, as well as leading members of the Tokyo chapter of the Indian Independence League. Bose was accompanied by a part of ......, including A. M. Sahay, Minister without portfolio, and upon stopping from the plane they exchanged greetings with Japanese leaders. Among those who anxiously watched the planes landing were two Indian girl students now studying at the Seishin Girls' School here who were waiting to welcome their father, A. M. Sahay. *Tokyo, English, 11.31.43*

Netaji Subhas Chandra Bose made an official call on Premier Tojo this morning and took his departure after remaining in conversation for forty minutes with the Japanese Premier. *Saigon, English, 11.1.43*

At the Hibiya Park Auditorium, a great lecture meeting for Mr. Subhas Chandra Bose was held. He explained the history of India in a sympathetic manner and condemned with furious rage the atrocities and exploitation of the British Government against India. *Tokyo, Japanese, 11.15.43*

Tokyo: On the first anniversary of Bose's assumption of leadership of the Indian Independence Movement, members of the Tokyo chapter of the League assembled to observe Netaji Week. Silent Prayers for those who lost their lives fighting for freedom of India were said and work was reviewed. A resolution was adopted: "Indians express joy and gratification over progress to date, they pay homage to heroes of Azad Hind Fauj, they pray for repose of heroic martyrs, they express profound gratitude to Japan for aid, they renew and reaffirm loyalty and allegiance to Netaji." *Tokyo, English, 7.4.44*

Rash Behari Bose

Rash Behari Bose, Supreme Advisor of the Indian Independence League, arrived in Tokyo yesterday. *Tokyo, Japanese, 9.21.43*

Forty representatives of the local Indian community, led by Rash Behari Bose, Supreme Advisor to the Provisional Government of Free India, met at the headquarters of the Japan Chapter of the Indian Independence League this afternoon to observe the 15th anniversary of the Declaration of Indian Independence from the British yoke by Mohandas Gandhi. *Tokyo, English, 1.26.44*

The Tokyo Branch of the Indian Independence League at this time decided to hold a great prayer meeting with Behari Bose, Supreme Advisor of the Free India Provisional Government, and a large number of others participating on February 21 in Tokyo in order to encourage the Free India National Army. *Tokyo, Japanese, 2.17.44*

The Japan Chapter of the Indian Independence League will broadcast special programs to the people of India between 12 : 15 and 12 : 45 every night, giving vital news and commentaries of Azad Hind's war effort. The first program tonight features an address by Rash Behari Bose, Supreme advisor to the Provisional Government of Azad Hind. Tokyo, 3.22.44

Tokyo: Rash Behari Bose, Supreme Advisor of the Indian Independence League, now in Japan, cabled message of folicications to Subhas Chandra Bose on anniversary of Netaji Week.

Tokyo, English, 7.5.44

Rash Behari Bose, who has been devoting himself to the anti- British independence movement from early days in Japan, welcoming Chandra Bose's arrival in Japan, beamed with joy and stated: "The Indian Independence Movement must be awaited..... All preparations are made and we can only await a strong prosecution. Thus the significance of having welcomed Chandra Bose is in need of no explanation. I am at complete ease and feel as though I had attained a million allies. The activities of the Indian Independence League will probably be opened with greater strength." *Tokyo, Japanese, 6.19.43*

Training for Leadeship

Thirty-five Indian youths who have been selected to be sent to Japan by the Provisional Government of Azad Hind Fauj from Shonan to receive an education in order that they may became future leaders of Free India, today made a round of courtesy calls on Government offices here, starting with a call at the War Ministry, where they were received by Maj. Gen. Kenryo Sato, Director of the Military Affairs Bureau. The Youths, whose ages range from 15 to 19, have already received 5 month' training in Nipponego and other preparatory courses in Shonan. After receiving final preparatory training at the New Asia Institute..... Gakuin here, they will enter the Military Academy, so that they may be thoroughly trained as worthy army officers and leaders of the Azad Hind Fauj in the historic battle for independence. *Tokyo, English, 4.13.44*

Indian National Army

Today the first batch of the Indian Independence League of Tokyo, consisting of Indian youths resident in Japan, is about to leave for Shonan to join the Indian Independence Army. Mr. D. W. Sardani (P. W. Sadani), of

Yokohama, who has lived in Japan for the last thirty years and has taken an active part in Indian Independence Movement along with Rash Behari Bose, is the man in Charge. *Tokyo, Hindustani, 7.18.43*

China Independence Movement

Hongkong: Five hundred representatives of the Indian population in Hongkong gathered at a temple on Sunday and held a mass prayer for the early realization of Indian Independence and liberation of Mahatma Gandhi and other arrested leaders. *Tokyo, English, 9.6.42*

Over 1,000 Indian Nationals in Canton, including prisoners, on Monday offered reverent prayers for Indian Independence bowing reverently in the direction of Mecca. Following this, many made speeches, shouting, "Down with Britain." *Tokyo, English, 10.12.42*

Nanking: A mass meeting to rally support for the Indian Independence Movement was held at the National Assembly Hall in Nanking on Monday. Mr. Wang-Ching-Wei, President of the National Government of China, issued a statement and speeches were delivered by Dr. Chu Min-Yi, Foreign Minister, Mr. Lin Powshong, Publicity Minister, Mr. Masayuki Yoshitomi, Spokesman of the Japanese Embasy in Nanking, and others. A declaration of sympathy was passed and a message of encouragement sent to Mahatam Gandhi and the people of India.

Tokyo, English, 3.1.43

Nanking: The establishment of the Indian Provisional Governnment is Shonan with the appointment of Mr. Subhas Chandra Bose as the President of the Indian Independence League was hailed by the National Governmemnt of China as the start of the long-cherished armed revolution of the Indian Independence Movement, to which the Nanking Government has extended active support during the past year. The National Government is resolved to extend all-out help in fostering the Indian Independence Movement and the close collaboration with the new Indian Government, toward the final goal of the liberation of the whole Asiatic race from the Anglo-American yoke. *Tokyo, English, 7.5.43*

Indian Independence League
Peking Branch

The President of the Indian Residents' Association here yesterday called on the Peking Office of the Japanese Embassy and expressed hearty felicitation on the brilliant achievements of the Japanese operations on the India-Burma border. In the course of the interview, the Indian leader expressed the firm conviction Indian is certain to acquire her long-cherished national independence and freedom from British oppression with Japan's support. He sought Japan's continued assistance in the cause of Indian Independence, stating the Indians in North China are determined to follow those who have already joined the Indian Independence Army and are fighting in Burma on the Indian border. *Tokyo, English, 2.14.44*

Shanghai Branch

Shanghai: Various Indian organizations here will go into one body, following a conference Saturday. The new central body included Independence Movement, National Society and others. Officials were named and the organization started immediately. Five hundred Indians gathered at the Raco Track discuss the death of Gandhi's secretory..... gave stirring addresses falling Indians to fight. *Tokyo, English, 8.25.42*

Inuraugral ceremonies of the Indian Independence League will be held this afternoon at the Race Track and the entire Indian community..... will be attended by high ranking Japanese, Chinese and Axis officials and other sympathizers with India's cause. The organizing committee of the League has asked the Indian employers to grant their emplyees leave to enable than to be present. *Shanghai, English, 31.3.42*

Acting in concert with the Bangkok Indian Independence Federation, preparation were being made among the 2,000 Indians living in Shanghai for the establishment of a Shanghai Branch of the Indian Independence Federation. As inaugural meeting consolidating six organizations was held at the Race Course and attended by over 1,000 people representing the factions and all Indians living here and will maintain close relations with the headquarters at Bangkok, China and Indians overseas. It will enter upon positive activities been attention. (Kotochin) has been made President. *Tokyo, Japanese, 11.4.42*

All minor differences have been ironed out and all Indian communities in Shanghai have been consolidated into one association.

Seigon, English, 11.4.42

With Gen. (Iwane Matsui), Vice President of the East Asiatic League, as the guest of honor, the Shanghai East Asia Society held a round table conference at the Opera House in Shanghai. To the conference were invited representatives from the Shanghai Chapter of the Indian Independence League and the Phillipines Assocation as well as Afghanistan. Gen. (Matsui) stressed the importance of establishing an Asia for the Asiatic through the close cooperation of various East Asiatic peoples. He also explained about Japan's justified stand as well as her true intentions. Mr. (Jarlemaru), Managing Director of the Shanghai Chapter of the Indian Independence League, said, "If we miss this Heavon-sent opportunity, the Indian people may lose forever the chance of becoming independent. We are firmly determined to achieve the long-cherished ideal of the Indian Independence with the support of Japan." *Tokyo, English, 11.26.42*

Taiping Branch

A huge increase was seen in the membership of the Taiping Branch of the Indian Independence League since the beginning of this year as streams of Indian men and women have been flocking to the promises of the League, membership has increased by nearly 100% compared with last year's figures. *Tokyo, English, 3.3.41*

Hankow Branch

Celebrating the entry of Japanese and Indian Independence Army Forecast into Manipur, as well as marking the inauguration of the Hankow Branch of the Indian Independence League, a mass rally was held here March 25 at the Asia Development ground, with 1,000 local Indian participating. The function which was held under the auspicious of the Indian Residents' Association in Hankow was also attended by representatives of the Axis countries, Japan, Germany, China and Italy.

Tokyo, English, 3.28.44

Hongkong Branch

On the 72nd birthday of Mahatma Gandhi, a rally held by the Hongkong Branch of the Indian Independence League, at which absolute obedience to the Gandhi was sworn to gain the complete independence of India. *Tokyo, English, 10.2.42*

More than a hundred members of the Hongkong Branch of the Indian Independence League at their office to hear the sensational speech of Mr. Subhas Chandra Bose which was broadcast Monday night.

Tokyo, English, 6.23.43

Welcoming the return from Shonan of Dr. Dejo Naidu, Chief of the Hongkong Branch of the Indian Independence League, more than 2,000 members of the branch held a mass meeting Monday and reaffirmed their determination to fight to the bitter end for Indian liberty. Dr. Naidu declared that the Indian Independence Army is rapidly preparing itself for a battle against Britain. The independence movement is progressing swiftly in Shonan according to plan. *Tokyo, English, 8.11.43*

On his retun from Shonan where he attended the Indian Independence League conference, Dr. (Nai Ding), Chairman of the Hongkong Branch, declared that the activities of the league and the national army are progressing rapidly. *Tokyo, English, 9.13.43*

All Indian shops and firms in Hongkong and Kowlon were closed today in observance of the Baisakhi Festival and they will be closed tomorrow for the mass meeting in connection with National liberation Week and the Jhallinwala massacre. All Indian were expected to make it a special point to attend and participate in this historic meeting. Meanwhile, the Independence League gave out the report in the local paper that it would be thankful to all employers for granting permission to their Indian employees for leave of absence on this day.

Hongkong, English, 4.12.44

The Indians of Hongkong celebrated the Provisional Government's (birth) yesterday by holding a mass meeting..... speeches were made by leading members of the Indian Independence League. A minute's silence in honor of those who have sacrificed their lives in the cause of freedom was observed. *Hongkong, English, 4.22.44*

A mass meeting was held at the Hall of the Indian Independence League by Indians in Hongkong in celebration of the fourth Provisional Government Day and for offering prayers for Mahatma Gandhi's quick recovery from illness. The meeting was enlivened by the singing of national songs by a trio from the Indian Youth Corps, followed by a speech by Dr. Naidu, Chairman of the meeting , who declared: “This day four months ago amid cheors of universal hope and rejoicing was celebrated by Indians throughout Greater East Asia with unfurling of the tri-colored banner of the Indian nation on the doorstop of every Indian home. On this day it was proclaimed to the world that the political ideals of the people without single exception are one and one only and as regards these ideals being brought to a realization in a tangible and substantial form, no Indian, will remain tongue-tied. On this day our entire nation took a firm resolve that as long as independence is not achieved, none will rest content but will go on fighting untill Delhi is reached.” *Hongkong, English, 5.22.44*

*A mass meeting of all Indians in Hongkong will be held under the auspices of the Indian Independence League at the Keenster Theatre next week to celebrate the commencement of the fight by the Indian National Army and the first victory achieved on the Arakan front in cooperation with the Japanese air arm. Meanwhile,...... will be paid to their leader, Subhas Chandra Bose, and the gallant fighting men on the front lines.

Hongkong, English, 2.20.44

Four thousand Indian residents attended a mass rally here this morning under the auspices of the Hongkong Chapter of the Indian Independence League to pray for victory for the Indian Independence Army which is now participating in Japanese operations in the Arakan factor on the Burma-India border. *Tokyo, English, 2.21.44*

The Indians of Hongkong held a mass meeting commemorating the martyrdom of the great Indian patriot, Bhagat Singh. After the singing of the national song by Jamedar Jagat Singh, a minute of silence followed.

Hongkong, English, 3.24.44

The Hongkong Indian Independence League held a meeting recently when the league was completely reorganized and Mr. (T. V.) Krishna elected the new Chairman. He declared: "We are now entering a very critical stage in the fight for independence and with the reorganization of the league the fight for freedom will be taken up with increased vigor. The present body elected is not going to sit quietly and talk. They are here to do somethings. The new chairman revealed that July 4 to 10 will be observed as Netaji Week, as it was on July 4 last year that Subhas Chandra Bose took charge of the Indian Independence Movement in Singapore. A special meeting will be held on the first day of the celebration when the new policies and aims of the league will be clearly stated for the benefit of the Indian Community and the meeting will be followed by a mass procession through the main city the meeting will be followed by a mass procession through the main city streets." *Hongkong, English, 7.3.44*

The Hongkong Indian Independence League is going to celebrate Netaji Week. Today, the first day, they held a mass meeting in the facade of the Japanese Club House, for all Indians in Hongkong to remember their Independence for the nation of India. They announced of their aim of their independence. Afterwards, there was a mass procession. All the Indians of the different organizations of Hongkong and those in Kowloon have joined this meeting. They again announce that they will ally themselves together politically to drive the British out of India. On July 9, the Japanese new pictures and Indian show will; be exhibited in the..... Theatre is Kowloon. *Hongkong, Cantonese 7.4.44*

Indian leaders in Hongkong recently held a meeting at the Indian Independence League Hall where impressive lectures and political addresses were delivered and a committee and it was decided to held weekly and fortnightly meetings in.... where he would deliver lectures on various subjects for the general education of Indian women. The committee will invite all Indian ladies regardless of caste or creed to attend the meetings regularly and fit themselves to take their places as leaders in the work of Greater East Asia. *Hongkong, English, 8.19.44*

Canton Branch

Members of the Canton Branch of the Indian Independence League on June 20 met at headquarters in (Shanghang) and adopted a resolution pledging wholehearted support to Subhas Chandra Bose, prominent Indian Independence Leader who recently arrived in Japan from Germany.

Tokyo, English, 6.22.43

Canton: A celebration of the creation of the Provisional Government of Azad Hind was held here this afternoon under the Canton Branch of the Indian Independence League. A street parade along the main streets of the city and a meeting in the public hall were the highlights of today's functions. *Tokyo, English, 10.25.43*

Hand in hand with the Japanese, all Indians are shouldering the sacred mission of overthrowing Britain, declared Dr. Nader Khan, chairman of the Canton Chapter of the Indian Independence League at a meeting highlighted by the report announcing the commencement of offensive oprations by Japanese forces in concert with the Indian Independence Army at the Indo-Burma border. Dr. Khan said, "You can't imagine how long we have been waiting for this day." He said that Indian residents last night gathered together to discuss until dawn the future of independence. He pointed out that many who gladly joined the Indian Independence Army are no doubt marching bravely on toward their mother country to the tune of roaring guns. He said,"We will continue the march until victory is won. Only glorious victory awaits us." *Tokyo, English, 2.8.44*

The Canton Chapter of the Indian Independence League held a rally here this afternoon to celebrate the participation of the Indian Independence Army in the current Japanese operations on the Burma-Indian border.

Tokyo, English, 2.21.44

The Canton Branch of the Indian Federation recently held a large.... meeting in conjuction with the great movement of Indian Independence. Besides expanding the structure of the Cultural Department, they elected now officers to fill the new posts. *Honkong Cantonese, 6.6.44*

........, Chairman of the Canton Branch of the Indian Independence League, recently came to Hongkong to strengthen the relation of the

Hongkong and Canton Branch offices... He said that the Government of Can.on is also very cooperative with the Canton Branch.

Contributions

Shanghai (Domei): It is already one year since the formation of the Free India Provisional Government and the 2,000 Indians residing in Shanghai held a commemorative rally and contributed 6,000 yen to the Indian Independence League. *Tokyo, Japanese, 6.22.44*

Indian National Army

The Canton Branch of the Indian Independence League on July 4 sent a large number of the volunteers to Shonan for the Indian Independence Army. The office of the league here is daily receiving numorous application from local Indian Youths who are impatiently waiting for the day when they will be able to take up arms for the cause of their independence. *Tokyo, English, 7.10.43*

The Hongkong Branch of the Indian Independence League decided to begin recruitment of volunteers for the Indian Independence Army. The registration of men between eighteen and thirty-five commenced on September and immediately applicants poured in.

Tokyo, Japanese, 9.16.43

In order further to bolster this movement and realize the independence even a day earlier, President Bose dispathced Lt. Col. (Nega Nadan) to the China area as representative. He arrived at Canton, Communicated his mission and examined volunteers at the Overseas Residence. *Tokyo, Japanese, 9.2.43*

Shanghai: All Indians, regardless of caste or creed, are enrolling for service with the Indian Independence Army in order to fight for......, says President (Chet Soon), of the Shanghai chapter of the Indian Independence League, who recently returned from Shonan after attending Burma's .... celebration for the formation of the Indian Independence Army.

Tokyo, English. 7.26.43

A batch of more than 400 Indians, consisting of Hindus and Muslims, is about to leave for Shonan to join the Indian Independence Army. Even the women have volunteered to serve the national cause as nurses.

Tokyo, Hindustani, 7.28.43

Indian volunteers, who are trained in Hongkong to....... among the first groups called into the Indian Independence Army by Subhas Chandra Bose, leave Hongkong as soon as they have acquired a..... knowledge of the arts of war to go it Shonan where they put themselves directly under

Bose's command, then to be sent to the front lines to fight against the allied forces, according to a Damoi dispatch from Hongkong. Because of this situation, the Branch of the Indian Independence Movement in Hongkong has decided to open a fully equipped training center for Indian volunteers on December 18 in Kowloon new Honkong.

Tokyo, German, 12.17.43

Hongkong: Observance of Indian Liberation Week here was brought to a successful close yesterday with a huge rally held by local Indian residents who pledged to offer everything for the liberation of their motherland. In line with various other parts of East Asia, local Indians observed liberation Week which started April 6 with colorful programs. Following the rally yesterday, memberes of the Indian Independence Army who are presently training here paraded thc streets of the city amidst the loud cheering of a crowd wildly waving the Indian colors.

Tokyo, English, 4.14.44

Shanghai: The local Azad Hind Fauj Training Camp was officially opened in a colorful ceremony held yesterday before members of the Indian Community and prominent Japanese, Chinese and German guests,. In the opening initiation program, Captain Boo Narain, Commandant of the camp, expressed his gratitude for the facilities granted for drilling purposes and informed the guests drills which would follow would be conducted by Reservists. These recruits gave a very impressive exhibition of marching and the executive of various military orders before the guests. Nanak Chand whose position as Chairman of the local Chapter of the Indian Independence League was approved by the Provisional Government President, gave a tea party after the opening ceremony. In his speech he pointed out inauguration of the camp is a fitting manifestation of the patriotism of the local Indian community and it was the first time in the history of Shanghai that such a schools has existed, as previouslsy it was not possible due to measures taken by the British to prevernt such a movement. Doctor Herest Ley, Director of the Ostatischer Lloyd, German Language School, also addressed the meeting stating that it was not only fighting for its right but also to aid in the liberation of India. He wished every success to the training school. *Tokyo, English, 6.20.44*

The Shanghai Institute for training Indian Independence Army volunteers opened this afternoon with ceremonies attended by Mayor Chen Kung-Po, of Shanghai, Uzuhiko Usami, Japanese Minister, diplomatic envoys of Axis countrious and others. It is learned that the Institute has an enrollment of 600 volunteers, selected from many applicants.

Tokyo, English 7.9.44

The Shanghai Institute for training local Indian volunteers had the assistance and support of the local Japanese and Chinese authorities who make its establishment possible. Six hundred Indian volunteers will be accepted for a three months's training course.

Tokyo, English, 7.9.44

Shanghai: More than 3,000 Indian residents will hold a rally celebrating the capture of Imphal with address by B. Bobby Chiod Fot El. liaison officer of the Shanghai Branch of Indian Independence League.

Tokyo English, 4.12.44

Azad Hind Dal

An extraordinary meeting of members of the Advisory Board of the Indian Independence League and representatives of all Indian association and socities will be held tomorrow at the League Hall in (China House) for the purpose of forming a (fighting corps) and organizing the Azad Hind (Jatha), the Indian Independence League announced.

Hongkong, English, 5.31.44

The Hongkong Branch of the Indian Independence League announced yesterday: By order of our Netaji, a new organization is being set up under the name of Azad Hind Dal, consisting of those who were not members of the Azad Hind Fauj. Indian Independence Army, It will participate in the fight for India's independence and will work in close cooperation with the Azad Hind Fauj during and after the campaign. The Azad Hind Dal will consist of those who will work in a civilian and semi-military capacity. Enrollment of applicants will begin at the League branches on June 19. The Indian public, except those who are already in the Azad Hind Fauj, are requested to enroll. *Hongkong, English 6.16.43*

A large number of Indians have already enrolled in the Azad Hind Dall, a new organization set up by order of Netaji Subhas Chandra Bose.... In Hongkong, the Azad Hind Dal is being created for the purpose of protecting the interests and property of Indian nationals in (time of emergency). *Hongkong, English 6.21.44*

Leaders

Subhas Chandra Bose

Nanking Damoi: Subhas Chandra Bose, President of the Free India Provisional Government, who is at present visiting China, called on Premier Wang, Commander-in-Chief Hata, and Ambassador Tani. He also called at the Government Embassy and the Manchukuo Embassy to pay his respects. Mr. Bose expressed his joy upon his first visit to China and stated that in order to liberate East Asia, first there must be unity of China and second, independence of India. Without these the liberation of East Asia cannot be completed. Thus he urged Chungking for profound reflection. *Tokyo, Japanese 12.18.43*

Nanking: Subhas Chandra Bose, head of the Provisional Government of Free India. In this morning received the return visits of Dr. Ernst Wormann, German Ambassador to Nanking. A citizens welcome meeting held in his honor at the National Public Hall, after which he was guest of honor at a luncheon given by Masayuki Tani, Japanese Ambassador to China, Bose conferred with Wang Ching Wei at his official residence and with Dr. Woernann. This evening Bose will be guest of honor at a dinner party tendered by Gen. Shunroku Hata, Commandor-in-Chief of the Japanese Forces in China. *Tokyo, English, 11.19.43*

Nanking Domei : The leader of the Free India Provisional Government, Subhas Chandra Bose, while sojourning in Nanking thrice conferred with Premier Wang and also with leaders of the National Government. The significance of his visit to China is great. The conference between Leader Bose and Premier Wang mutually reaffirmed the enthusiastic assistance of the National Government towards the Indian Independence Movement and the sincere desires of the Free India Provisional Government relative to the unity of China in accordance with the fundamental rule of equality and friendship, which is the ideology of the establishment of the Greater East Asia. Thus the fundamental relationship of the two nations has been established.

Tokyo, Japanese, 11.21.43

Shanghai: The 47th birthday of S. C. Bose. was observed yesterday by the entire local Indian community. *Tokyo, English, 1.24.44*

Indian Independence League
Mukden Branch

A branch of the Indian Independence League, whose headquarters are located at Bangkok, was opened here Sunday morning before the Mukden Shrine. The branch will be open to all Indian residents in Manchukuo proper and the Kwantung Loased Territoryand will work for the emancipation of the East Asia from the Anglo-American imperialism.

Tokyo, English 9.13.42

Mukden: Responding to the enthusiastic Indian Independence Movement under the leadership of Subhas Chandra Bose, the Mukden

Chapter of the Indian Independence League has decided to form an all-Maunchukuo India Youth Corps. These youths will be trained militarily and spiritually so as to be qualified to join the Indian Independence Army is case of emergency. *Tokyo, English, 7.23.43*

Mukden: Denouncing the tyrannical rule of the British in India, which is responsible for the starvation of thousands of his follow Indians, Nichaelman Boolchand, President of the Mukden Chapter of the Indian Independence League, in an interview today declared: "Indians is East Asia have not...... time arrived to bear arms in a fight for the righteous cause and free our countrymen who are suffering torture unheard of in this history of the world at the hands of vicious Britishers."

Tokyo, English, 10.5.43

Mukden: News of the establishment of the Provisional Government of Free india was received with jubilation by members of the local chapter of the Indian Independence League, whose members unanimously reiterated their determinaiton to forge ahead to attain the goal of Indian Independence under the able leadership of Subhas Chandra Bose. In an interview, Nachaldas Boolchand, President of the local league chapter, expressed the belief that the cherished desire of the Indians to gain independence is not far distant. He added that it will not be long before the Indian Independence Army under the banner cry of "On to Delhi" crosses the Indian frontier to sweep the British from Indina soil.

Tokyo, English, 10.23.44

Heinking: Chollarom Arlwani, Secreatory of the Manchukuo Chapter of the Indian Independence League in a radio address directed to follow Indians in Hindustani, today drew a vivid contrast in conditions between Manchukuo and India and urged determined continuance of the Indians' fight for freedom and independence. Alwani outlined the fast progress made by Manchukuo from conditions of benditry and chaos to modern... and declared this had been made possible by establishment of the state on lofty ideals of racial concori and amity. He declared that Manchukuo owed much of her present prosperity to Japanese united moreal and matorial support based on Japan's principles of enabling all nations and peoples to enjoy their rightful place under the sun. He concluded this is in direct contrast to the "Fency promises" given by Anglo-Americans to the Indian people, and urged Indians to rise with greater determination in their fight against the hated enemy of Asia and humankind.

Tokyo, English 6.17.43

Burma Independence Movement

Two millions Indians residing in Burma hastened to hold a big rally to renew their determination to fight with the leader until liberation of the fatherland is achieved and also to find means in order that Mr. Gandhi may not die as a consequence of his ıast. *Tokyo, Spanish, 2/21/42*

Rangoon: "Establishment of new Burma means an establishment of a read for the transfusion of blood into India" this idea in mind, the Indians in Burma had been striving for an organization of Burma Estanblishment Service Corps. However, recently the organization of the corps has started, so that many comrades gathered in Rangoon and held a ceremony for the corps organization in an elaborate manner on July 26. noon.

Tokyo, Japanese 7/26/43

Rangoon: Indian residents in Burma, on Monday organized an Indian Services Corps in Rangoon with the object of helping to construct the new Burma as a vital blood transfusion route for Indian Independence. The head of the corps, (Sadi Lee) said that Indian in Burma will do all in their power for the construction of the new Burma (on the side) of the Indians. *Tokyo, English 7/26/44*

Indian Independence League

Rangoon: Independence League branch of Burma passed a resolution to support Gandhi's demands and fight until British rule is driven out of India will support Bose proposal. *Tokyo, Japanese, 8/11/42*

Rangoon: Echoing the...... of ...... Independence Movement, approximately 50 representatives of the Burma branch of the Indian Independence gathered at the city auditorium in Rangoon for five day conference on September 17. The conference is expected to map out a systematic plan for the Indian Independence Drive to be carried on....

Tokyo, English, 9/15/42

In order to rally Indian Nationals in Burma for the independence of their mother country, a meeting was held in Rangoon on Thursday by the Burma Chapter of the Indian Independence League. The gathering was attended by Dr. Bahmo, Chief executive of the Burmese Government, as well as by high Burmese officials, Speeches were delivered for the immediate liberation of India and overthrow of the British empire.

Tokyo, English, 9/18/42

Dr. U Ba Moung said that the people of Burma are fully aware now of this war,, why and the aim,... The leader of the Indian Independence League in Burma said that all their doubt in Japan's aim is gone. They believe the intentions of Japan and hope to be independent some day......

Tokyo, Malayan, 2/24/43

The Burma Committee of the Indian Independence League make a radio address on the night of February 23, directed to Burma and India, demanding a great stirring up of spirit on the part of all Indian people with respect to Gandhi's wishes. *Tokyo, Japanese, 2/24/43*

Rangoon: Upon the occaion of the.......Independence Preparatory Committee for Burmese Independence, the spokesman of the Rangoon branch of the Indian Independence League issued a statement in which he declared all Indians residing in Burma will extend their assistance in the rebirth of new Burma. *Tokyo, English, 5/9/43*

Rangoon: The establishment of the Free Indian Provisonary Government has decided the course of the Indian Independence Movement, declared the chief of the Rangoon Branch of the Indian Independence League, after listening to the radio speech of Mr. Subahs Chandra Bose..... Chief of the Rangoon Branch stated, "Now is the time for the Indian people to rise in arms, for (there) is the task of (storming) into India. The Indian residents in Burma should immediately launch the war of bloodhsed regardless of their (rank)" *Tokyo, English, 7/5/43*

Indian Independence League

Rangoon: In a message congatulating Burma on its independence (Mr. Payan Gamee), Chairman of the Burmese Chapter of the Indian Independence League, stated that Burma has had the glory of being an independent country (thru) the sincere support of Japan. The glory of Burma will...... accelerate the independence movement in India. The Indians have renewed their determination to fight it thru until India can enjoy the day of complete freedom. *Tokyo, English, 8/3/43*

Rangoon: Mr.(Harimal) Canis, President of the Burma Territorial Committee of the Indian Independence League, on Saturday expressed his gratitude in behalf of the Indians is Burma over the Burmese Government's declaration that the Indian-British subjects ir. Burma will be accorded treatment of a friendly third power and will be permitted in future to become maturalized Burmese citizens. He said that the present declaration is clearly a great help to the Indian Independence Movement.

Tokyo, English, 8/21/43

Rangoon: A rally, celebrating the independence of Burma, was held on Sunday under the auspicious of the Indian Independence League.

Mr. Karim Chani, chairman of the Burma Branch of the Indian Independence League, said that the new people of Asia have been encouraged by the independence of Burma. *Tokyo, English, 9/13/43*

Rangoon: On the 2nd day of Burma's Independence Festival, Sunday, prayer was offered by the Indian Independence League for the liberation of the India. Teh prayer was offered at the graveyard of King Bahadur Shah, who died a Rangoon after years of active service as the leader of the anti-British movement. *Tokyo, English, 9/27/43*

Rangoon: ..... Representatives of the Indian Independence League branches throughout Burma met this morning int the initial session of a three day conference to formualte and put into immediate action measures for the total mobilization of resources of the Indians in Burma for the successful conclusion of the struggle for Indian freedom, which neared a decisive stage with the Indian Independence Army waging war on the enemy on Indian soil. Netaji Bose said, "of course the government and people of Nippon have been giving and are ready to give all-out (wd) against the Anglo-American Armies in India, but until we mobilize ourselves to the last man to the rupee, to the last grain of food for our own army, we have no moral right to expect more aid from Nippon. The Netaji urged the assembly to apply itself to the sacred task of strengthening..... night and day to translate the decisions of the conference into action."

Tokyo, English, 4/8/44

Rangoon: A Council Meeting of the representatives of the Burmese Branch of the Indian Independence League, which had been in progress since April 8 at an undisclosed place in Burma, came to an end on April 11....... Regarding among the various representatives of the branches of the Indian Provisional Government in connection with the mobilized and vigorous movement of the Indian people will be commenced.

Tokyo, Japanese, 4/13/44

Women Members

Rangoon: Indian mothers are active in the Independence Movement under the slogan of "Indian Mothers for Independence," several hundred Indian women gathered Monday afternoon in (Ilances) sponsored by the Burma branch of the Indian Independence League. Manifesting full sympathy with Mahatma Gandhi, the Indian Mothers passed a resolution pledging all-out efforts in the drive, "India for the Indians."

Tokyo, English, 8/17/42

A group of 70 Indian women of all ages, representing provincial districts in Burma, held a demonstrations meeting Tuesday in support of the Indian Independence Movement. The rally was the first to be sponsored independently by the Indian women since the recent organization of the Burma branch of the Indian Independence League urged the complete collaboration of the Indian women in the present struggle to free India from British domination and achieve freedom for India. The group promises to be the nucleus of and achieve freedom for Indina. The group promises to be the nucleus of auxillary women's organizations within the Independence League of Burma. *Tokyo, English, 10/8/42*

In Burma, on the occasion of greeting the birthday of Queen (name)[2] an inauguration ceremony for Women's Corps aiming at the destruction of Britain was held on October 20 at Rangoon. AT 6:30 p.m. Lt. Col. (name) who was dispatched from the Indian Independence League Headquarters at Shonan, was met by the Women's Corps and arrived at the location of the ceremony, Lt. Col. (name) spoke before his audience on the admirable achievements of Queen (name) who in 1858 mobilized an army to fight desperately against a powerful army of 600,000 British forces in an attempt to protect her country. The Lt. Col encouraged the members of the Women's corps to bravely and enthusiastically follow in the footsteps of the Queen. *Tokyo, Japanese, 10/22/43*

Youth's Training Movement

The Rangoon branch of the Indian Independence League, in order to cultivate the combative spirit in independence movements in their homeland, recently established a Youths' and Boys' Training Institute. One hundred Indian youths ranging from 17 or 18 to about 25 on a schedule of approximately one month, will be givern spiritual training and when dispathced to various regions, will promote the Indian Independence Movement throughout Burma. Every region will have branch offices established and, rallying round the rising strength of youths there is keen interests to complete the independence. *Tokyo, Japanese, 9/19/42*

Japanese Cooperations

Berlin: The Indian National residing in Burma (will evacuate) to their mother country in accordance with an agreement reached among the Governments of Britain, Burma and India, according to a broadcast from Delhi, India intercepted by the D.N.B. news agency. However, it is not known (the approximate) under of Indian Nationals they will actually evacuate. *Tokyo, English, 1/24/42*

2. Rani of Jhansi

Rangoon: All Indian residents in Burma expressed profound joy at the sympathy expressed by Prime Minister Tojo in his adminstrative speech made before the Imperial Diet on Wednesday afternoon. In which reference was made to the Indian people 's painstaking efforts towards attainment of independence. *Tokyo, English, 6/17/43*

Free Indian Provisional Government...... has now moved into Burma ... Premier Tojo declared that Japan is ready to give Andaman and Nicobar to Free India. Andaman is important location for India's patriots for many of them were imprisoned here and died. This is now selected as stronghold for India Independence. *Tokyo, English, 6/17/43*

Free India Provisional Government.... has now moved into Burma.... Premier Tojo declared that Japan is ready to give Andaman and Nicobar to Free India. Andaman is important location for India's patriots for many of them were imprisoned here and died. This is now selected as stronghold for India Independence Movement. Nicobar will be renamed as "Swaragi". *Tokyo, Japanese 1/20/44*

In a statement to Domei on Premier Tojo's statement of Nippon's determination to spare no efforts in extending all possible assistance for India's liberation and that all the territories of India into which the Indians National Army will advance will immediately be placed under the administration of the Provisional Government of Free India. The Netaji said, "My governement and army and Indians in general are profoundly grateful for the statement which His Excellency General Tojo issued to the world....." *Tokyo, English, 3/24/44*

Burmese Cooperation

Rangoon: It was decided in the cabinet meeting, held the day before yesterday, not to treat Indians who cooperate in the establishment of GEA as enemy nationals; however, in Burma this principle had already been in application since the beginning of military administration enforcement. and the Indians residing in Burma are expressing their deep gratitude for our measures..... However, as actually the majority of Indians cooperated with our forces, the policy of the army was not to regard the assets of these Indians as enemy assets..... It was decided to have the Burma Indian Residents Association control absolutely all the assets of owners who do not reside in Burma and have our army supervises and lend guidance. *Tokyo, Japanese, 2/27/43*

The Burmese Governement declared on August 21 that the Indians who are British subjects would not be considered enemy nationals but would be treated as friendly people. With Burma as the foothold, the people of Rangoon welcome this news, that hereafter the Indian Independence Movement will progress briskly. Among them, chairman of the committee in Burma area of the Indian Independence League, (Karim) Gani, stated in resume as follows: "State Representative of Burma, Ba Maw, previously stated that the Burmese Government and its people would not begrudge any aid to the Indian Independence Movement, and the recent declaration is clearly one of the constructive moves."

Tokyo, Japanese, 8/22/43

Rangoon: Extending wholehearted Burmese hospitality, Deputy Prime Minister Thakin Mya, speaking at the civic reception accorded the Provisional Indian Government, in unmistakable terms, linked the destiny of Burma and India, declaring, "The Indian Peoples' War is the Burmese Peoples' War for independence." *Tokyo, English, 1/23/44*

Rangoon: Major General Aung San, Burmese War Minister, welcoming Netaji S. C. Bose and members of the Provisional Government of Azad Hind, declared that India "must fight for her own freedom" but will have the active sympathy and support of the whole of East Asia led by Nippon. The War Minister called on all Indians in an outside India to march forward to their own independence. The War Minister warned the attendants at the rally, we must not take things easy, we must not think that we can achieve easy victory..... Our enemies are still unconquered and they remain entrenched on the other side of us, toying with the idea of a counter offensive against us every now and then.

Tokyo, English, 1/23/44

March 25: In conformity with the statement issued by Adipadi Ba Maw, wherein he declared Burma and India must join together at this juncture for the overthrow of their common enemy, Gotaro Ogawa, Supreme Adviser to the Burmese Government, asserted "The Burmese Government is extending its utmost assistance to the Provisional Government of Free India in their fight to regain their full sovereign rights," Ogawa, who returned to Tokyo to confer with governmental authorities, at today's press interview recalled that the Burmese and the Indians in the past were bitter enemies due to Britain's crafty policy of divide and rule. He asserted that through the efforts exerted by the Adipadi, a friendly feeling is now prevailing between the two nations. Praising the fighting spirit of S.C. Bose, head of the Provisional Government of Free India. Ogawa called him "the greatest hero India ever produced". He recalled Ba Maw's statement wherein he asserted that if Netaji Bose has not been leader of the Indian

Provisional Government, cooperating between Burma and India might not have been effected so soon. Recalling the careers of the two leaders, Ogawa said both of them were natives of countries subjected to British oppression, both studied law in England, and both were imprisoned due to their anti-British agitation. He added further, both are men of action based on zeal and will-power. *Tokyo, English, 3/24/44*

Free India Provisional Government

Rangoon: It is announced that Lt. Col. Alagappan (will be) Administrator of the Advance Headquarters of the Provisional Goverment of Free India and in supreme commnad in Rangoon.

Tokyo, Japanese, 11/8/43

Information has recently been received from Burma that all arrangements for the transfer of the Provisional Government of Free India Headquarters to Burma have been completed. The Indian Independence Army which is already on the move, is itching for action and is only waiting for the zero hour from their commander, Netaji Bose. Then will begin the battle which will only end in the victory of the Azad-Hind Fauj the Free Indian Army...... powerful backed by the invincible Japanese and Burmese forces. The initiative in India's struggle against Britain has certainly passed into the hands of Netaji Bose. *Shonan, Hindustani, 11/21/43*

S.C. Bose head of the Provisional Government of Free India, from a broadcasting station in Burma, on January 8 announced that the Headquarters of the Provisional Government of Azad Hind have been shifted from Shonan to Burma and he revised the preparatory measure of the government. The Indian leader, who arrived in Burma this noon, disclosed that en route to Burma he stopped off at Andaman and there discussed preparatory measures with the Nippon authorities for transfer of the islands to the Provisional Government. He said, likewise, he discussed his appointement of Lt. Col. Loganadan of the Indian Independence Army as Chief Commissioner of Andaman and Nicobar Islands.

Tokyo, English, 1/8/44

Takashi Kaide, Manager of the overseas Bureau of the Momoi News Agency, said: The Free India Provisional Government has advanced. Geographically the Provisional Government is now nearer to its motherland, India. It was just 10 years ago, from the present up to the year 1934, Burma was placed under the British Government as part of India. It is an unforgettable, a so called state or member of the motherland, feeling for the Indians. The Supreme Adviser to the Free India Provisional Government,

Behari Bose..... states as follows: "India and Burma are lands which cannot be severed or divided. The advance into Burma of the Free Indian Provisional Government is the same as an advance into its own motherland. The Indians within the homeland of India can join with us (when we advance a little further). The raid on (name), the heart of India....... is like preparing its position for the enemy's sudden death." This is the comment. I believe that these words vividly clarify the feeling of the Indians top wards the land of Burma. For the Indians, Burma and India homeland is a land where there is no division. They have finally arrived on this land. Consequently, it is not merely that they have come one step nearer the India homeland. It is more correct to state that the Free India Provisional Government has advanced to the very front line in the battle in which they will liberate their homeland from the British.

Tokyo, Japanese. 1/12/44

S. C. Bose, Head of the Provisional Government of Free India, announced the appointment today of Shri Nambiar, Chairman of the Indian Independence League Committee in Europe, as Minister without portfolio. Shri Nambiar succeeds Lt. Col. A. D. Loganadan who was appointed Chairman of the Preparatory Committee to take over the Andaman and Nicobar Islands. The announcement said the newly appointed minister will remian in Europe while serving in the new official capacity. It is recalled that while head of state Bose was in exile in Germany, Minister Nambiar, as his right hand man, exerted all-out efforts toward uniting the Indians in the fitht against British oppression. After Bose left Germany for East Asia, Nambiar assumed, in his stead, leadership in the work of the Indian Independence Committee, in the establishment of which he participated actively. *Tokyo, English, 1/14/44*

Bose announced that the Chairman of the Indian Independence League in Europe would be Nambiar. *Tokyo, Japanese, 1/14/44*

The Provisonal Government of Free India has issued a communique standardizing the language to be used among Indians, the form of salutation, and the kind of colours to be adopted as the national emblem, and other matters......" The Council of Ministers decided that Hindustani shall be the common greeting and salutation between Indians. The present tricolor shall be the national flag of India; the song beginning with the words'Such Sukh Chain' shall be India's national song; the tiger will be India's national emblem; 'Chalo Delhi' will be the national war cry till successful conclusion of the revolution; Azad Hind Zindabad, Inquilab Zindabad, Netaji Kijai will be the national slogan till the victorious conclusion of the revolution. The plan for natonal unification in the matter of food, dress, etc., is subject to consideration by the Provisional Government of Azad Hind and its decisions will be announced in due course. In the first instance the plan so far approved by Provisonal Government......... recommendation to Indians of East Asia for adoption in their daily lives."

Tokyo, English, 2/2/44

A Headquarters Provisional Government Azad Hind communique, issued yesterday, disclosed that adequate pensions will immediately be given to families, living in East Asia, of Indian civilians who lose their lives while participating in military operation. The communique said, "A meeting of the Council of Ministers of the Provisional Government of Azad Hind was held at the official residence of Bose, Saturday, Feb 19. The advisers were also present, Bose presided .The Council of Ministers unanimously decided to award adequate pension to families of the Indian civilians who lose their lives when participating in military operations, although they are not members of the Azad Hind Fauj. The Council further decided that in the case of these Indians who had already lost their lives, and whose families happen to be living in East Asia, pensions to their families should be given immediately."

Singapore, 2/23/44

Netaji revealed that the Provisional Government shortly will organize the "Azad Hind Bank" to strengthen the government's financial positions.

Tokyo, English, 3/20/44

The Provisional Government of Azad Hind today established its own bank at a certain Burmese city, with two prime tasks of mobilizing the financial resources of Indians for India's war of freedom, and of contributing to the interests of Burma. Opening of the new bank is particularly significant in that it serves as a pivotal organ, materially and financially, for mobilizing the resources of Indians for supporting the cause of the Provisional Government Azad Hind, as well as enhancing the financial standing of the government and implementing its aims. The new bank will be under the management of four Indian directors, headed by Dina Nath.

Tokyo, English, 4/5/44

It is reported from Berlin that Mr. Nambiar, Minister without portfolio of the Provisional Government of Free India, who is now on a visit to Germany's capital delivered on April 13 a significant radio address. In his address, the speaker affirmed that the campaign for the liberation of India has already entered its decisive phase, thanks to the driving operation being carried out by the Japanese and Indian National Forces, and that all

Indians are going forward resolutely to put an end to Minister British Imperialism in India, which is not far off. *Tokyo, Portguese, 4/15/44*

In a special communique issued by the Provisional Government of Azad Hind yesterday, it announcement that five new members of state have been appointed, They are: (Lakshu Kownlaviya), Ishar Singh, (N. Ranganadhan), Lt. Colonel (Z. R. Mohan) and (Hadi Barama). Mr. (name) Alagappan will cease to hold the post of Adviser to the Provisional Government of Azad Hind and Lt. Colonel S.C. Alagappan, Minister without portfolio, will be in charge of the Ministry of Supplies in addition to his other duties. *Singapore, English, 4/23/44*

Kuala Lumpur: Another prominent local Indian (left) recently to take up a post with the advance headquarters of the Provisional Government of Azad Hind. He is 45 year old Dr. M. K. Lukshimeyah, a native of the Tanjore District in South Indian and a well known medical practitioner. When the Indian Independence League was organized, over two years ago, he was among the first to join the movement to fight for India's freedom. He became the first chairman of the Selanger Branch of the Indian Independence League and later was commandant of the Indian Independence Army Training Camp. Two other Indians also left for Burma. *Tokyo, English, 5/20/44*

Twelve months ago when the Indian Independence Movement in East Asia received new impetus, all activities converged towards one main objective. That objective was to prepare for and launch an armed struggle for the winning of freedom That objective has now been fulfilled. The Azad Hind Fauj has crossed the frontier of India and the battle for freedom new is being waged on Indian soil. This new development opened up a new sphere of activity. Previously our activities were paractically confined to East Asia. Now the situation has altered considerably. The liberated area of India has brought up new problems concerning administration and reconstruction. Further, military operations that have been launched with much success have created now problems how to ..... on with operations inside India and how to work up a revolution in the country. Consequently, we shall have in the future three spheres of activity. (1) East Asia, which will continue to be a base for our political activities and military operations; (2) the liberated areas, where problems to be faced will be mainly these of administration and reconstruction, as well as preparation for further operations; (3) enemy occupied Indian territory where the revolution has been (planned) and to which our army will have to penetrate. Since October 21,1942 the Indian Independence Movement in East Asia has been conducted by the Indian Independence League. The Azad Hind Fauj, Indian Independence Army, was the military organ of the League. Since October 21, 1943 the Provisional Government of Azad Hind took over leadership of the Indian Independence Movement and therefore of the Indian Independence League and of the Azad Hind Fauj. Till recenlty, activities of the Provisional Government of the Azad Hind have been virtually confined to East Asia. Now that the situation has changed considerably, the Provisional Government will have to look after three spheres of activity East Asia, the liberated area and enemy occupied India. Minister and advisers of the Provisional Government will therefore have to be allotted difinite responsibilities in their three spheres. One group will have to look after the work in East Asia, another in the liberated territory, and a third group in enemy-occupied India. The first group working in East Asia will be called the East Asia committee of the Cabinet. The second group working in liberated India will be called the Liberated Area Committee of the Cabinet; while the third group will be called the War Committee of the Cabinet. In East Asia the mobilization of men, money and materials will have to be expanded in order to cope with new problems...... A new ministry, called the Ministry of Manpower, will have to be created for recruiting and mobilizing more men and women of various categories for different tasks..... for the Azad Hind Fauj, for the Rani Jhansi Regiments for the Azad Hind Dal, as well as for day to day work of the Indian Independence League. The ministry of Supplies, which has recently been created, will have to be enlarged. While other ministries which may already be in existance or may be set up hereafter, will have to carry may already be in existence or may be set up hereafter, will have to carry on their work, the main responsibility in the future will devolve on the Ministries of Finance, Manpower and Supplies, The East Asia Committee of the Cabinet will be responsible for directing the work in East Asia and will be composed of those ministries and advisers who ordinarily work in East Asia. For the liberated area in India, plans for administration and reconstruction already have been prepared and they will be given effect as the opportunity comes. The necessary staff of the Azad Hind Dal already had been detailed for the purpose of......members of the Azad Hind Dal already inside India or near the frontiers., The Liberated Area Committee will consist of minister and advisers who have been especially detailed to work in these areas and such ministers and advisers as may happen to there. The War Committee of Cabinet will consist of those ministers and advisers who will deal almost exclusively with problems concerning further military operations in enemy occupied India, as well as with problems pertaining to propaganda, revolutionary activity, administration and reconstruction in that territory.

Tokyo, English. 7/3/44

The Provisional Government of Azad Hind announced details for the seven days celebration which will be held on the occasion of Netaji Week, beginning July 4. The program follows: July 4: Flag hoisting ceremonies at League branches Netaji conference with pressmen, mass rally, radio broadcast by Netaji; July 5: Public lectures at various Indian communities; public lectures at various communities; July 7: Military sports, ladies mass meeting; July 8: School children's meeting, visit to wounded at Indian National Army Soldier Hospital by Netaji and entertaining patient by Netaji Fund Committee, radio broadcast by Netaji July 9: Merchants' meeting; July 10: Public meetings, also League Branches.

Tokyo English, 7/3/44

The Provisional Government of Azad Hind and the Indian National Army are carrying on daily broadcasts from Burma on the wave length of 35.5 meters. Here are the timings of the various important items from the Provisional Government of Azad Hind Headquarters in the broadcasts from Burma News and commentary, in Hindustani, beginning at 10 minutes past 8:00 Indian standard time. News and commentary, in Bengali beginning at 21 minutes past 8:00. News and commentary in English, beginning at 45 minutes past 8: 00 Indian standard time. Special feature at 55 minutes past 8: 00 Indian standard time. The Indian National Army located in Burma broadcasts every evening on the wave length of 35.45 meters. The program begins at 9:45 p.m. and lasts until 10:00 Indian standard time. Listeners in India, don't fail to tune into the Provisional Government of Azad Hind and the Indian National Army headquarters broadcasting station, operating from Burma on the wave length of 35.54 meters in the evening. The program begins shortly after 8:00 p.m. and ends at 10:00 p.m,. Indian standard time.

Singapore, English, 8/17/44

The Provisional Government of Free India announced the creation of new decoration, "Tamgha-Eshatru Nassh" There are two classes of the new decorations. The first class decoration will be presented to Indian officers and men who render outstanding service or display exceptional bravery in the line officers and men, but also to Indian civilian joining the fight for the liberation of the motherland, and who kill or imprison Anglo-Americans.

Tokyo, English, 8/31/44

Women's Organization

Rangoon: Extending a warm welcomes to Capt. Lakshmi, the Minister of the Women's Organization of the Provisional Government of Free India, (Daw Kinna Ma), wife of Dr. Ba Maw and President of the Burmese Women's National Service Association, yesterday afternoon assured Capt. Lakshmi that the Burmese women will do everything in their power to assist their Indian sisters in the coming great struggle for India's independence. This statement was made by Burma's first lady at Ba Maw's official residence, where the Commander of the Rani of Jhansi Regiment called to make a courtesy visit following her arrival in Burma on January 7 with S. C. Bose, Head of the Provisional Government of Free India.

Tokyo, English, 1/14/44

Chandra Bose, Commander-in-Chief of the Indian National Army, accompanied by Swami Nathan Lakshmi Head of the Women's Organization of the Provisional Government of Free India. This morning inspected the Indian Women's Corps. Impressed by the intensive training carried on by the Women's Corps, Bose encouraged the women members to continue to fight for achievement of the ultimate goal of liberation of India from Anglo-Americans. *Tokyo, English 1/12/44*

Indian National Army

The India Independence Movement in India had completed its preparation when the Indian National Army advanced into Burma and leaders of the Provisional Government of Free India, including Chandra Bose, have arrived in Burma; thus; along with the coming of the third year of the decisive war, the first step of the historical march toward New Delhi has been commenced. The fact that the Provisional Government of Free India has advanced to Burma is inevitable, in view of the facts that Chandra Bose arrived at Tokyo in June, last year, and following this, on October 21, the declaration of the establishment of the Provisional Government of Free India was made at Shonan....... The advance of the Provisonal Government of Free Indian to Burma is the best opportunity for the government to make a direct call upon the people of India who are making frontal resistance against Britain. Therefore, the anti-British antagonism of thee Indian soldiers in India will be further instigated. In addition to this, the fact that the Indian National Army and the Provisional Government have advance to Burma will extend more hidden force in aiding not only the Indian soldiers who are posted along the India-Burma border but also various secret anti-British organization in India, and will instigate the activities of these organs. *Tokyo, Japanese, 1/8/44*

The indomitable and fighting determination to liberate the motherland was keyonoted in the fiery, one hour address by Subhas Chandra Bose, given yesterday afternoon before the troops of the Indian National Army which advanced into Burma along with the Provisional Government of Free India. With the sweeping march to Delhi imminent, Bose reminded his soldiers again that the 3,000,000 Indians living in East Asia, as well as 380,000,000 Indians in India, and the powerful Axis nations stand firmly and solidly in back of them.

Tokyo, English, 1/11/44

An Indian meeting, celebrating the Independence of India was held on Wednesday at the advanced base of the Provisional Government of Free India in Burma. President S. C. Bose, head of the Azad Hind personally inspected the troops under his direct command at the ceremonial grounds, packed with the pick of the international army and Burman troops, as well as of the thousands of people. President Bose and Dr. Ba Maw representative of the Burmese state, gave inspiring addresses.

Tokyo, English, 1/27/44

The Indo-British Army is now said to total about 1,403,000 of which there are 600,000 irregulars. Most of the latter troops are Indians. The drive on Delhi by the National Indian Army not only will affect these troops but their long cherished dream of making India for the Indians. The anti-British movement which is fast spreading throughout the land, is expected to become doubly active as soon as our armies advance into India crying: "India, the liberation Army is Here."

Tokyo, Japanese, 3/21/44

Subhas Chandra Bose received congratulations from Mussolini on brilliant achievements Indian National Army. Duc extended wishes for further success and added he always cherished pleasant memories of his interview with Netaji in Rome few years ago.

Tokyo, English, 4/15/44

Shonan: Subhas Chandra Bose's recent announcement that units of the Rani of Jhansi Regiment have been moved to the front lines has sent a fresh wave of enthusiasm among Indian women throughout East Asia. Following the announcement, the recruitment, the recruiting offices have been flooded with eager applicants determined to further swell the ranks of the Indian women fighting for the freedom of their motherland..... these women soldiers were well disciplined and showed no sign of feminine excitabitlity or nervousness. Proud and war like, their faces proclaimed their burning enthusiasm to go into battle against the British....

Singapore, English, 5/4/44

Rangoon: The Manipuris residing in Burma have broadcast an appeal to the people in Manipur, asking them to give fullest support and cooperation to the Indian National Army and the Nippon forces now at the gates of Manipur in order to expel the enemy and save Manipur from the clutches of British Imperialism. The message points out: "We in Burma, irrespective of caste or creed, whether we are Khattiyua or Brahmans. have been fortunate enough to enjoy, since British evacuation, under the Nippon Military Administration as well as after attainment of Burmese independence. Such blessings as complete religious liberty, with absolute freedom to practice ones own ancestral rites and rituals, equal rights and privileges with all other brother Asistics no matter whether we are white, yellow brown or black and unlimited trade facilities without any racial or class discrimination and freedom from all kinds of restraint so common under the British." It says the Manipuris in Burma, therefore , have been, all along, cooperating with their heart an soul with the government in Burma as well as Nippon and India military authorities in fighting this war and in building a new order. Recognizing that Manipur is still under the British yoke and the people are not yet free, but still are oppressed , deprived of privileges and national rights, the message asked the Manipur people to give their fullest support and cooperation to the Japanese and Indian forces "so that you may soon enjoy all the blessings of independence as we in Burma are already enjoying now."

Tokyo, English, 8/5/44

Leaders

Subhas Chandra Bose

Rangoon: By the recent conference between Ba Maw and Bose in Shonan, the part that Burma is to play in the Independence Movement was promised that Major General On Sane..... issued statement leader. Now Chandra Bose has risen as a political and military leader for liberation and independence of India.... There is no doubt that the Indian Naitonal Army, with such a leader , will certainly in the near future reach its goal.

Tokyo, Japanese, 7/24/43

Rangoon : S. C. Bose, head of the Provisional Government of Free India, arrived at the undisclosed base in Burma, by air, this morning. Bose was given a hearty welcome at the airfield by a number of Burmese and

Japanese officials and civilians, including Adipadi Ba Maw and Ranzo Sawada, Japanese Ambassador to Burma, as well as India representatives. After his arrival, Bose inspected troops of the Indian National Army and then.... (Pawa) court on Adipadi Ba Maw at the latter's official residence and on the Commander-in-Chief of the Japanese forces in Burma.

Tokyo, English, 1/7/44

Immediately after Bose moved his government to Burma, he made a radio broadcast address to the people of India, making clear his visit to the Andaman Islands, and announced the appointment of Lt. Col. Rogananadan as Chairman of the Administrative Preparation Committee for the Andaman Islands.

Tokyo, Japanese, 1/10/44

According to a Demei wire from an undisclosed base in Burma, Subhas Chandra Bose, head of the Provisional Government of Free India, issued the following statement in the name of the supremo commander of the Indian National Army. 'Ever since the formation of the Indian National Army was announced several months ago, the propaganda of the enemy has been frantic in deceits directed to the Indian people and to the British Indian Army to the effect that the Indian National Army does not exist, and that amounts to nothing more than propaganda. However, although I made no promises whatsoever heretofore in opposition to the propaganda of the enemy, I fulfilled all the promises I made to my countryman in the mother country and drove home the fact that they would be fulfilled when the time came. Moreover, I declared to the whole world that during the past two months we were native according to plan... It is a fact that our allottted time has become somowhat (shortened). We will be active according to plan and have firm confidence in fulfilling the solemn pledge of liberating our mother country when the times comes. We have absolute trust in our allied and unlimited confidence in our ultimate victory."

Tokyo, Japanese, 2/7/44

Speaking before a mass rally of Indians, in celebration of actual participation in the battle of Azad Hind. (Netaji) S.C. Bose, in his capacity of Supreme Commander of the Indian National Army, declared, that with the Indian Indepenedence Movement having entered a new phase, all Indians are awakening to the significance of the latest developments and must newly resolve to fight the battle for India's freedom to a successful conclusion. He stressed this is the last fight for the Indians and the first victory in that final battle has already been achieved.

Tokyo, English, 3/20/44

The second giant mass meeting since the establishment of the Free Indian Government was held on the 19th with Subhas Chandra Bose, the Netaji, who has just returned from an inspection tour of the front lines, as the principal speaker. *Tokyo, Japanese, 3/20/44*

The Free India Provisional Government, in the name of Subhas Bose, head of the Provisional Government and Commander-in-Chief of the Indian National Army, made the following announcement: "The Provisional Government Azad Hind hereby solemnly swears that it will fight through to the day of absolute liberation, with the friendly aid of Japan. It is therefore this government's sincere desire that our brethren render all aid directly or indirectly for the advancement of Japan-India Army. Moreover, the Free Indian territory and guarantee, the administration of general affairs. This government advises all our Indian brethren to stay out of American and British army barracks, factories, harbors and other military establishments to avoid being injured, as these will be subject to destruction by our troops." *Tokyo, Japanese, 3/21/44*

In the name of Bose, the Indian Provisional Government issued statement. It says, "The Indian National Army is now able to march on to India and into Delhi. The army members are resolved to march (onward) with the Japanese Army." *Tokyo, Japanese, 3/21/44*

Profound admiration for the hard fight of President De Valera and the Irish Government for maintenance of the neutrality of Eira was expressed by the Netaji, Subhas Chandra Bose, Head of the Provisional Government of Azad Hind, in a message addressed to the Irish nation through "Domei" news agency. The message reads, "In the history of our fight against British imperialism there perhaps is no other struggle which has influenced us so much and for which we have had so much sympathy as the struggle of the brave Irish nation for their birthright of liberty. Having boon a close student of Irish history and having been in Eire myself, I know that this sympathy is fully reciprocated from the Irish side. The other day the question of recognizing our Provisional Government was raised in the Irish Parliament. I read with deepest interest the proceedings of the debate. Though the government of Azad Hind and I know for fact that the sympathy of the entire Irish nation is with us in our struggle against the common foe, and having the privilege of knowing President De Valera and his cabinet ministers personally, I am fully aware that in their attitude toward India there is no difference whatsoever between the government and the people of Eire." *Tokyo, English, 3/27/44*

Mr. Subhas Chandra Bose, on Thursday, is issued a message regarding the inauguration of a National Liberation Week. Now this new week is to be observed in place of the former Indian National week, which began on April 6th every year. The Netaji asked all his countrymen, especially those in Greater East Asia, to observe this National function in such a manner as befits the historical significance.

Tokyo, Japanese, 3/31/44

The Provisional Government of Free India, in a news bulletin issued yesterday morning, disclosed that Netaji Subhas Chandra Bose, Head of the Provisional Government of Free India and Supreme Commander of the Indian National Army, has arrived at his Headquarters in Burma. The bulletin also disclosed that the most elaborate proparations are being made at the Burma Headquarters to celebrate "Netaji Week" from July 4 to 10. This marks the first anniversary of Bose's assumption of the leadership of the Indian Independence Movement in East Asia as Supreme Commander of the Indian National Army. *Tokyo, Japanese, 6/30/44*

On July 4, the opening day of the Netaji Week, Subhas Chandra Bose issued a statement revealing the future plans for the 3,000,000 Indians in the Greater East Asia for their independece. The content of his statement is as follows: ".......In conclusion allow me to indicate three points in our future policies. Firstly, we must continue to win battles and advance farther and farther into India. To this end, we must strengthen the fighting front with both man and material. Secondly, reconstruction activities will surely increase in the liberated areas. Therefore, we must increase the personnel for reconstruction work. Thirdly, we must strengthen the home front; and to meet this, it is necessary to exert our efforts towards the mobilization of manpower, resources and capital." *Tokyo, Japanese, 7/4/44*

An enthusiastic mass rally, highlighted by spontaneous demonstrations for the patriotic government supported by determination to free India, marked Provisional Government Day held here yesterday. The gathering, which was held in a spacious hall profusely decorated with the national colors and flowers, was attempted by prominent Indians in Burma as well as high officials of the Azad Hind Government. A martial aspect was lent by guards of honour who lined all corridors and approaches to the hall. Stressing the iron determination to continue the armed fight until India is free, no matter how long the struggle may last, Netaji Subhas Bose again reminded his audience freedom cannot be won unless all Indians units give their utmost, and also called for continued total mobilization of men, money and materials. *Tokyo, Japanese, 7/22/44*

The 6th mass meeting commemorating the establishment of the Free India Provisional Government was held somewhere is Burma. At this conference Subhas Chander Bose emphatically stated that now is the time to mobilize the total material and manpower resources of the Indian people to build up war power, and demanded a strong unification and action on the part of the people. Resolutions emboyding the common will of the 500,000,000 people of India were passed and read before the gathering by Subhas Bose. Thus the unshakable determination of the East Asia Indian people to wrest the victory for the sake of liberating India was manifested. The gist of the resolutions are as follows: This conference pays its heartfelt respect to the officers and men of the Free Indian Nationa Army....Today the Indian National Army is waiting for another battle with the enemy. The responsibility which rests upon the shoulders of the Indian people in East Asia is to use this opportune time to the best advantage and make strong preparations for the coming compaigns. With this goal in mind, the mobilization of all material wealth and manpower should be carried out to completion... The conference pays homage to the spirits of these who have fallen in this war of liberation and also felicitates the brilliant records made by our fighting men. This meeting resolves that it will face all situations shoulder to shoulder with Japan and her allies, and will continue to fight in the face of all difficulties until victory is obtained and India is freed from the oppression of foreign powers. *Tokyo, Japanese, 8/22/44*

Behari Bose

Behari Bose recently said, "India and Burma are two inseparable countries. The move of the government to Burma was like moving to its home country." This means that the Indians have a strong feeling toward the Burmese. The Indians can hardly distinguish between Burma and India.....Kawabe, Commander-in-Chief of our forces in the Burma area, said the Indian Army is growing stronger. *Tokyo, Japanese, 1/10/44*

Indian Independence Movement

A momentous conflab of Indians is now in session in Bangkok. The inaugural meeting, held on Monday, the 15th, was attended by an impressive gathering of Indian representatives from all parts of East Asia. This is the largest and most significant meeting of Indians over to have been held abroad, and had the singular distinction of having among its foreign guests the Ambassadors of three active powers, Japan, Germany and Italy, and the respresentatives of the Thai Government. Messages of great and far reaching significance were addressed to the meeting by Premier Tojo of Japan, Premier Bipul Songram of Thailand and the German and Italian envoys at the Thai Cabinet. These messages reiterated friendly greeting entertained by the three powers, Japan, Germany and Italy, towards Indian and the Indian people.... Mr. Rash Behari Bose addressed ..... inaugural message, paid the highest tribute to Mahatma Gandhi for preventing India from being involved in the present war as a (tomb) of Britain. Expressing the need for India's whole-hearted cooperation with Japan in exterminating British power, Mr. Bose asserted, "India's freedom in the true sense of the word is a problem which can be solved only by the challenge of Japan against British Imperialism." The Indian patriot added, "India should not lose any time in the fight against Britain." Appealing for immediate action, Mr. Bose told the conference, "Now let us stand up together.....preparation to work for India's independence for which Mahatma Gandhi has fought for the past 20 years."....Foreign Minister Togo and Ambassador (Taubogami) expressed to the Indian conference the full cooperation and support of the Japanese nation. Foreign Minister Togo asked the leaders of India to forget their minor differences of opinion and unite in getting their countries to stand as a body.....and exert themselves to bring about the collapse of British Imperialism.

Tokyo, English, 6/19/42

Bangkok : A mass meeting of Indian residents of Bangkok and Thenburi was held today at the Wathnakorn Theater Hall, in commemoration of the "Quit India" resolution adopted in 1942 by Indian National Congress. The gathering was addressed by Daljit Singh of Manila and Lieutenant Colonol Hussian of the Indian National Army, after which three resolution were adopted. They are as follows : "1. We express our profound pleasure that Mahatma Gandhi has voiced his emphatic assertion in a recent statement that the "Quit India" resolution of 1942 stands good in letter and in spirit, and that it cannot be altered even by .... and he has further advised Indians to hold demonstrations throughout India today to record reaffirmation of the resolution; 2. that we, on this day, renewed our determination to follow Netaji Subhas Chandra Bose in his onward march toward the promised land of free and happy India until the enemy is forced to "Quit India" through the collaboration of forces from within India and without it; 3. that we take this opportunity of congratulating the Japanese and Thai both of whom our extreme pleasure has been expressed for continuation of the same.....which has been beneficial to our cause."

Anti-Britian Statement

The Bangkok Indians stated they must take arms to achieve independence of their fatherland. The homeland of India must extreminate British and Americans and build an India for Indians.

Tokyo, Japanese, 8/11/44

Bangkok : Addressing the Indian people at home, a member of the Bangkok Branch of the Indian Independence League broadcast from Bangkok, on Tuesday night, to the following effects: "The British authorities once proudly declared that they would be able to suppress an anti-British movement in a cleared that they would be able to suppress an anti-British movement in a few days if it ever occurred in India. Despite the cruel and inhuman British oppression, the anti-British movement in India is becoming more aggravated. The distrubance in India are assuming serious proportions and, despite the ceaseless activities of the British Army and police, Indian youth and labourers are giving their all for the emancipation of their race. *Tokyo, English, 9/9/42*

Propaganda by Radio—In order to assist the patriotic Indian at home, the Indian residents of Thailand have begun a private radio broadcast, directed to India through the Bangkok Radio Station, every evening for an hour, from 8.00 to 9.00 Indian standard time. *Tokyo, English, 5/4/43*

Bangkok Branch, Activities—The Bangkok Branch of the Indian Independence League broadcast to all Indian, on the evening of September 8, encouraging them: "There is no possibility that the great spirit of Indian for India's independence and British imperialism will agree. Hold strong encouragement that the British imperialism will be thrust out from the land of India. Brethren of our motherland, prosperity is near"

Tokyo, Japanese, 9/9/42

Several thousands of Indian residents in Bangkok celebrated the birthday of Mahatma Gandhi at the Bangkok Headquarters of the Indian Independence League. Fundamental ideals of the Independence Movement were discussed. *Tokyo, English, 10/3/42*

Bangkok: The Thailand Branch of the Indian Independence League, on the occasion of the first anniversary of the GEA war, yesterday hold a commemorative rally at the (Silver Cone) Theatre. At the rally a resoultion was decided upon, stating the Japan's victory is India's victory and....Japan's brave fight they would fight their uttermost for the restoration of their mother country, India. *Tokyo, Japanese, 12/8/42*

Today the Bangkok Indian Independence Federation is to hold a ceremony of prayer for Gandhi *Tokyo, Japanese, 2/24/43*

Bangkok: On the occasion of the birthday of Mahatma Gandhi, the Thai Chapter of the Indian Independece League, on Saturday, held at its office a rally of Indian residents in Bangkok. Before 2,000 Indians the chairman of the Thai Chapter delivered a stirring address, urging all-out effort of the local Indians to fight for crushing Britian. After the rally all participants paraded the streets. *Tokyo, English, 10/2/43*

The (Wd) committee of the Bangkok Indian Independence League held a ceremony this morning to pay allegiance to the national flag of Independent India in order to felicitate the establishment of Provisional Government of Free India. About 2,000 Indians assembled at the (grounds) of the league. There a people's rally was held at the (Namo) Park, at which time (Name), chief of the Publicity Dept. of the Indian Independence League, and (Name), Educational Dept. Chief, gave speeches. A people's felicitation rally will be hold in a grand manner this evening also. Tomorrow a.m. a review of the Indian Volunteer Corps is scheduled to be held.

Tokyo, Japanese, 10/25/43

Bangkok: Commencing today, the Thai chapter of the Indian Independence League will observe Netaji Week. A mass metting was held this morning, following a flag raising ceremony. A message of appreciation and encouragement was adopted to be forwarded to Bose.

Tokyo, English, 7/3/44

Bangkok: Netaji week celebrations opened here this morning with a rally attended by more than 1,000 Indian residents headed by Sardar Singh, new Minister without Portfolio of the Provisional Government of Free India. The headquarters of the local Indian Independence League, where the rally was held, was decorated with the Indian tri-colour. The programme included singing of the Indian National songs and passing of resolution renewing the resolve to fight out the battle against Britain to victorious finish. A massage of gratitude and encouragment was sent to Netaji Bose. *Tokyo, English, 7/4/44*

Bangkok: A mass meeting and parade by Indian residents here highlighted the last day of Netaji week today. At 9.00 a.m. more than 1,000 Indian residents here assembled in front of the headquarters of the Indian Independence League in Thailand. After parading the main streets of the city, the Indian residents held a mass meeting at the local theater. The meeting opened with an address by the chairman of the league who spoke on the Indian Volunteers' Training Institute. Events included the reading of partriotic poems, composed by Indian youths, and also speeches by committee members. *Tokyo, Japanese, 7/10/44*

Contribution

The head of the Free India Committee, who recently visited Thailand, gave 25,000 baht to take care of wounded Thai soldiers and 35,000 baht to Chulalongkorn University. *Bangkok, Thai., 8/22/43*

Shonan: It was learned here Saturday that Subhas Chandra Bose, President of the Indian National Army, made a donation of 50,000 bahts to the Thai Government on onc of his recent visits to that country. This donation was meant partly for the aid and comfort of wounded Thai soldiers, and partly as a contribution to the (wd) university.

Tokyo, English, 10/17/43

Free India Provisional Government

Bangkok: Subhas Chandra Bose had named (Ishaaru Sin), chairman of the Thailand Branch of the Indian Independence League, as the new State Minister of the Provisional Government of Free India. The new minister is one of the outstanding Indian figures in the (Honneian Uuyonsas) commerical circles. He has long been active in the anti-British movement, and prior to this was prohibited from returning to India by the British Government. Since the establishment of the Indian Independence League in Bangkok in 1942, he has been very active within the organization. He was appointed advisor to the provisional government with its inception....

Tokyo, Japanese, 4/22/44

Cooperation of Thailand

Bangkok: The Thailand Government announced tonight over the radio that it has extended official recognition to the Free India Provisional Government headed by Chandra Bose. *Tokyo, English, 11/19/43*

Bangkok: The propaganda Bureau announced on April 8 that Premier Pibut Songgram had sent a telegram to Subhas Chandra Bose, Commender-in-Chief of the Indian National Army, congratulating him and his men on the recent invasion of India by praying for their success. The telegram reads as follows: "Beloved Indian friends—the recent invasion of the homeland by the National Army under the leadership of Subhas Chandra Bose indeed has caused much rejoicing among the Asiatic people. At this time, in behalf of the people of Thailand, I wish to extend my sincerest congratulations to the National Army on its recent invasion of the motherland and pray for its further advance and ultimate victory in this was of righteousness." *Tokyo, English, 7/4/44*

Leaders

Subhas Chandra Bose—Bangkok—Greatly elated over the sudden advent of Mr. Bose in Tokyo, the Bangkok Headquarters of the Indian Independence League held a welcome rally for Mr. Bose on Monday, and it was attended by some 2,000 Indians. *Tokyo, English, 6/22/43*

Bangkok: Hailing the new post of Mr. Subhas Bose as president of the Indian Independence League, Indian residents in Bangkok, on Monday, voiced their confidence in him as a man of action, who is the only man in India able to bring the present complicated international situation to a successful conclusion. The Indian residents pointed out that the menace to the British by the Japanese forces on the Indo-Burma border has been doubled by the entrance of Mr. Subhas Bose on the scene, especially in view of the fact that he is strongly supported by the people of (Assam) and Bengal on the Indian frontier. *Tokyo, English, 7/5/43*

Subhas Chandra Bose, who is now visiting Bangkok, in a joint interview with reporters on July 27, expressed the firm determination to overthrow Anglo-American policy from India by mobilizing the total strength. He said: " .....When Burmese independence is realized, we will win a strong ally of Burma, which is a neighbouring country of India, and I am firmly convinced that our independence movement will be further pushed forward in a cooperative manner." *Tokyo, Japanese, 7/30/43*

Bangkok: Subhas Chandra Bose, President of the Indian Independence League and concurrently Commander-in-Chief of the Indian National Army, again visited Bangkok on August 4, on route from Burma to Shonan. During his second visited here Mr. Bose called on Premier Pibul Songgram and had a freindly talk with him. He deepended his acquaintanceship with Japanese and other Axis organs on the sport. Mr. Bose held an Indian rally at the (Name) University as a prelude to the anniversary of the suppression of the Indian Independence (wd), which falls on Monday, and exhorted all Indians in Thailand to direct their efforts toward the Independence of India. *Tokyo, English, 8/9/43*

Bangkok: President Chandra Bose of the Indian Independence League, after spending several days at Rangoon participating in the Indian Independence rally held there, arrived at Bangkok on September 30 and gave a rally speech on October 5 on the occasion of the celebration of the date of birth of elder Gandhi. He encouraged the people.

Tokyo, Japanese, 10/4/43

Rash Behari Bose—Independece Movement of Bangkok—In view of the coming conference, Behari Bose made speech through radio, encouraging those at Bangkok to do their best. *Tokyo, Japanese, 8/6/42*

Women's Corps

Bangkok: There have been many among the Indian women residents of Thailand who have expressed their desired to join the Indian National Women's Corps which was established in Shonan. The Indian Independence League, Bangkok Branch, which was impressed by this enthusiasm, immediately chose 9 women including (Mrs. Surubayaru Tuuru) as first volunteers and decided to send them to Shonan. The party left Bangkok for Shonan on December 21 with a send-off by a large number of persons, including (Basu), Adviser to the Free India Provisional Government. *Tokyo, Japanese, 12/23/43*

Bangkok: The activity of the Women's Corps of the Indian National Army in Shonan greatly inspires Indian women living in Thailand, and volunteers to join the corps are increasing steadily daily. The Bangkok section of the Indian Army, deeply moved by the eager desire.....number of....women to be sent to Shonan and a party left Bangkok for Shonan on Wednesday morning with a hearty send-off by the Indian residents.

Tokyo, English, 12/23/43

Bangkok: On Friday some Indian women, under Mrs. Narain's leadership, from the Bangkok Branch of the Indian Independence League will join the Rani Jhansi Regiment somewhere on the Indian-Burma border to celebrate the (Eighteenth) Freedom-week with great pomp. Rani Jhasi Regiment is under the command of Mrs. Lakshami.

Tokyo, Urdu, 4/8/44

Indian Independence League
Saigon Branch : Activities

Today, the Indians held a big meeting at (the Headquarters of the Indian Independence League in Saigon). The president of the meeting said— "Today is the most important for the Indians, because in 1857, on this every day, the foundation-stone of the Indian freedom was laid." After the meeting a thousand Indians tooks the oath that they were ready to make every sacrifice for the freedom of India, and they will help with life, heart and everything to destroy the British. *Saigon, Urdu, 5/10/43*

The Saigon Branch of the Indian Independence League, representing the 3,000 Indian residents in southern French Indo-China, donated a considerable amount of money to the Provisional Government of Free India as an expression of their enthusiam towards the independence cause, and a Volunteer Corps for the Indian National Army has been dispatched. A second Volunteer Corps is being already organized.

Tokyo, English, 11/8/43

Cooperation with Japan

The Indian Society in Saigon held a mass meeting on Tuesday to commemorate the first anniversary of the GEA war. The following resolution was passed at the meeting and sent to Premier Tojo: "We Indians residing in Cochin China, on the first anniversary of the GEA war, wish to convey our heartfelt thanks and compliments to the Japanese Government and its people for the brilliant victories achieved by the Imperial forces and for their efforts in costing all Anglo-American influence from East Asia. We believe that freedom and prosperity of Japan and India can be obtained only by complete victory over the United State and Britain. In order to accomplish the foregoing objects we desire that we shall spare nothing in cooperation with Japan."

Tokyo, English, 12/10/42

Free India Provisional Government

The enthusiasm of the 300 Indians living in the southern part of French Indo-China has been boosted by the establishment of the Provisional Government of Free India. The Saigon Branch of the Indian Independence League contributed 2,500,000 rupees to the provisional government as a fund for the Indian National Army, while 16,000 piastres have been contributed to the Indian Red Cross. The Saigon Branch of the Indian Independence League dispatched, yesterday, its first contingent of men who are volunteering to the Indian National Army.

Tokyo, Japanese, 11/8/43

Indian National Army

Expressing the jubilation of 6,000 Indian residents in French Indo-China over now of the Indian National Army's participation in the current Arakan operations, Sheik Mohamed, head of the French Indo-China Chapter of the Indian Independence League, is a statement issued today, voiced full confidence in the victory of Indo-Japanese forces.

Tokyo, English, 2/10/44

Saigon: 3,000 Indians residing here held a mass meeting yesterday on the occasion of "Azad Hind" day, and adopted a resolution pledging to further continue work for the cause of complete independence and freedom of the motherland. The resolution declared that the Indian National Army has completed its first stage of operations in its fight for the independence of the motherland and, presently, is preparing for the next phase of operations. All Indians residing in French Indo-China will mobilize their total power for such operations, which the Indian National Army is fully ready to carry out. In conclusion, the resolution expressed the determination of Indian residents in French Indo-China to overcome any difficulties and to fight out the current war in close cooperation with Japan and other allied nations for the attainment of the common objective of liberating East Asia from Anglo-American aggression.

Tokyo, English, 8/22/44

MALAYA

Indian Independence Movement

Youth Movement

To do their duty and liberate their sacred land from the yoke of the British....." *Saigon, English, 3/9/43*

Addressing the enormous Indian youth rally held in Shonan Sunday, Rash Behari Bose, the President of the Indian Independence League in East Asia, declared that there can be no compromise or halfway settlement in this fight against the British. It is the united effort of the Indian youth that will bring victory and glory to India. *Tokyo, English, 4/1/43*

Shonan: Symbolic of patriotic fervour, a 17 year old girl, a Sikh, Jit Kour, on Friday offered 1,000 yen to the Indain Independence League; and has offered her name to be enlisted as a volunteer in the Rani Jhansi Regiment. It may be of interest to note that the Jit Kour had only 1,000 yen with her and she gave here all for national freedom.

Tokyo, Urdu, 10/3/43

Shonan: The Provisional Government of Free India, on Thursday, announced that Indian youngsters are under training to participate in the administration and construction of Free India in various districts to be relieved from Anglo-Amercian oppression. *Tokyo, English, 11/6/43*

Shonan: Boys and girls of the Indian National School here formed themselves into a "Balak Sena" youth corps in response to Netaji S.C. Bose's appeal to Indian youth to raise themselves into an effective body to serve the motherland. It is understood the "Balak Sena" will function under the Shonan Branch of the Indian Independence League. Already members of this new organization have started to work for the national cause, having so faı collected among themselves $250.00 as a donation towards the Independence Movement Fund. Plans for training in the role they are to play in the independence struggle are going to be drawn up. It is recalled the first of such organizations was formed in Johere Bharu at (wd) of National Liberation Week celebrations, April 13.

Tokyo, English, 4/22/44

Local Indian boys and girls have formed themselves into a (Balikpemah) or (New Corps), in response to the appeal of Netaji Subhas Chandra Bose. The decision to form this corps was carried out on May 10, when....anniversary of their counry's first war of independence.

Manila, English, 5/17/44

Indian Independence League East Asia Headquarter in Shonan

Shonan City: It is reported from Shonan City that the Shonan Branch of the Indian Independence League will hold their Independence Rally on September 2nd at 5.50 p.m.

Tokyo, English, 8/31/42

30,000 Indians rally here Wednesday night to support India's Independence Movement. Moslems resolve and join the Independence League. Tokyo, 9/2/42

Shonan: India Independence Federation, Shonan Branch, held a rally at the ground in front of Izacc Club in Shonan City yesterday, 5.00 p.m.. First, (Goh Ho), the President of India Independence Federation, Shonan Branch, and (Dagahan), the president of Senang Branch, delivered greetings and the 30,000 attendants shouted, "Freedom or Death!", revealing their enthusiastic support for the independence of India. As the resolution of the rally, the chairman announced that the resistance strength and morals will be boosted in opposition to the British suppressions and resolved to fight to the bitter and for the independence of India, supporting the India National Congress Party. The rally was adjourned in eathusiastic manner .... The Indian soldiers who had capitulated to the Japanese volunteered to server as members of the police force and are doing good work in restoring peace and order. These Indians are permitted to act as police, revealing the perfect trust existing among the East Asiatic people.

Tokyo, English, 12/25/41

750,000 Indian residents in Malaya, in the main cities, firmly decided to fight until liberation of Indians. *Tokyo, Japanese, 8/11/42*

Oath of Allegiance

Shonan: Indian residents here will take their independence pledge in a mass meeting to be held next. Wednesday in the (Farror) Park. A procession, consisting of detachments of the Indian National Army, (of) volunteers and civilians, will start from the headquarters of the local branch of the Independence League of Free India and go to the Park, while speeches on the day and its significance will be made on this occasion (by) Indians in the Tamil language. This meeting will end after it passes a resolution (reaffirming) Indian determination to fight to their complete independence.

Tokyo, French, 1/25/44

Shonan: More than 30,000 Indians last evening reaffirmed their determination to exert their utmost for the attainment of their independence at a mass rally held at Farrar Park on the occasion of the 15th Indian Independence Day. Highlight of the meeting was the mammoth procession, consisting of a detachment of the Indian National Army, Women volunteers from the Rani Jhasi Regiment, military trainees, school children and others. An army brass band led the procession, which started from the premises of the Indian Independence League and proceeded to the mooting place.

Tokyo, English, 1/27/44

Shonan: Thousands of Indians flocked to the six extra centers, which were temporarily opened on Tuesday and Wednesday in various parts of the city, to take the Oath of Allegiance to the Netaji, Subhas Chandra Bose, and the Provisional Government of Azad Hind. These centers were opened in addition to the Branch of India Independence Leauge, is connection with the observance of National Liberation Week, with a view to making it easier for them to take the oath near their place of residence. Though official figures of those who have taken the oath are not available yet, it is learned that the number tops the ten thousand mark.

Tokyo, English, 4/13/44

Women's Service

Firmly pledging their determination to cooperate with Japan's crusade to liberate Asiatic peoples from the Anglo-Saxon yoke, Indian women of the newly established Shonan Branch of the Indian Independence League sent a message to the Japan Woman's Association on March 28 on the occasion of the inaugural meeting of the branch office in Shonan.... A message of similar nature was also sent by Indian youth to Japan's young Men's Association on the same occasion.

Shonan: Malai and local Indonesian women, under the sponsorship of the paper "Fajar Asia", will hold a rally at the Shonan Kokaldo on March 6, Chikyuseta, or the birthday of Her Imperial Majesty the Empress of Japan, Lectures on the war of Greater East Asia and women's duty in the present wartime situation will be delivered by leading Malai women.

Tokyo, English, 3/2/44

Youth Movement

The Youth India, the organ of the Indian Youth Movement, made its first appearance in Shonan yesterday. The paper editorially declared, "we are confident we will maintain Mahatma Gandhi's spirit and we urge all Indians at 8.30 p.m. *Tokyo, Japanese, 9/2/42*

Shonan: The Malai Branch of the India Independence League, ever since its establishment last spring, has led the Independence Movement for 700,000 Indians residing in Malai as the influential body of the south and has continued to call reassuringly to the homeland Indians. To keep in accordance with the recent urgent situation in India in order to further strengthen the activities of the league, a general Shonan Movement has been decided upon to be carried out with Shonan volunteers such as the Prsident of the Shonan Indian Association (Kumaratini), and the manager of the Shonan Indian Newspaper, (Yaja Yanchi).

Tokyo, Japanese, 3/8/43

Shonan: The India Independence League headquarters, which has mobilized the Indians throughout the Greater East Asia sphere and is working towards concrete realization of their independence, comments.....that the appointment of Wavell, former Commander-in-Chief of the British forces in India, is but the revelation of the British plan to oppress the Indians who are becoming quite restless throughout the whole nation. *Tokyo, Japanense, 6/19/43*

Penang: Welcoming President Subhas Bose of the Indian Independence Movement Federation, the Indian National Convention of Penang was held on September 5 at the stadium. The gratitude and enthusiasm of Indian people in Penang, who for the first time welcomed their leader, reached to the climax..... *Tokyo, Japanese, 9/5/43*

Under the leadership of Subhas Chandra Bose, the Shonan Indian People's Rally to express felicitation on the Philippine Independence was elaborately staged at the Ala Park in Shonan.

Tokyo, Japanese, 10/18/43

The Central Headquarters of the Indian Independence Federation has decided to hold the All-Asia Indian people's Rally on October 25 and to start a gigantic movement for freedom and these instructions were sent to all branch associations throughout East Asia. This movement is to be carried with the objective of putting into full swing the resolution which is to be decided at the conference of representatives from all East Asia to be held on October 21 in Shonan. It is believed that, as a result of the above, the Indian Independence Movement will be further accelerated.

Tokyo, Japanense, 10/18/43

Shonan: The Indian Independence League All-East Asia Representatives Conference was convened at 10.30 at the Greater East Asia Theatre at Shonan. Indian representatives from Malai, Japan, Manchukuo, Thailand, French-Indo-China, Jawa, Boraeo, Sumatra, Burma, Hongkong, the Philippines, Colobes, Canton and other places throughtout entire East Asia, as well as staff members of the women's Corps of the Indian National Army attended. After the Indian national anthem was sung, President Subhas Chandra Bose delivered an important speech, lasting for about one hour, on the present condition of the Indian Independence movement and the world situation. Lastly he declared forcefully, "I shall announce the establishment of the provisional government in the meeting this afternoon." ..... In the afternoon meeting President Subhas Chandra Bose submitted the important bill for the establishment of a Free Indian Provisional Government. As all the respresentatives Subhas Chndra Bose as head of the Government has as its object, as a stronger unified organ for the Indian Independence Movement, the winning of independence... The structure of the provisional government will be as simple as possible and will consist of only five departments. The organisation will have, under the president, five departments, namely; The Military Affairs Department, The Financial Affairs Department, The Foreign Affairs Department, The Propaganda Department and the Women's Department. In addition there will be a small number of the minister without portfolio and government advisers who are Indians. The seat of the government will be in Burma, which is appropriate as the main base for the struggle against Britain.

Tokyo, Japanese, 7/5/43

Connection with Moslem League

Kuala Lumpur: The Moslem League of India in Malaya announced that it had dissolved itself to become merged with the Independence League of Malaya. The announcement was issued on August 21st and added that the act was approved by all the Indians of the Moslem League in all parts of the peninsula. The movement for the Independence of India, in Malaya will now be placed under one central control. *Tokyo, English, 6/25/42*

The spokesman of the Indian Independence League in Shonan, in a broadcast yesterday, made an impassioned appeal to Mr. Mohammed Ali Jinnah, leaders of the Moslem League in India, to rise again as a national leader at this crucial hour in India's struggle for independence. The.....Moslem League and the India....Moslem League of New Delhi the spokemans declared that there can only one be one resolution for any of the Indians who want the name and that resolution is to plunge themselves into the fight for Indian Independence.

Tokyo, English, 4/23/43

Shonan: "We must vow today to liberate India from the bonds with which her tyrants chained her," declared Abdul Aziz, leader of the East Asia Indian Muslims, in a message to his compatriots on the occasion of the birthday anniversary of Prophet Mohammed.....He said the participation of a Muslim detachment of the Indian National Army is yesterday's procession, as well as the face that thousands of Indians, irrespective of caste or creed, are mingling in mosques and eating the same food, are regarded as a sure indication the unity of all Indians is here. Pointing out that those who in any way try to bring discord among them would be branded traitors and tried as such, Aziz concluded, "Let us march unfaltering forward along the road of independence under the banner of the Provisional Government of Free India and sacrifice everything we have for the glory of our motherland."

Tokyo, English, 3/7/44

Shonan: The 23-day conference of Mohammadan priests of Menangkabo, for the purpose of furthering cooperation of Mohammedans in Sumatra with the Japanese Administration, was opened July 8 on the occasion of Ascension Day. The day's meeting, held at the Taishokan (Imperial Rescript Hall) was attened by 500 priests. The conference will formulate appropriate measures for furnishing collaboration among the populace in order to give impetus to the program for strengthening Sumatra's defenses, increasing food-stuff production and other self-sufficiency measures. Mohmmedans, not only in Menangkabo, but throughout Sumatra, will be requested to support the measures adopted at the conference. Much as expected to be accomplished at...., which is being held at the instance of the Menangkabo Mohammedans themselves.

Tokyo, Japanese, 7/10/44

Propaganda by Radio

Centered around the Malay Branch of India Independence Movement Federation, the Indian Independent Movement in Shonan and Malaya has doubly grown recently. The comrades of Independent Movement is Shonako will start a daily broadcast from Shonan Broadcasting Station to the people of their native land, India. It will be given daily from 10.30 p.m. (JCT) till 1.40 a.m. (JCT). Today, on the first day of the broadcasting schedule, Mr. Koshi Sei Manao, the propaganda chief of the Malaya Branch, will send the first voice, beginning with this, it is scheduled that very active broadcasting compaign to Indian will be carried out.

Tokyo, Japanese, 8/1/42

The headquarters of the Indian Independence League in East Asia, in Shonan, has begun radiocasting towards India for two hours, between 8.40 and 10.40 Indian standard time, every evening on the wave length of 25.3 meters. *Tokyo, English, 5/4/43*

Shonan Branch : Activities

The Indian Independence League Branch of Shonan, in the afternoon of September 9th, held a memorial service at the Nishi Hongwanji Temple in honour of the souls of the Imperial forces who have given their lives in the Malayan campaign. About 100 Japanese people concerned and a great number of the Indian people attended the srevice to offer their prayers of gratitude to the souls of the soldiers.

Tokyo, Japanese, 9/9/42

In Shonan city..... a branch office of the Indian Independence League was opened today. The opening ceremony was perform by General (Long Singh) who declared that....of the Indian soldiers have pledged to give their lives for their motherland. *Tokyo, English, 11/24/42*

Shonan: The Indian Mass Rally, in order to recall for Indians the notorious Amritsar massacre, was sponsored by the Shonan Branch of the Indian Independence League here Tuesday evening, which is the last day of the Indian Nation Week.

Shonan: The Shonan chapter of the Indian Independence League had a lecture at the GEA Theatre, Sunday, on the occasion of the third (Udnam Sing Azad) day. Films depicting the occasion were also shown at the theatre..... Events took place to commemorate the day set aside for (Udnam Singh Azad) who, on Time 13, 1940, assassinated Michael O'Dwyer, former Governor of Punjab, to avenge the Amritsar Massacre.

Tokyo, English, 6/14/43

Shonan—Today, on the commemoration day for the establishment of the Free Provisional Government of India, The Shonan Branch of the Indian Independence League sponsored a street parade, participated in by the National Army, Women's corps and general public.

Tokyo, Japanese, 2/21/44

Kuala Lumpur Branch : Activities

Kuala Lumpur Indian Independence League Branch starts sympathetic fast. *Tokyo, Japanese, 2/18/43*

Penang Branch : Activities

Penang: The local Indian community is greatly enthusiastic over the news of the inauguration of the Provisional Government of Free India. The spokeman of the Penang Branch of this Indian Independence League said that ever since Subhas Chandra Bose's announcedment in July, after his arrival in Shonan, that he was striving to establish such government, Indians all over East Asia were expecting such news. He added....It is the government which, under the leadership of Bose, will command confidence of Indians in the whole of East Asia. Meanwhile, a mass meeting to express the heartfelt enthusiam and pride in allegiance to the provisional government will be held here October 25.

Tokyo, English, 10/23/43

Penang: "Loyality to the Provisional Government of Azad Hind means increased responsibilites and a greater extent of coopartion and assistance with all Japanese authorities with whom the members come in contact." declared Dr. N.K. Menon, chairman of the Penang Indian Independence League, in an address at a ceremony of taking the oath of allegiance to the provisional government at the League's headquarters attended by the Indians of Penang Province. He revealed the Ceylonese in Penang, although numbering no more than 100, have already contributed $20,000 to the Netaji's fund. He emphasized that the war aims of Japan and the provisional government are exactly the same and complete liberation of India from bondage will not be possible without Japan's help. Similar ceremonies were held in Butterworth, Prai Bukit, Martajam, Nibong and Tebal.

Tokyo, English, 1/4/44

Ceylon Branch: Activities

Stockholm: At Ceylon Island an Independence Movement is growing. The Indian National Congress Party has resolved for Ceylon Island Independence.

Tokyo, Japanese, 12/25/42

Shonan: Arrangements are being made to organize a Ceylon Branch of the Indian Idependence's League, according to Perera, President of the Singhalese Association of Shonan, who issued a statement today.

Tokyo, 11/9/43

Shonan: A public meeting of Ceylonese residents here is scheduled to be held January 24, at the promises of the Indian Independence League, under chairmanship of Pillai, member in charge of the Ceylon Department of the League. Full attendance of both men and women is expected. Meanwhile Pillai and other Ceylonese leaders throughout Malai have issued a press statement urging their community to take full advantage of the opportunity afforded by the opening of the Cylon Department within the Fabric of the leagues and particularly on calling Ceylonese youths to shoulder the task with other Indians, for the common freedom of India and Ceylon are destined to form together an imprtant entity in the new order of Asians. Culture, language, religion and other environments bind them together to such an extent that no right-thinking Ceylonese can allow himself to be led astray by the cursed British divide-and-rule policy. It is therefore up to us Ceylonese in East Asia to cooperate sincerely with the movement by subscribing fully to the total mobilization demanded of us.

Tokyo, English, 1/22/44

Shonan: The Ceylon Department of the Indian Independence League, this evening, held a mass meeting in the plaza in front of the Independence League Building to encourage the Ceylon islanders in the fight for independence. (Sawvan) Anuttu, acting chief of the Penang Chapter of the Independence League, and several Ceylon young men who recently graduated from the Azad School were vehement speakers at the mass meeting. *Tokyo, English, 3/25/44*

The fervor of Ceylonese youth who are trying to escape from British Bondage had deeply impressed Bose, the head of the Provisional Government of Free India. A Ceylonese Branch of the Federation for Indian Independence was recently established and its members are new engaged in anti-British activities. The Ceylon Branch, celebrating the advance of the Indian National Army in the motherland, hold a mass meeting at 6.00 p.m., March 25, in the open square before Independence Hall for the purpose of appealing to those unify the young Ceylonese who have escaped from Ceylon. From far Penang came (Soavanamut), representing the leaders of the Penang Branch of the Independence Federation.

Tokyo, Japanese, 3/26/44

Penang: "Ceylonese in Malai fully realize that without the independence of Indian there can be no free Ceylon," declared (Yo Yoh

Do) Alawala, Secretary of the Ceylon Department, at the Indian Independence League Headquarters in an interview here today. Alawala, at present on tour of Malai, stated, upon his return to Shonan after visiting Thailand and Burma, he will hold an all-Malaian conference of Ceylonese leaders. He added he found great enthusaism among the Ceylon community at various Malaian centers he visited. *Tokyo, English, 5/26/44*

Andaman Islands Branch: Activities

Among Indian Nationals here, the Independence Movement of the home country is very strong. 7,000 compatriots are united under the leadership of the esteemed Dr. (Wong Shun) who was formely (a certain captain). They are building huge rafts on which they intend to cross the Indian Ocean to join in the fight for Indian Independence.

Tokyo, English, 9/30/42

Shonan: 200,000 Indians in the Andaman group are now singing their way to the independence of India. "The Independence of India" is the name of a song widely sung among Indian partiots today. It was once prevalent among the prisoners in the famous Andaman Prison and soon all the Indians were singing it throughout the Andaman Islands. Later the British authorities censored the major part of this patriotic song for obvious reasons, but now, under the Japanese protection, they are free to sing this song again to their hearts contents.

Tokyo, English, 10/1/43

Welfare Association

The Indian Independence League in Shonan at this time established a welfare Association and will engage in welfare work of the Indians residing in Shonan. Up to now, the Indian Independence League had heen taking charge of the welfare problems of the Indian residing in Shonan. However, as the Independence League become in the most part of political and military organ of the anti-British struggle, it's activities increased. Therefore, an Indian Welfare Association has been established, with Indian residents as members, which will be active in social work, employment and....

Tokyo, Japanese, 4/14/44

Shonan: Besides contributing $4,000 to the Patients' Fund, a party of leading Indian ladies here paid a visit to the Indain National Army Hospital to comfort recuperating soldiers. The party, headed by Mrs. K.R. Assomull, entertaind the soldiers with food, music, songs and dances.

Tokyo, English, 5/1/44

Shonan: The Indians Destitute Home was officially opened in the city with President (Ana F. Pelai).... of the Indian Welfare Association as its first director. The some is to take care of sick and destitute Indians and will be supported by the local Indian community.

Tokyo, English, 7/12/44

Study of Japanese

The Fire Insurance Bureau of Shonan had decided to grant to members of the Indian Independence League desiring to study Japanese, German, and Italian...... *Tokyo, Japanese, 4/21/43*

In order to encourage the Indians residing in Shonan whose ideal has been realized in the course of the war to study foreign languages, particularly Japanese, the Bureau of Welfare of the Special Administration of Shonan decided to loan money to these Indians. The generous action on the part of the Japanese authorities has pofoundly moved the population. *Tokyo, Franch, 4/21/43*

Colonial Settlement

Shonan: The Bintan island settlement scheme for Shonan Malaians and Indians has received the whole-hearted support of the two communities. The first group of settler formers made all necessary arrangements to leave for their new homes. Though the first batch of colonists was limited to 100 families, over 150 families are on the waiting list with some more applications pouring in. The settlers will take up farming in the island to attain food self-sufficiency.

Tokyo, English, 5/10/44

Shonan: The agricultural settlement for Indian families at Bintan Island, in the southern part of Shonan, is now ready to receive pioneers, according to a statement issued by the Indian Welfare Association. The settlement, which was sponsored by government auhorities here, among other advantages offers each settler and family four acres of land for foodstuff cultivation, and quarters, as well as a subsidy of 300 yen. The statement added that the official of the association who was sent to study conditions on the island is of the opinion the aspect is favorable and soil extremely fertile. *Tokyo, English, 6/7/44*

Indian National School

Shonan: Catering to children as well as adults, an Indian National School, under the auspices of the local Indian Independence League, has been opened here. The object of the school is to impart education in Indian culture, national spirit, Hindustani music, handicraft, gardening and other subjects. *Tokyo, English, 11/16/43*

Shonan: The graduation ceremony of an entire batch of cadets who have undergone training for posts of administrators in the liberated areas of India was held last evening in the presence of Subhas Chandra Bose and high ranking officers of the Indian National Army as well as members of the Provisional Government of Free India. Presenting certificates to the graduates, Bose exhorted them to be prepared to surmount all difficulties even at the risk of their lives in carrying out administrative and reconstruction duties in the areas of India that would soon be liberated from British occupation. The graduates completed the minimum standard of military training as well as administration and reconstruction courses.

Tokyo, English, 12/3/43

The patriotic spirit which the Shonan Indian National School inspired has become evident (of) many Indian homes in Shonan. The school has provided lessons in Indian history, cultural subjects, and specially in study of Hindustani. The school has been established to teach young children born in Shonan who know nothing of the suffering of their countrymen in their motherland. *Tokyo, English, 1/7/44*

Japanese Cooperation

On the occasion of the fall of Singapore, the Finance Ministry has added 76 Indians who are making sincere efforts for the Independence of India to the rest of those Pro-Japanese Indians who are exempted from the application of the freezing order.

Tokyo, English, 2/17/42

Shonan: "A new era has dawned in East Asia when age-long British imperialism will ultimately be wiped out of India and the long cherised independence will be acheived by Indians," declared Prime Minister General Hideki Tojo in his congratulatory message sent to the Indian mass rally held in Shonaan today. "With the Outbreak of the GEA War, all the Indian leaders rose up and have spiritually completed preparations for Independence.... Japan has not frequently declared its desire that India for Indians wi!l be established as early as possible. In other words, Japan is firmly determined to do everything in its power to help Indian attain the long-looked for freedom.....I am firmly convinced that it is the only way for the Indian to achieve their independence to cooperate with the Tripartite powers in their fight against their common enemy by taking advantage of this God-given opportunity," Prime Minister Tojo concluded.

Tokyo, English, 7/4/43

Contributions

Panang: ....The contribution by the people have already reached as high as $ 2,000,000 even immediately after the convention (Indian National Convention at Penang, Sept, 5th) was opened.

Tokyo, Japanese, 9/5/43

Malacca: Contributions to the Indian Independence League Fund have already passed the 300,000 yen mark, it was revealed by the secretary of the local branch. Including 48,000 yen collected during the visit of Subhas Chandra Bose of Malacca, the total now amounts to 364,000 yen. The general secretary pointed out that Malacca's full quote of 1,250,000 will be attainable soon. The largest contribution to the League Fund was made by Chettiar community, which contributed 269,000 yen, followed by Bombay merchants with 30,00 yen.

Tokyo, English, 10/9/43

Penang: "The response in men, money and material of the Indian community all over Malai to the appeal of Subhas Chandra Bose has been truly remarkable," declared Dr. N.K. Menon, chairman of the local Indian Independence League, in an interview on his return from a tour of Malai.

Tokyo, English, 10/15/43

Shohan: "The 2,000,00 Indian soldiers mobilized by the British will to be our side when we begin our historic march to Delhi. They will join us with all the supplies taken by the British," declared S.C. Bose, Commander-in-Chief of the Indian National Army, in his stirring addressed before a mass meeting of more than 20,000 Indians who jammed (name) park last night to congratulate the Filipions on achieving their independence. He said "Today we meet for the purpose of congratulating the Filipines on having become independent." .....Stressing that the Indians cannot attain everlasting independence with the sacrifices of their allies and friends, Bose declared, "We must fight for it ourselves, shed our own blood. If we (are) a small people, there we could get freedom at the hands of others, but we are 380 million people and, if it will be with our own sacrifices, we shall become a free people. Our fight will begin this year."....expressed confidence that a nationwide revolution will break out in India to spell doom for India's British domination.....At the conclusion of the meeting the garlands presented to Bose were auctioned, fetching over 125,000 yen. The donations in the form of cash as well as jewellary, by hundreds of Indians present, were handed to Subhas Chandra Bose.

Manila, English, 10/16/43

Firm determination and growing enthusiasm of the Indian residents in Malai to devote themselves to the cause of India's Independence is seen in the even-incresing amount of donations pouring in everyday. In the two mass rallies held in Shonan on Monday and Tuesday, a total of 20,000,000 yen was donated in cash and good to the Provisional Government of Free India. *Tokyo, English, 10/27/43*

It is reported from Shonan that within 24 hours after Netaji Subhas Chandra Bose, head of the state of the Provisional Government of Free India, had asked for $ 100,000,000 as a first installment to carry on the war against the Anglo-Americans, $13,500,000 were subscribed by the Indians in Shonan. *Saigon, English, 10/27/43*

Singapore: A "Bomb the British out of India Fund" was launched here last evening by Appavar Yellappa, chairman of the local branch of the Indian Independence League. Within a few minutes of the inauguration ceremoney, substanial sums were received from leading Indians who have promised full support. Meanwhile, Indian officers workers themselves took the initial start in collections and at the same time promised to give a portion of their salaries, monthly, for contributions towards the fund.

Tokyo, English, 2/15/44

Shonan: The Indian Press Association here has contributed the sum of 2,150 yen to the Imperial Nippen Army War Wounded Fund. This amount represents the proceeds of a dramatic performance staged here last Monday under the auspices of the association. The director of the association declared the motion is only a small token of Indian gratitude for the gallant part of the Nippon forces in conjuction with the Indian National Army for the cause of motherland emancipation.

Tokyo, English, 2/18/44

Shonan: A purse of 6,500 yen was presented to members of the Rani of Jhansi Regiment by the Indian citizens of Shonan at a women's mass meeting held Saturday in connection with National Liberation Week. Prior to the meeting the Indian women soldiers in their smart khaki uniforms marched from their camp to the league grounds, accompanied by an Indian National Army Band. *Tokyo, English, 4/10/44*

Johore Bahru: More than $200,000 in case, as well as a fresh batch (sic) of men and women volunteers for active service, were results of a vigorous campaign for the total mobilization of Indian men and material resources conducted during National Liberation Week celebration here. According to an official of the Johore Indian Independence League, the campaign will be kept up until all available resources of the Indians here have been mobilized to carry of India's war of Independence. The official disclosed that the largest contribution received were from Butupahat and Muar Districts.

Tokyo, English, 4/18/44

More than $1,000 was netted by a dramatic play staged here last Saturday at the ..... theater, under the auspices of the local branch of the Indian Independence League. This amount has been donated to the Indian National Army wounded Officers and Soldiers Fund.....

Manila, English, 5/12/44

Free India Provisional Government

It appears that the Independence Movement is to be carried on under the unified supervision of the Provisional Government, which is newly established, based under Mr. Bose's supporters. It is thought quite natural as soon as this movement for independence.....what Mr. Bose calls (routine)....It will naturally be recognized internationally as being carried on by the beligerent (party) and we think its present from such as the Indian Independence League would be inadequate.

Tokyo, English, 7/8/43

Shonan: Beginning with the materialization of independence for Burma and the Philippines, the objective of the GEA war of liberation of the various nations in Asia is steadily being realized.....As all preparation to obtain independence for India has been completed, a Provisional Indian Government will be established, it has been decided, on October 21 at Shonan and Chandra Bose will head this government. At the same time it is also expected of the new government to declar war upon America and Britain.

Tokyo, Japanese, 10/19/43

.....Issued the following statement concerning the establishment of the provisional government: "The provisional government has prepared its own individual qualities and has a truly independent character. The Free Indian Provisional Government is simply a wartime government. It is also an exile government separated from the mother country because of the war. It has just the one mission of (wd) the enemy camp and to liberate the people of (members). (Its organization) will be further strengthened (hereafter).... Under the command of Subhas Chandra Bose, Commander-in-Chief of the Indian National Army, this revolutionary army will....of New Delhi. 'On to Delhi! On to Delhi!'....The free Indian Provisional Government (has received) the aid and sympathy of the National Government of China, the Manchukuoan Empire, Thailand, and Philippine Republic which was newly born. In the same manner, Germany and Italy announced the sympathy and aid would be given when the Indian Independence began in East Asia. Japan has stated at every opportunity that politically and economically and also militarily she would not begrudge aid to India.... Subhas Chandra Bose today assumed office as President of the Provisional Government of Free India and took the following oath of office, 'I, Subhas Chandra Bose, in the name of God here vow to liberate Indian and the 380,000,000 people of India from their fetters....' When the objective of driving British power out of India is completely achieved, the provisional government will transfer all to the Indian Government which should be established in India in accordance with the total will of all Indians.....President S.C. Bose assumed office as Minister of Military Affairs and Minister of Foreign Affairs (Ameel) Chandra Chatterji, Finance Minister, S.A. Ayar, Publicity Minister, Madame Slakshmi, Women's Minister." *Tokyo, Japanese, 10/21/43*

Shonan: Lineup of the Provisional Government of Free India....head of state, Prime Minister and concurrently Miniter for War and Foreign Affairs, Subhas Chandra Bose; Publicity Minister, S. A. Ayer; Finance, Lt. Col. A.C. Chatteriji; Woman's Organizations, Swami Nathan Lakshami; Secretary with Ministerial Rank, A. M. Sahay, Supreme Adviser, Rash Behari Bose. Other advisers are—Karim Gani, Debanth Das, D.M. Khan, Ayellappa, J. Thivy and Sardar Ishar Singh. Legal Adviser is A.N. Sarkar, whil representatives of the armed forces includes Lt. Colonels Aziz Ahmed, N.S. Bhagat, J.K. Bhonsle, Gulzara Singh, M.Z. Kiani, A.D. Loganadan, Ehsan Quadir and Shah Nawaz. *Tokyo, English, 10/21/43*

Shonan: The Headquarter of the Provisional Government of Free India announced today that the first meeting of the Council of Ministers of the Provisional Government of Free India was held last night at the official residence of the head of the government, Mr. Subhas Chandra Bose, who presided. The first item on the agenda was a resolution paying homage to all those who are carrying on the heroic struggle against the British inside India, undergoing tremendous sufferings and making tremendous sacrifices, and to all those who have laid down their lives for the cause of India's freedom. The council of Minister also discussed the political and economic situation in India. *Tokyo, English, 10/23/43*

Shonan: At a mass rally of Indians held here this evening, the first since Subhas Chandra Bose returned from Tokyo, a resolution was passed expressing gratitude to the Japanese Government for its promise to cede the Andaman and Nicobar Islands to the Provisional Government of Free India and congratulating Bose on his successful completion of the recent tour of East Asia. This meeting also expresses its profound joy at the decision of the Government of Japan to hand over the Andaman and Nicobar Islands to the Provisional Government of Free India as announced by His Excellency, Premier Gen. Tojo, at the Assembly of GEA Nations, and offers its grateful thanks to the Government of Nippon for the same. The meeting reiterates its firm resolve to go on fighting shoulder to shoulder with Nippon and other allies under the leadership of Subhas Chandra Bose till our common victory is achieved and India is completely liberate from the British Yoke."

Shonan: The Provisional Government of Free India announced yesterday that it approved two systems in its cabinet meeting held on December 9, the (compensation) system and the (wd) system. Under the (wd) system, (wd) will be given to the members of the family and to (bereaved members) in the event of death in action. It will be applicable first to the Indians residing on the islands. *Tokyo, Japanese, 12/11/43*

Recognition of Government

The recognition of the Provisional Government of India by Imperial Japan is entirely different in significance from the customary recognition in accordance to the international law. That is to say, the Provisional Government of India is not a government of an indepentent nation, it is a government established primarily as an organ through which independence may be obtained. The Imperial Government of Japan recognition the Provisional government so that independence may be achieved as quickly and smoothly as possible. Therefore, diplomatic relationship ordinarily maintained among independent nations will not be made, i.e. exchange of diplomatic officials will not take place but close relationship will be maintained through the eexisting outpost organs on the spot. Following are the points that bear notice in regard to the recognition of the provisional government: This recognition declares now to the world that the Government of Japan considers her aid to India in the Movement of Independence is one of her national policies. Therefore, Imperial Japan will not stint in the least in giving her aid to India until the final glory of independence shines over India and her people. Through the request of the Provisional Government of India our government immediately reported her recognition of the India Government of friendly nations Germany, Italy, Manchukuo and the National Government of China at Nanking. Manchukuo has already declared that its government will not limit itself in giving all the aid possible to the Provisional Government of India.

Tokyo, Japanese, 10/23/43

Shonan: Subhas Chandra Bose meeting, Head of the Provisional Government of India, declared today that a notification from the Burmese Goverment of the recognition of the Indian Provisional Government arrived.

Tokyo, Japanese, 10/24/43

The Indian people's mass meeting,commemorating the establishment of the free Indian Provisional Government, was held Octobor 4 in Shonan... Bose arrived at the place of the meeting where he was not by the chief of the provisional government. Following the review of the National Army, flag railsing ceremony of the national flag was held in a very impressive manner.Then, as Bose stood up before the ceremony grounds, a (service award) was put on the president's neck by the Indian people.... In this way the announcement of felicitation wires from Manchukuo, Thailand and other natons was made. *Tokyo, Japanese,10/24/43*

Nanking: The National Government of China today, on Monday, formally announced the recognition of the Provisional Government of Free India. *Tokyo, Japanese.11/1/43*

The Provisional Goverment of Free India today formally was recognized by the Fascis Republic of Italy, which decided to recognize the provisional government November 2 and instructed Col. Omero Principini, who is incharge of Italian interests in Japan, to formally inform the provisional government. It has been recognized by 6 nations, including Japan, China, Burma, Manchukuo and the Philippines.

Tokyo,English, 11/9/43

Shonan: Heartily reciprocating the message of felicitations from the Irish Republic, Subhas Cnandra Bose head of the Provisional Government of Free India, in a press statement today said, " I herewith sound a word of cheer in reply—our cause in just. Our demands are out birthright. We are prepared to pay the price. We shall therefore triumph. Freedom will come." Declaring it has given him the greatest pleasure to receive the message, Bose stated, "Of all the freedom movement we Indians have studied closely. and from which we have derived inspiration, there is perhaps none that can equal the Irish struggle for independence. .... the nation has had the some oppressors and exploiters as ourselves. It has had the same experience of ruthlessness, brutality and hypocrisy as we have."

Tokyo, English, 12/2/43

Declaration of War

Shonan: The Government of Free India decided to declare war on British and the U.S.A. according to a communique issued this morning.

The decision was reached at a meeting hold yesterday by the Council of Minister of the Provisional Government of Azad Hind, which met at the official residence of Subhas Chandra Bose. *Tokyo, English, 10/23/43*

Grant of Territory of Japan

Bose's message to the 3,000,000 Indians in East Asia and to the 350,000,000 of India.... Bose told Domei, in as exclusive interview, "For the Indians, the return of the Andamans represents of the first territory to be liberated from the British Yoke. By acquisition of this territory the provisional government has now become a national entity, in fact as well as in name." Liberation of the Andamans has a "Symbolic significance", he said, because the Andamans always were used by the British as a prison for political prisoners. "Like the Bastille in Paris, which was liberated first in the French Revolution, the setting free of the political prisoners on the Andamans, where our patriots suffered much, is the first to be liberated in the Indians fights for independence. Part by part the Indian territory will be liberated but it is always the first plot of land that holds the most signficance.".....The return of the Andamans, he added, will have an "emotional moral appeal to the Indian people in the fact the prison house of India has been liberated." *Tokyo, English, 11/7/43*

The declartion of Premier Tojo to the effect that the Andaman and Nicobar Islands will soon be returned to the Provisional Government of Free India has deeply impressed the 18,000 Indians who comprise the majority of the local inhabitants of the Andaman Islands and is further deepening their attitude toward the Japanese Government. According to a report from a naval correspondent in the Andamans, this reaction has first of the all manifested in the first national defence contribution in the Andamans. Then, too, as a result of a meeting hold in the office of the Military Administration on November 12, the Andaman branch of the Indian Independence League resolutely carried out a reorganization of the executive staff and decided to establish a volunteer army under the direction of the branch director. A committee for the establishment of the army has already been formed and it has been decided to select a total of an undisclosed number of men, 20 to 40 years of age, from the villages in the island.... *Tokyo, Japanese, 11/14/43*

Shonan: When the islands of Andaman and Nicobar became territory of the Free Indian National Government, in accordance with the declaration made by our Preimer Tojo at the recent CEA conference, it was decided to change the names of the two islands. Andaman Island will be called (Karido) or (wd) island and the Nicobar Island will be called (Suwaya) or (wd) island[3]. *Tokyo, Japanese, 11/26/43*

Shonan: At a mass rally of Indians held here this evening, the first since Subhas Chandra Bose returned from Tokyo, resolution was passed expressing gratitude to the Japanese Governemnt for its promise to cede the Andaman and Nicobar Island to the Provisional Government of Free India and congratulating Bose on his successful tour of East Asia, as well as reiterating determination to fight till victory is attained.

Tokyo, English, 12/2/43

The Tokyo Branch of the Indian Independence League held a (wd) meeting in Tokyo on December 2 and ..... in regard to the transfer of the two island of Andaman and Nicobar to the Free Indian Provisional Government by Japan. The Indian Independence League (Council) in Japan decided to have its headquarters in Tokyo and establish branches in Yokohama, Kobe and Osaka for the purpose of.....

Tokyo, Japanese, 12/2/43

Members of Indian Independence League of Japan met here this afternoon and adopted a resolution expressing profound gratitude for Premier Tojo's promise to transfer the Andaman and Nicobar Islands to the Provisional Government of Free India. They also despatched telegrams to Subhas Chandra Bose, Head of the Provisional Government of Azad Hind, and Premier Tojo, expressing their determination and appreciation.

Tokyo, English, 12/2/43

Immediately after Bose moved his government to Burma. He made a radio broadcast address to the people of India , kaking clear his visit to the Andaman Islands, and announced the appointment of Lt. Col. Regananadan as Chairman of the Administrative Preparation Committee for the Andaman Islands. *Tokyo, Japanese, 1/10/44*

Subhas Chandra Bose recently appointed (Chiri) (Neme) as (Governor) of the Andaman Islands. He was in Germany and has been heading the Independence Committee.

Tokyo, Japanese, 1/4/44

The Free Indian Government, under the leadership of Subhas Chandra Bose, has completed all the preparation for the attack on India... with regards to Andaman Islands, Chandra Bose declared that the Japanese Government has promised that these islands will be returned to the Indian Government at the close of hostilities. *Tokyo, English, 11/9/43*

---

3. They were named as Saheed and Swaraj

Shonan: Lt. Col. A.D. Loganadan, who was recently appointed chief commissioner of Andaman and Nicobar Islands left here today for Port Blair, Andaman, to take up his post(sic). The Andaman and Nicobar Islands are scheduled to be transferred soon to the Provisional Government of free India by the Japanese Government. *Tokyo, Japanese, 2/21/44*

Love to Burma

Free India Provisional Government ... has now moved into Burma. *Tokyo, Japanese, 1/20/44*

National Holidays

Shonan : Indians all over East Asia will observe Indian Independence Day, January 26, with mass meetings at which speeches will be given stressing the significance of the day. Resolutions, pledging the allout effort of the 3,000,000 Indians of East Asia for the attainment of Indian's emancipation are expected to be passed. It was at Johore on January 26, 1939 that the Congress, at the proposal of Pandit Nehru, supported by Subhas Chandra Bose, decided to take the uncompromising stand of complete independence and not a dominion status within the British Empire. Since then, Indians have renewed this pledge on January 26 each year. This year's observance will have the added significance not only in East Asia but also in India, that Indians now have a free government and their own army in their fight to realize that pledge.

Saigon, English, 1/23/44

Shonan Domei : Upon the passing of Madme Kasturibai, Mrs. Gandhi, the Free India Provisional Government has decided to observe March 1 as National (Affection) Day to commemorate eternally the seventy year old life of the Madame. *Tokyo, Japanese, 2/24/44*

Shonan: The 109th anniversary of the birth of Sri Rama Krishna, famous Indian Saint will be observed at Rama Krishna Mission tomorrow. Prayers will be offered and a public meeting held, at which A.C. Chatterji, Minister of the Provisional Government of Free India, will deliver a speach on the life and work of Rama Krishna. *Tokyo, English, 2/26/44*

Indian Liberation week began on April 6 in Shonan. Almost every day student parades and victory prayers are being held. The joy of the Indians was never as great as when the National Army recently invaded the homeland. The Azad Hind, "a newspapar published by the Independence League in Shonan, sold but every issue... In view of the strong interest of the Indians in Japan, the Independence League had M.R. (Naizu), member of the Shonan Propagarda and Information

Committee, translate Professor Kooya Nakamura's "History of Japan" into Tamil. His book sold out immediately. In the streets, the marching of the Indian women's regiment, which is in training is attracting more and more attention. It is the custom of the Chinese and Malayans to bless these woman. These people have shown sincere cooporation.

Tokyo, Japanese, 4/9/44

Penang: One of the most impressive procession in Penang took place yesterday when more than 6,000 local Indians, led by Doctor M.K. Menon, chairman of the Penang Chapter of the Indian Independence League, participated in a march along Penang's principal streets in commemoration of Indian Liberation week. Headed by Menon and members of the local Indian Independence League Committee, the procession, which was about two miles long was participated in by members of the civil volunteers, the Indian National Army and Indian women. *Tokyo, English, 4/11/4*

Shonan: During National Liberation week, celebrated by all Indians in East Asia, the Indians here did not forgot to comfort the wounded Japanese and Indian soldiers who had played a great part in the fight for India's liberation. A group of Indian school children and women visited the hospitals with their (wd) entertainment. The patients enjoyed the children's songs, dances and concerts besides the cakes .. cookies showered upon them..... *Tokyo, English, 4/11/4*

Shonan: The Provisional Government of Azad Hind Day, which falls on April 21, will be observed by the Indians here and all over East Asia. The celebration this month is expected to attract special public attention, in view of the tremendous successes achieved by the Azad Hind Fauj and its press Association here will sponsor special cinemas and lecture meetings in which brief speeches will be made by prominent Indians.

Tokyo, English, 4/19/4

Shonan: The Indians here, in conjunction with their compatriots (wd) East Asia, paid tribute today to the memory of the heroic sepoys who gave their lives 87 years ago in India's first war of independence. The Indian national tricolor and rising sun flag flew side by side at every Indian home. Thousands packed the Indian places of worship early in the morning to pray for the reponse of the gallant sepoys and for te success of the Indian National Army. A two mile long procession through the principal streets of the city highlighted the day's proceedings. Officers and men of the Indian National Army, woman of the Rani of Jhansi Regiment, looking trim and soldierly, school children and others marched jauntily through the city to the municipal square, where a mass meeting was held. Speaking to some (80,000) gathered there, Thivy, newly appointed Vice-President of the rear headquarters of the Provisional Government of Azad Hind, paid a glowing tribute to the memory of tens of thousands of sepoys who died in 1857 for emancipation of their motherland. Calling upon all those present here to emulate their noble example and sacrifice all for the independence drive launched by the Netaji, he assured them success was bound to be theirs. Amid enthusiastic scenes, the gathering unanimously resolved to carry on the fight for Indian independence under the leadership or the Netaji to and at the same time vowed to avenge the deaths of the sepoys who fell in 1857 and other martyrs whom the British have killed during the intervening years. *Tokyo, English, 5/10/44*

Shonan: Momories of India's first war of independence, and the in human treatment meted out to the unfortunate Indian nationalists ever since then, are today goading the 3,800,000 Indians all over East Asia to make greater sacrifices to wrest their independence from British hands, competent Indian circles here stated today. May 10 has been a red letter day to all Indians ever since 1857, when J.H. Mangal Panday fired the first shot and unleashed the countrywide revolution which has, till today, never been suppressed despite British boasts to the contrary.

Tokyo, English, 5/10/44

Shonan: Observance by the Provisional Government of Azad Hind Day here by the Indians today was marked by grim determination to carry on the present struggle for successful liberation of their motherland and by their firm resolve to sacrifice their all in that noble cause. The Indian national tricolor flew side by side with the Rising Sun flag from every Indian house while special prayers were offered in all places of worship by the Indians for complete victory of the Indian National Army and its allies and for the repose of the souls of those gallant men who have fallen for this cause on the battle fields of Burma and India. Glowing tributes to the war dead and to the valour of those fighting now on Indian soil were paid at mass meetings held in four centers of this city. The special feature of this day's observances was taking on the oath of allegiance to their provisional government by thousands of Indians here.

Tokyo, English, 5/21/44

Shonan: Starting Netaji week, Indian National Army met at barracks, residents paraded, held mass rally unfurled flags, prayed and broadcast. Throughout the week the Indian Tri-coloured flag will be unfurled alongside the Rising Sun. *Tokyo, English, 7/4/44*

National Songs

Shonan: National songs portraying the true martial spirit of the sons and daughters of India today, are enjoying immense popularity among Indians throughout Malai. Soldiers of the Indian National Army sing stirring verses during their gruelling marches, while volunteers sing..... on parade and even little Indian boys and girls popular airs in praise of the glory of their motherland and the cause for which their fathers and mothers, brothers and sisters are now fighting. Through the medium of Indian songs, especially Hindustani patriotic marches, national consciousness and a burning desire to win freedom has been born in the hearts of every Indian, young and old. *Tokyo, English, 11/30/43*

Awards

The Provisional Government of India, at this year's first cabinet meeting, decided upon complete plans for awarding medals and orders and for providing annuities to officers and men after the termination of India's war of Independence. The plans published on Tuesday are as follows: After the termination of the war, all officers and men living will be conferred the order of the war of Independence, and in case they are killed they will be honored with order of the (Martyr). Moreover they will be conferred the order of the Indian Knight, the order of the Great Hero, and the order of the Battlefield leader together with their annuities in recognition of their respective merits. The bereaved families of the war dead will be provided with subsidies. Wounded soldiers will be conferred annuities and will be given first consideration for official posts. Privates will be specially accorded 1,000 0r 500 rupees or a plot of ground worth 500 rupees.

Tokyo, Japanese, 1/5/44

Ever since Subhas Chandra Bose appeared in GEA, India's Movement for Independence has become more active. The India Independence Headquarters issued a declaration to the effect that the Indian Independence League has formed an Indian National Army for Independence. The Indian National Army is composed of several thousands and in undergoing intense training day and night. This army makes no distinction of religion and classes.

Tokyo, Japanese, 7/8/44

Shonan: The Indian National Army was reviewed by Chandra Bose and by Tojo. Bose first stood up and expressed his gratitude that they are to fight for independence, then the first review was held. The review ended after 20 minutes. Tojo then left the stand with Bose. Bose on July...

declared that he would not stop fighting until the Indian National Army marches into New Delhi and independence is attained.

The organization of the Indian National Army is viewed in Tokyo and other Asiatic political circles as a momentous step toward the long-desired goal of India's independence. .....This Indian National Army, unlike the Indian forces organized under the British is an independent Indian army organized and led by the Indians themselves. The officers and men of this army are all ardent young Indian patriots ready to shed their blood in this (life or death) struggle... The members ... of superior arms are undergoing training daily and have already made much progress in the mechanical line. *Tokyo, English, 7/8/43*

While the Movement for Indian Independence in the hand of the Indians themselves is progressing in the lands of East Asia, the reconstruction of the Indian Independence League has resulted in the rapid development of the Indian Voluntary National Militia, which created its nuclei in May of last year in various parts of Malaysia and East Asia. This Indian militia, armed with excellent modern arms, has already reached a stage of perfect technical discipline, following the closing of the great..... on July 5 reviewed the Indian Voluntary National Militia, which is a dependency of the league. *Tokyo, Italian, 7/8/43*

The headquarters of the Indian Independence League, at 3:00 O'clock, Thursday afternoon, issued the following communique regarding the organization of the Indian National Army: To fight for complete freedom from British rule in India, the Indian Independence League has organised a National Army to be know as Azad Hind Fauj or the Indian National Army. The aim of this newly organized army is to drive out the British from India and to create an India for the Indians. *Tokyo, English, 7/9/43*

....One of these great events of this week was the official debut of the Indian National Army that took place on Thursday. You had better put it down in your notebook. From now on, Indian National Army means this is a powerful and magnificent army of the Indian volunteers who will fight actually fight for the independence of India. They are formidably equipped with all modern weapons. They are fully trained to use these weapons effectively. The organization of this army started in April, last year. It was read for action in September of the same year. Last Monday a part of this army assembled in a large force for the first time in public for a military review in the city of Shonan. All the customs and daily routine of this army are conducted in accordance with the custom of the Indian people, all the drills being conducted in their own language. It is the Indian own army. It in eager to throw itself into battle for India's independence.

Tokyo, English, 7/9/43

On Friday, the Indian Independence League at Shonan began to accept applications of Inidan volunteers for the Indian National Army. More than 2,500 Indian youths offered for enlistment on Friday. Next day large crowds came for enlistment. Chandra Bose came to supervise things and made a vigorous speech to the Indian youths.

Tokyo, Hindustani, 7/18/43

Johore Bahru: An additional batch of 75 volunteers left here for the Indian National Army training camp in Shonan yesterday, to undergo military training. The group was seen off by many friends and relatives, as well as officials of the local chapter of the Indian Independence League.

Tokyo, English, 1/17/44

Kuala Lumpur: Eager youths from all stations of life have already enlisted at the recruiting office here in response to an ... announcement that a fresh batch of volunteers is required for the Azad Hind Fauj center. Judging from the number registered since yesterday, the requirement quota is expected to be filled within the next few days.

Tokyo, English, 2/7/44

Outside Volunteers

Shonan: A large nunber of Indian volunteers have already arrived in Shonan from Thailand and Canton in order to join the Indian National Army, organized under the leadership of Mr. Subhas Chandra Bose.

Tokyo, English, 7/9/43

A batch of Indian volunteers from Sumatra are on their way to Shonan to join the Indian National Army. A second batch of volunteers from Sumatra will also be dispatched shortly. A large contingent of Indian youths are at present being given military training at severnal centers in Sumatra, prior to being sent to Shonan. *Tokyo, French, 10/21/43*

Shonan: The third batch of Indian recruits from Borneo arrived here, enroute for one of the Indian National Army training camps somewhere in Malai. Looking chearful and healthy, three recruits are representatives of many Indian races, the prominent among them being Sikhs. The leader of the group is a 6-footer, Niranpa Singh Gill, who stated the Indian living in Borneo are united with the common purpose of freeing their motherland. It is revealed that besides volunteering for the Indian National Army, the Borneo Indians are also contributing substantial sums for their country's cause. *Tokyo, English, 1/13/44*

Training Schools

Shonan: In the presence of Mr. Subhas Chandra Bose, President of the Indian Independence League, the first graduation ceremony of the famous school of the Indian National Army officers was held on Tuesday. Those graduating Indian officers will be immediately commissioned to the Service.

Tokyo, English, 7/21/43

Shonan: In view of the daily increasing applicants for joining the Indian National Army, the headquarters of the Indian Independence League has decided to open a training institute for those Indian young men who wish to be officers among the volunteers . The committee men in charge of the entrance examination, which was held on Wednesday, were agreeably surprised to see more than 1,000 enthusiastic Indian youths rush to take the examination for the enrollment of 30 students.

Tokyo, English, 1/30/43

By Sapuran Singh, Domei Staff Correspondent, Shonan : Racial and religious differences have vanished overnight with the clarion call of Subhas Chandra Bose for total mobilization of Indian wealthy men in East Asia. Today with the disappearance of artificial barriers, the Indians now are joining together in brotherly accord as various part time training centers on the Island. So far, 15 centers have been opened by the local branch of the Indian Independence League, while 5 more are proposed for the near future Training, which began with ordinary marching, develops into use of the rifle and other firearms, while long route marches and vigorous physical exercises build up the body stamina of the trainees. Lectures are given daily on Indian history and politics to instill courage and patriotism, a spiritual force that will withstand all trials and hardships and keep up morals in the hour of battle.

Tokyo, English, 10/9/43

Penang: Dr. N.K. Menon, chairman of the local Indian Independence League, declared in an interview on his return from a tour of Malai that many new training centers of the Indian National Army that have been established and the new volunteers eager to join the colours are extremely gratifying to headquarters.

Tokyo, English, 10/15/43

Shonan: The Indian National Army Headquarters here is preparing to open, under the personal leadership of Subhas Chandra Bose, a training institute for women volunteers, which will be named after the Queen of Jhansi, an Indian woman patriot who had fought against British rule during the first independence war in 1857.

Tokyo, English, 10/16/43

At Johore, in southern Malai, a large number of prominent Indians were present at the (Central) Valley Railway Station yesterday to give a hearty send-off to over 100 Indian volunteers to the Indian National Army who are proceeding to Kuala Lumpur for training at the Bharat Youth Training camp. Another group of 200 Indian volunteers left for Epoh on Thursday to receive military training there at the newly-established Bharat Training Camp. *Saigon, English, 10/16/43*

Klaung, Monore State: A group of Indian women left here for Johore Bharu prior to proceeding to Shonan to join the Rani of Jhansi Regiment and undergo military training. Devaki, leader of the group when Lakshmi was head of the women's organization, addressed them last month and said they were filled with the desire to amulate her noble example and volunteer for the women's regiment. Their one desire is to share in the struggle for Indian liberation and to stand side-by-side with their menfolk to the very end. It is understood the husbands of these women volunteers already have joined the Indian National Army.

Tokyo, English, 10/23/43

Shonan: With patriotic Indian women gathered from throughout GEA, the Indian Women's Volunteer Training Camp, which opened here October 21 under the leadership of Dr. Swaminathan Lakshmi, director of the Women's Dept. of the Provisional Government of Free India and concurrently commander of the Women's Volunteer Corps, has had continuous stream of loyal Indian woman from Shonan and various Malaian Provinces, including Penang and Malacca as well as Salangor and distant Thailand, pouring into the camp. Following reveille at 7:00 a.m., Japan time, the trainees pay respects to the Indian National Flag and then they go through Physical and military training, nursing and study of Hindustani and Japanese language. *Tokyo, English, 11/19/43*

Shonan: Education should be part of the means of making Indian youth worthy sons of Mother India, declared Mr. S.C. Bose, head of the Provisional Government of Free India, in his address at the graduation ceremony of the Indian National School here on Sunday evening. In his address to the students, Mr. Bose said that he had two reasons for attending the ceremony. He wanted to express his thanks for the good work of the institution and at the same time he wanted to thank the municipal authorities for the help they have been rendering not only to the school but also to the cause of India's independence. *Tokyo, English, 12/29/43*

Kuala Lumpur: A graduation ceremony for a group of Indians of the Bharat Youth Training Camp was held this afternoon in the presence of a huge crowd which filed the Plaza in front of the government building here. Immediatly after the ceremony, graduates proceeded to barracks to join their comrades at Training Schools in the Indian National Army.

Tokyo, English, 2/1/44

Ipoh: Completing an intensive 3-month military training course, the first batch of volunteers in the Azad Hind Fauj Training Camp, situated "somewhere outside Ipho," gave an impressive display of matrial drill at the graduation ceremony held on the camp grounds recently. Paying tribute to the camp officers for the efficient manner in which the camp has been run, a high ranking officer from headquarters of Azad Hind Fauj declared he had soon for himself what proper training methods could do to Indian youths who three months ago were just raw recruits. The ceremony was climaxed by march......with the camp commandant taking the salute.

Tokyo, English, 2/2/44

Kuala Lumpur: A large number of members of the Rani of Jansi Regiment passed through Kuala Luumpur on their way to the Indian National Army's advance posts and were greeted by the local Indian community at the railway stations. There was eager excitement among the crowd waiting on the platform, among them many relatives or friends of members of the Rani of Jhansi Regiment, as the train steamed in. Trim in their military kit and unable to hide their determination by their confident smiles, these women fighters for India's freedom, after their months of strenuous training, looked in fine fattle despite the tedious rail journey. Joyous greeting were exchanged as the train arrived. Leaders of the Selangor India Indepencence League entertained the Ranis to dinner, while several citizens supplied the women soldiers with..........

Tokyo, English, 6/12/44

Training in Japan

Penang: The Indian National Army will select 25 youths from all parts of Malai and, after they have been given a short term training at Shonan, they will come to Japan in the near future.

Tokyo, Japanese, 11/13/43

Liaison with Japanese and Burmese Armies

.......A report from an undisclosed base in Burma discloses that with the object of perfecting the liaision among the Imperial Japanese forces, the Burma Defense Army and the Indian National Army, a permanent joint liaison organ has been created, composed of members of the staff of the three armies, ...it is certain to enhance the already smooth and cordial liaison among the three armies, since members of the staff of the Burma Defense Army and the Indian National Army will be sent to the General Headquarters of the Japanese forces in Burma to map out common operation jointly. ....Netaji Subhas Chandra Bose, head of the Provisional Government of Azad Hind and supreme commander of the Indian National Army, has returned to headquarters after a flying visit to the front. Lieutenant-Colonel (H.E. Algappan) has been appointed as the (representative) of the Provisional Government of Azad Hind. Lieutenent-Colonel A. C. Chatterji, Finance Minister of the Provisional Government of Azad Hind and (General Secretary) of the Indian Independence League (wd) Headquarters, was transferred to the Headquarters in Burma (on Saturday). Lieutenant -Colonel (H.E.Algappan), the new (wd)Minister of the Provisional Goverment of Azad Hind, is transferred from Headquarters in Burma to the (wd) Headquarters in Shonan and will take over the duties of Lieutenant-Colonal A.C. Chatterji, Lieutenant-Colonal (H.E. Algappan) is continuing ....the post of Minister of ....Supreme Commander, Azad Hind Fauj.

Singapore, English, 3/3/44

Women's Corps

It is reported from Shonan that as the call to arms of the Indian liberator, Sr. Chandra Bose, who has decided to organize woman's legion as an integral part of the Indian National Army, has had such a formidable repercussion among the Indian women of East Asia, several thousand Indian women, in a meeting hold on the 18th in Waterloo Street, Shonan, offered themselves for military service as regular Indian soldier.

Tokyo, Spanish, 7/15/43

Futher bolstering the fighting front of the Indian Independence Movement, a women's Corps in organized by the (Solangore) Branch of the Indian Independence Leugue at a ceremony which is slated to be held today... The now Women's Corps aims at the training of women leaders who will become the mainstay in women's independence activities.

Tokyo, English, 7/25/43

Dr. N.K. Menon, chairman of the local Indian Independence League at Penang, declared that the response of Indian women to join the Women's Regiment has been especially enthusiastic. He disclosed that new centers for training women will shortly be established in Shonan, where they will be taught military as well as Red Cross work. We shall soon be sending a pioneer unit of 50 women from Penang : "he declared." these women have already volunteered to leave their homes, to sacrifice their all for the cause of their motherland. Also within a week's time we are sending over 5000 women for military training . "In conclusion, Menon said that what struck him most during his trip was the patriotism that exists among the poorer sections of the community. *Tokyo, English, 10/15/43*

Shonan: It is revealed that large numbers of women volunteers, desiring to fight side by side with the men for the Indians' Independence, continue to join the women's Division of the Indian National Army through branches of the Indian Independence League in East Asia. The Women's Division of the Indian National Army is under the capable leadership of Dr. Lakshimi. *Tokyo, English, 10/16/43*

Shonan: "We give you our word that we will fight bravely against the alien oppressors of our motherland, with complete faith in victory," declared Miss V.M. Chinnammu, a member of the Rani Jhansi Regiment Training Camp, in a radio broadeast to Indian last night.

Tokyo, English, 1/12/44

Shonan: "The Indian National Army is already knocking on the Eastern Gate of India and the Rani Jhansi Regiment is eagerly awaiting the signal from S.C. Bose to go into action on the battlefield," declared Baljit Kaura Sikh, an Indian woman volunteer, in a radio broadcast to the Indians at home. *Tokyo, English, 1/22/44*

Pensions

Shonan: Pension and compensation for soldiers of the Indian National Army who may be injured or disabled or may lose their lives in the coming campaign was discussed by the Council of Ministers of the Provisional Government of Free India at its 3rd session yesterday evening... A committee, consisting of Lt. Cols. J.K. Bhonsle, N. Z. Kiani, N.S. Bhagat, A.C. Chatterji and Mr. D. M. Khan, was formed to go through a scheme already drafted by the supreme command of India with the purpose to make final recommandation on the same lines as are in vogue in free countries. A committee was also empowered to consider recommandations of the supreme command headquarters regarding medals and other rewards to be conferred on member Indians who distinguish themselves in the coming campaign. It is expected the official decision of the government will be announced in the near future. *Tokyo, English, 10/23/43*

Subhas Chandra Bose

Subhas Chandra Bose, your beloved leader, arrived today in Shonan, the former British fortress of Singapore. This day marks a new epoch in Indian's fight against British imperialism. ..... Subhas Bose has arrived in Shonan to take an part in the Indian Independence Movement in East Asia. *Singapore, English, 7/2/43*

Shonan: Rash Behari Bose, President of the Indian Independence League in East Asia, and the great Indian patriot and (revolutionary) leader Subhas Chandra Bose arrived in Shonan from Tokyo on Friday afternoon. At the airport the Indian leaders were received by members of the headquarters of the Indian Independence League the Malai Branch of the League, the President of the Shonan Branch and prominent members of the Indian community in Shonan ....A crowded program of engagements, beginning with courtesy calls on the high Japanese officials, has been arranged for the Indian leaders, Subhas Chandra Bose will take a leading part in the Indian Independence Movement in East Asia.

Batavia, English, 7/3/43

On the inauguration of Chandra Bose as the President of the Indian Independence League, the Chief of the Information Board of the Southern Army issued the following statement: Mr. Chandra Bose had held a conference with the Army Supreme Commander and he expressed his firm determination to serve for the Independence Movement .... At this moment, the Indian Independent Movement League, which is very.... and active organ, welcomed Mr. Chandra Bose, who is very highly regarded by the people. The 2,000,000 India people outside of India in the Southern Regions enthusiastically welcomed him. Mr. Chandra Bose, who left his motherland under the cruel and cunning suppression of Britain although he was burning with a land. His appointment to the presidency, I firmly belive, has an important and great signficance for the acceleration of a great independent movement development for the sake of India by taking more righteous path and discarding trival matters and by calling together all the comrades under, with a firm conviction that to fight through by playing a role in this Sacred War with confidence in the sincerity of Japan and her Axis friend nations and to accelerate their strids in the Independent movement under the epoch making cooperation under the command of Mr. Bose is the only way to reach their glory." *Tokyo, Japanese, 7/4/43*

Singapore: Mr. Chandra Bose .... spoke for about 15 minutes from the Shonan Broadcasting Station last night in Hindustan language and Indian language. *Tokyo, Japanese, 7/4/43*

Shonan: The headquarters of the Indian Independence League in this city officially announced today that the league members unanimously elected Mr. Subhas Chandra Bose as President of the League. It is recalled that this great Indian leader recently came to Japan from far-off Cermany and now, with the assumption of leadership of the Independence League by Mr. Subhas Bose the activities of the Independence Movement will definitely intensify both in fervor and in scope. *Tokyo, English, 7/4/43*

Upon the nomination of Mr. Subhas Chandra Bose as president of the Indian Independence League by its headquarters in Shonan today Mr. (Nobuyuke) Abo, the President of the Imperial Rule Assistance Political Society, sent the following message: "... On the occasion of your appointment as President of the Indian Independence League, the IRAPS, representing the entire people of Japan, hereby wishes you and your colleagues every success in the noble fight for Indian freedom."

Tokyo, English, 7/4/43

The news that Chandra Bose has boldly stood on the front line of the anti-British movement has filled the 2,000,00 people living outsides of India proper, in the various parts of the GEA, with great repture of happiness and the Malay Branch leader of the Indian Indedependce League stated the following: "when Chandra Bose was visiting Tokyo a few days ago , I was travelling thru various places in Malaya but when this message was once related, every Indian was full of great enthusiam. Again today Bose has lated, every Indian was full of great enthusiam stood on the front line of our Independence Movement. He is an exceptional revolutionist who does not know compromise. All the Indians with standfast determination are ready to follow this great leader." *Tokyo, Japanese, 7/5/43*

Shonan: Mr. Subhas Chandra Bose, newly appointed president of the Indian Independence League, called on the Commander-in-Chief of the Imperial Forces at the letter's headquarters yesterday afternoon and expressed his thanks for the efforts of the Imperial Forces.

Tokyo, English, 7/5/43

Subhas Chandra Bose returned to Shonan, had been gone since July or June 25. Had conferred with Commander in Chief of Japanese forces... Also in Bangkok he saw Premier Songgram.....conferred with local civil and military officals in Franch-Indo-China, also saw Yoshinzawa.

Tokyo, Portuguese, 8/12/43

Shonan: Mr. Subhas Chandra Bose started on a travel around the Malai peninsula on an important mission. He is expected to hold a series of discussions with the leaders of the Indians Independence Movement in

Malai on the preparations for advancing the Indian National Army into their mother country. *Tokyo, English, 9/1/43*

The Indian Independence League will not be abolished with the establishment of the provisional government, and it will take part in practical application of the Independence Movement measures in cooperation with the policy of the newly established provisional government. As Chandra Bose is the Prime Minister of the Provisional Government, he will also be the Governor of the Indian Indepdence League. Prior to this time, the Indian National Army came under the supervision of the Indian Independence League but in the future will come under the supervision of the provisional government. Prime Minister Bose will be the supreme commander of the Indian National Army. *Tokyo, Japanese, 10/21/43*

The Head of the provisional Free India Government, Mr. Chandra Bose, after visiting the assembly of the East Asian nations at Tokyo, visited the capitals of China and the Philippines, arrived on November 23 at Saigon, French-Indo-China. In the afternoon he attended a meeting of Indian residents. According to a dispatch from Shonan, Mr. Bose arrived on November 25 in this city. *Tokyo, Spanish 11/25/43*

Shonan: First anniversary Bose's assumption of leadership Indian Independence Movement finds all Indians here ready to carry on with increased vigor the struggle for freedom of their country and extermination of Anglo-Amercians. At present, 10 wartime training centers functioning in Shonan. A steady increase in membership of Indian Youth Corps being maintained. *Tokyo, English, 7/3/44*

Speeches and Interviews

Resume of address by Chandra Bose, Shonan: The people of India are now becoming dissatistied with the Civil Dis-obedience Movement and their determination to appeal to other means of attaining the goal of independence had increased......regardless of party we must make all preparations under one leadership..... From the standpoint of mobilizing effectively part of our effort, it is our aim to establish a temporary Free India. To lead and carry the revolution to perfection is the very purpose of the new temporary government....... The temporary government may prepare our follow men inside and outside of India for military combat and this will show the climax of nationlistic effort which has been within the hearts of all the Indians over since 1885...... What is to come will be left to the will of the people of India; a permanent government will be established and the temporary government will pass over the administrative powers to the new government. As soon as our preparations are completed thoruly, the battle of Indian Independence will be joined with the powers of the Axis nations of Japan, Germany and Italy. With the joining of India with the above combined power we will gain the eligibility of freedom and independence. *Tokyo, Japanese, 7/4/43*

Commenting on the great responsibility of Babu Subhas Bose: .... Subhas Bose, arriving in Tokyo from Berlin, said during the course of press interview that the enemy has unsheated his sword and our answer must be by the sword. The Civil Disobedience Movement should be converted into an armed revolt.....Under the present set-up of delicate world situation, when the rarest of opportunity is before us, this sacred mission and message is given to Subhas Bose by Himself. The blessing of God and Divine Order is given to Bose to terminate the slavery of Indian forever...The state where Subhas Bose is standing today has been set and reached by the precious blood of his predecessors among Indian patriotic leaders. Also, we know that Babu Subhas Bose, under the presence imminent circumstances, will not consider it necessary to follow the thoughts of his revered predecessors stop by it necessary to follow the thoughts of his revered predecessors step by step.....The Indian leaders failed in their fight for freedom according to the circumstances of those times. The method with which they carried out their struggle in those days never brought them nearer to their goal of independence. The path of Indian freedom is paved with thorns. They tried to clear off this path and draw Britain on to their side by truth and negotiation, but it is impossible to kick out a strongly-entrenched power like that of the British by these methods. Therefore, Britian cannot be driven out of Indian expect with the sword. Babu Subhas Bose considers it a matter of prices and possibility to achieve Indian freedom by armed forces."

Tokyo, Hindu, 7/5/43

Shonan: Subhas Bose leading the movement, the Indian Independence Movement has become vigorous. The Indian Independence League Branch of Malai held a rally today. On this occasion Bose encourage the people, saying: "You people of Shonan and Malai are able to take the leadership for the independence of India. The reason I left India is to give aid for independence from the outside. We must receive military aid from the outside in order to destroy the British. As for receiving aid, we have reached this. You must be prepared to give all sacrifice for India."

Tokyo, Japanese, 7/9/43

Chandra said: "Today is the most glorious day for us, the Indians. We have had the privilege this day to make known to the world our intentions. Today, with the formation of this army of our own, much is anticipated in the future. Before Singapore became Shonan, the Japanese forces cried, "To Singapore, to Singapore." Let us now cry out, "To Delhi, to Delhi." The faith that the Indians have towards their new army is absolute. A truly great episode is taking place. At the time of announcement of the establishment of the army, even the elderly Indians came running to the recuiting office to offer their services." *Tokyo, Japanese, 7/9/43*

Subhas Bose in his first press interview in Shonan, said that the Provisional Government of Free India will soon be in existence. Describing this new government, he said it will not be a normal peacetime government. It will be fighting organization to organize the Indian people and lead them to victory...... the new slogan that (Subhas) in saying, "The total mobilization of all our resoureces." The phase of mobilization will naturally include the expansion to the utmost limit of the strength of the Indian National Army. Mr. Bose has declared that approximately 300,000 soldiers, under Indian officers, would take the field when the first offensive begins. The Provisional Government of Free India will also direct the training of these soldiers.... In addition to a high standard of military training, the soldiers of the Natinal Army will aso be given an intensive moral and spiritual. training so as to turn them into a highly efficient force... Once that victory is won and India is again free, it will cease to exist as a govrnmetn, end the Indian people will have to decide for themselves what form their new government should take...... With regard to Japan, he has said, "I am convinced of the sincerity of the Axis countries regarding Indian independence and particularly of the sincerity of Japan, and if that wore not enough has not General Tojo, the Japanese Premier, assured us time and again that Japan has no territorial , military or political amunitions whatever in India? Has he not, on the other hand solemnly promised all-out aid to India in her struggle so that she might attain full independence in the true sense of the term? Has not complete independence been pledged to Burma and the Philippines within this year?"

Saigon, English, 7/12/43

Subhas Chandra Bose, President of the Indian Independence League, made the following speech at a mass meeting at (Farar) Park in Shonan. On Aug. 15 on the occasion of the first anniversary of the Anti-British Resistance: The Indians in various parts of the GEA are holding this meeting, first, to felicitate the independence of.Burma, and second, to reaffirm our determination to continue with the struggle until British are driven out from Indian and until complete independence is achieved."

Tokyo, Japanese 8/15/43

Chandra Bose, President of the Indian Independence League, returned from a tour of Burma Thailand, and French-Indo-China and on August 17, in a presss interview in Shonan, stated as follows: ".... The Indian problem does not necessarily depend upon the world situation... Even in the event that the Anti-Axis forces attain some kind of success somewhere in the world, this true determination in Indian will not weaken. Rather, the victory of the Anti-Axis forces will further strengthen their imperialistic policy, but we must may that the Anti-British sentiment in Indian will be increased that much more." *Tokyo, Japanese, 8/18/43*

Bangkok: Statement of Subhas Chandra Bose—"A simulataneous outbreak of war in Europe and in Asia has been a dream I have had for the past 20 years, German authorities judged in the pst at that time that America would be defeated if war broke out. I also firmly believed in Japan's victory . After the GEA war boke out, the successive great war results confirmed my convition fully." *Tokyo, Japanese, 12/7/43*

Shonan: "Indians are now ready to commence their last assault on British power in India and the year 1944 will not only be a fateful year in Indian history out will also mark the turning point of this war toward victory ," declared Subhas Chandra Bose, head of the Provisional Government of Free India, his New year message to the peoples of East Asia ...... Declaring that in the last six months Indians in East Asia numbering nearly 3,000,000 have been welded into one solid revolutionary organization, Bose pointed out "All of them are ready of sacrifice all their worldly possessions and very lives in the coming fight for India's independence. With the sanction of forces behind them, the Indian National Army is well trained, well trained, well equipped and ready to light the spark that will start a country wide conflagration in Indian which will reduce which will reduce the British Empire to Ashes.

Tokyo, English, 12/29/43

Rash Behari Bose

Mr. Rash Behari Bose, noted Indian Independence leader stated to the press at undisclosed place, on Sunday, that 30,000 Indian overseas residents have now joined the India Independence Movement. He stated that the more strengthened the British pressure is, the more will the resistance of the Indian People increase. Mr. Bose declared that the day when their resistance is at its height is the day when the British influence makes wholesale withdrawal from India. *Tokyo, Japanese, 8/31/42*

Mr. Rash Behari Bose, President of the Indian Independence League, arrived at Shonan last night after an extensive tour of Burma. Mr. Bose is expected to stay in Shonan for a week to meet the other members of the (Council of Action) of the Independence League in order to arrive at the important decision regarding the Independence movement.

Saigon, English, 10/10/42

Shonan: The President of the Indian Independence League, Rash Behari Bose, during the course of his radio address, said , "A new Asia is in the making now and the Anglo-Ameican course is removed therefrom; but this Asia not be free, nor can there be any peace in the world as long as Indian is not free..... Our Anglo-American enemies are sandwiched between our fight for freedom on the one side and the Japanese power on the other. The day is not far off when the White Imperialists' rule shall be terminated. Out side help is necessary to drive out the Ango-American armies from Indian, and Japan has promised to render this aid."

Saigon, Urdu, 5/3/43

Shonan: The nomination of Mr. Subhas Chandra Bose as the new president of the Indian Independence League brought joy to his lifelong friend and cooperation in the Independence Movement. Mr. Rash Behari Bose, a former president of League. As a noble gesture and compliment to his co-worker, Mr. Behari Bose voices the following words at a grand rally here of the League members: "I have brought here to you one of the most outstanding, if not the greatest, personality of our beloved motherland., With the news of his arrival in Japan, the 2,000,000 Indians in East Asia who are free from the talons of British rule, rose up in one body and welcomed his arrival. This aptly speaks of the confidence the India people have for this brilliant man. Under his leadership, I am confident that you will march onto victory however difficult and ..... that may be too our final liberation. Of Course, I will always be at your side, sharing your suffering and your triumph." *Tokyo, English, 7/4/43*

Shonan: Following the mass meeting of the Indian Independence League yesterday, Mr. Rash Behari Bose former president of the League, gave a press interview..... He declared that the real battle for Indian Independence is about to begin under the personal command of Subahs Chandra Bose. the sporadic outbursts of the past have merely been skirmishes, Mr. Bose said, but now we are prepared to launch a major war against the British... Mr. Behari Bose pointed out that Mr. Subhas Chandra Bose is the most ideal leader in the coming struggle because of his relative usefulness and his fearless record as the foremost champion of India's absolute independence. *Tokyo, English, 7/5/43*

Indian Independence League
Sumatra Branch Activities

Independence meeting held at Medan. Medan, Domei: Inauguration to be held on July 31. Subject will be ousting of British and American influence from India. *Tokyo, Japanese, 7/30/42*

Medani: The Sumatra Branch of the Indian Independence League on Sunday observed here a colourful rally in commemoration of the first anniversary of the foundation of the Branch Renewed pledges were make to crush the British Empire. *Tokyo, English, 8/29/43*

Bukit Tinggi: In response to the establishment of the Provisonal Government of Free India, leading Indian Residents in Padang. yesterday morning at the Central Theater of Padang, held a ceremony for the organization of a branch of the Indian Independence League of the West Coast Province of Sumatra. At the ceremony 1,000 members unanimously adopted a resolution to extend all out support to the new Provisional Government in the struggle for freedom India. Following the meeting the members paraded in the streets demonstrating their spirit.

Tokyo, English, 11/6/43

Java Branch Activities

Batavia: Following the mass meeting of the Indian residents in Java, which has been held throughtout Java since August 8, the leaders of the Java branch of the Indian Independence League are now making preparations for driving forward the wholesale independence movement.

Tokyo, English, 8/25/42

The Java branch of the Indian League for Independence gathered at a mane rally to observe the birthday of Mahatma Gandhi and spread the news of the determination to fight for the freedom of their homeland. The rally want on record to support the anti-British fight.

Tokyo, English, 10/3/42

In order to encourage Gandhi, the Java Indian Independence League held a meeting on Feb. 15 and speeches were given. Telegrams of encouragement came from Bangkok. A resolution of determination of the Jakarta Branch was passed. *Tokyo, Japanese, 2/16/43*

Jakarta: Putting a finishing touch to the "Crush Britain and America" rallies held at various places in Java since August 3, the Java Chapter of the Indian Independence League held a grənd island-wide rally at the special municipal theatre at Jakarta on Wednesday.

Tokyo, English, 8/26/43

Jakarta: The Branch of the Indian Independence League sent congratulations to the Philippine Republic.

Tokyo, English, 10/18/43

Jakarta: Approximately 300 Indians of this city adopted a resolution expressing condelence over the death of Mr. Gandhi giving went to indignaton over British inhumanity, which caused that undeserved death in prison, at a rally held this evening in the headquarters of the Indian Independence League of Jawa. *Tokyo, English, 2/26/44*

Jakarta: August 24: 2000 guilders have been donated by Indian Residents in Jawa to the Jawa Military Administration as a war plane construction fund. Assamull, Chairman of the Java Chapter of the Indian Independence League, accompanied by Akbani and Tejomall, Chairmen from the Jakarta and Bandoeng branches of the league respectively, called on the director of the People's Affairs Bureau of the local administration Tuesday to donate the sum which was collected by 3000 Indians. Determination to fully cooperate with Japan until Asia is finally liberated from the Anglo-Saxon yoke was also discussed.

Tokyo, English, 8/24/44

200,000 guilders were donated by the Indian Residents in Java to the Java Military Administration as a war-plane construction fund, (Attu Mall), Chairman of the Java branch of the Indian Independence League, accompanied by Ghani and Teji Hall. Chairman of the (local branches), called on the Director of the People's Affairs Bureau of the local administration on Tuesday, and donated the sum in a taken of gratitude for the...... of India. They also expressed the determination of the Indians to fully cooperate with the Japanese until Asia is finally liberated from the Anglo-Saxon yoke. *Saigon Hind – 8/25/44*

Borneo Branch Activities

The 75th birthday of Mahatma Gandhi was celebrated on Saturday by Indian Residents throughout GEA. On this occasion, according to a report from Kuching, the No. Borneo Chapter of the Indian Independence League decided to make a monetray donation to the Indian Independence Army for their airplane fund. *Tokyo, English, 10/2/43*

Kuching: The Indians in Borneo, like their blood brothers throughout East Asia believe that independence for India likewise signifies freedom for the whole of Asia, declared S.C. Bose. Rak Ravarty, President of the Indian Independence League in No. Borneo...... Outlining the Indian Independence Movement No. Borneo Rak Ravarty said the Indians in Kuching organized the Independence League on March 13, 1942, under the leadership of J. Lalchand, when permission was received to start activities. With the arrival of Bose in Tokyo the Indians here were spurred to further activities and his arrival in Shonan gave added courage and enthusiasm to our hearts. He said the Indians could not help but feel gratitude toward the Japanese Government for bringing Bose safe and sound all the way from Germany to Shonan.

Tokyo, English, 11/2/43

Celebes Branch Activities

400 Indians from Makassar had sent money to the Military Administration to help the Dai Nippon with the establishing of a GEA. In the newspaper "Pewarta Celebes" we published all the names of those who donated money already for this movement. Not only from the Indonesian people in this area, but also from all Asiatic people who live in Makassar we received money. *Makassar, Malay, 9/24/43*

Malacca Branch Activities

From Malacca rows report says that the Indian boys between the age of 7 and 14 will join the Youth Brigade, now being formed by the local chapter of the Indian Independence League......

Tokyo, English, 4/28/44

Free India Provisional Government

Jakarata: Hailing the establishment of the Provisional Governement of Free India., every Indian resident in Jawa is showing a grim determination to offer everything for the cause of their fatherland... The Indian Independence Army would advance into India in the due course of time. Yesterday, nearly 90 representatives of the due course of time. Yesterday nearly 90 representatives of the Indian Residents in Jawa including Kundandas, Chief Branch of the same league in Western Jawa, assembled here and discussed effective measures concerning their.... toward the new Indian Government .... Donations to the Indian Independence Army by local Indian Residents to date have reached 700,000 guilders.

Tokyo, English, 10/23/43

Subhas Chandra Bose – Speeches

Jakarta: Subhas Chandra Bose, head of the Provisional Government of India, in a radio address prior to his departure for Shonan yesterday, highly commended the determinations of the Indian residents of Java anu Sumatra to play their part in the coming struggle for India's freedom. Bose exhorted his countrymen to gird up their loins and prepare at once for the coming struggle which will be life and death a struggle for the Indians, but a struggle that will ultimately bring victory and freedom.... "Another fact came to my notice immediately after my visit to Sumatra and Java; .... inhabitants these territories have no desire to go back to the former regime which existed two years ago. To the past is a chapter of servitude, humiliation and exploitation which they would like to forget once and for all. What is particularly gratifying to me as an Indian is that my countrymen in these parts are politically wide awake and determined to play their part in the coming struggle for India's freedom." *Tokyo, English, 12/14/43*

Bose, who is visiting here for the first time, said it is difficult to imagine the Great War is at present raging when he sees normal life carried on busily and cheerfully on clean-swept Jakarta streets. Smilingly he added, "I had never been permitted to land in Jawa durimng Dutch days because of my political career. I recall our poet Rabindranath Tagore was allowed to land in Jawa in 1930 only after promising not o engage in political activities".

Tokyo, English, 12/13/43

Indian National Army

Jakarta: Keenly alive to the growing importance of the situation, more Indian youth in Jawa have voluteered for service in the Indian Independence Army under the leadership of Mr. Subhas Chandra Bose. Meanwhile, throughout Jawa, monetary donations for the independence movement are being brought in day by day to the branches of the Independence League by older Indians who are unable to offer their services directly for India's freedom. *Tokyo, English, 9/4/43*

Jakarta: Firmly determined to join the Indian Independence Army in its marcxh to Delhi, youthful Indian residents in Jawa are daily undergoing vigorous military training. It is recalled that the anti-British movement in Jawa was started in May last year when the Indian residents sent five representatives to the Indian Independence League. In the course of one and a half years since than 200 of the 3,000 Indian colonists in Jawa have volunteered for service in the Indian Independence Army and a sum of 700,000 rupees has been donated to its. *Tokyo, English, 11/28/43*

Jakarta: Upon receipt of news of the march of the Indian Independence Army in concert with Japanese Army forces .... D. T. Assesmul, Chairman of the Jawa Indian Independence League declared (that thousands of .... Ed.) Indian residents in Jawa, upon hearing the news of the commencement of the new offensives of the Indo-Burma border, are now fervently awaiting results of the drive. He continued that although the number of Indians residing in Jawa is relatively small, their loyalty and love for their country is just as high as any of their other follow men who are shedding their blood for the cause of India and GEA. As a striking example, he recalled how local Indians raised 3,000 yen all at once after learning the Japanese Administration would donate to the Indian Independence League the entire prodeeds from the news film of the Indian Independence Army which was shown to local Indians. He further declared, "At last our compatriots have started the drive into the motherland and our fighting spirit will so ar high upon the viage of victory with them."

Tokyo, English, 2/9/44

Philippine Islands

Indian Independence League

The president of the India Independence group in the Philippines stated: We must do everything for Gandhi. The independence move has begun. Gandhi is our blood and soul. We are away from our land, and cannot be in India in body. but through some method we are resolved to go forward for the Independence of India. Until the independence is achieved riots will be repeated occurrences. *Tokyo, Japanese, 8/11/42*

Brisk activities designed for the complete independence of India have been started by several thousands of Indian residents in the Philippines with the Independence League branch as its center. President (Doibe Suan) of the Independence League branch on the night of August 12 made a radio speech in Manila over station KZRH beamed at India in which he said that now is the time for all the Indian people to rise and launch a decisive fight against brutal Britain. He clearly expressed the strong determination of the Indian people in the Philippines to support India in its fight for independence. *Tokyo, Japanese, 8/14/42*

Manila: The battlecry of the Indian Independence is resulting into an organized movement by the Indian residents in the Philippines with the opening of the Indian Independence League offices in Manila. The three room headquarters will be known as the branch office of the league in charge of all activities concerning the fight for India freedom from British rule, Mr. B E. (Saiwanichi), the President, formally presided at the inauguration of the headquarters which was... with the flag of the Indian National Congress and that of Japan. *Tokyo, English, 8/25/42*

The authorities of the Indian Independence League in the Philippines decided on a one weed period from Feb. 20 to 28 as a Gandhi week, during which the Indians of the Philippine Islands will hold prayer meetings for the prolongation of the life of Mahatma Gandhi, to enable him to accomplish his 21-days fast. The first prayer meeting was staged on a large scale in the Manila Hindu Temple on Saturday. *Tokyo, English, 2/21/43*

Indians in Manila joined in celebration of Indian First War of Independence Mass meeting held with 400 Indians attending. President of Indian Independence League in Philippine Islands declared "We have not forgotten how horrible British treated Indians. With these memories fresh in our minds, will chase out the British from soil of India."

Tokyo, English, 5/11/43

Manila Domei: The President of the Indian Independence League in the Philippine Islands (Devi Dewari) prior to the Declaration of Independence in the Philippine Islands, spoke as follows: "Upon the honor of a grant of independence to the Philippine Islands, we extend our heartfelt felicitation and similtaneously offer our profound gratitude to Japan who liberated our East Asiatic Asia" *Tokyo Japanese 10/12/43*

Commencing on the beginning of the Indian March "On Delhi". He said the local Indians are enthusiastic and following closely on the news report of the progress of fighting are flooding the office with inquires. Emphasizing it is "Indeed good news," Sehwani asserted "Every Indian in the Philippines feels with heart and souls that the Indian Independence Army is march to Delhi under the inspiring leadership of S. C. Bose will be climared with victory." *Tokyo, English, 2/8/44*

Manila: In memory of Mrs. Mahatma Gandhji, who died on Feb. 22 while incarcerated in Poona Prison, the Indian community here held memorial services everning at the Sikh People. While Indians throughout the world mourn the death Mrs. Gandhi, all Indian (Shops) and establishments in the Philippines were closed with the Indian Independence emblem displayed at half must today of respect for the great woman leader.

Tokyo, English, 2/24/44

Manila: Enthusiastically following the progress of the victorious Japanese and Indian National Army troops which are reducing one British fortress after another, the local Indians are presently actively observing liberation Week which began from April 6 with a new drive to raise funds to aid the Indian National Army drive to Delhi. On April 13 a mass meeting is scheduled, marking the climax of National Liberation Week and, at the same time, commemorating the 25th anniversary of the Amritsar Massacre. Throughout the week the Indian National Flag is being displayed in all Indian Independence League headquarters to hear the latest news falshes from the fighting front, supplied by "Domei" news agency. Meanwhile, it is learned the Indians are planning to offer voluntary later service in order to aid the administation's food drive and, at the same time, contribute their share toward winning the war of GEA. *Tokyo, English, 4/11/44*

Manila: Indians in the Philippines will join the rest of their countrymen in East Asia in celebration of "Netaji week" beginning July 4 to commemorate the first anniversary of the assumption by Subhas Chandra Bose of the chairmanship of the Indian Independence League and the leadership of the Indian Revolutionary Movement in East Asia. Local observance will be held at the Medical Pharmacy Hall here at which the chairman of the Philippine chapter will speek. The program will include the adoption of the resolution of congratulations which will immediately be cabled to Bose, raising the Indian National Flag, and soliciting funds and volunteers for the Indian National Army. A special radio program will be broadcast over the local station PIAM with Kara Singh Gill. spokesman of the Philippine League, speaking. Meanwhile, on the eve of the celebration, spokesman Gill issued a statement explaining the significance of "Netaji Week" to all Indians. He said the dramatic appearance of Netaji in the orient a year ago "brought a well of jubilation among Indians in the East Asiatic countries and instilled in them pregnant hopes for the eventual release of Mother India from the British." *Tokyo, English, 7/3/44*

Foreign Minister Claro M. Reoto, in a message to the opening ceremony of local observance of "Netaji week" held this morning at the Medical Pharmacy Hall here, under auspices of the Philippine Chapter of the Indian Independence League expressed the hope that leadership of Subhas Chandra Bos, 'Indian may advance India's freedom nearer yet to realization." *Tokyo, English 7/4/44*

Manila: July 27 Carrying a message from President Jose P. Laurel, an Indian jouranl titled "On to Delhi" came off the press yesterday. Published journal is dedicated to Netaji Subhas Chandra Bose, "Fearless Champion of the Indian Independence Movement and Uncompromising Exponent of the Cause of the Motherland (Dosei asterisks), whose Unexcelled Patriotism and Firm Conviction coupled with his Defialnce has Instilled fear and Terror in the British Hierarchy". The jouranal also carried messages from Foreign Minister Claro M. Recto and Shozo Maroto Japanese Ambassador to the Philippines. Indian Independence League the 148 page jouranl, through well-organized contents consisting of pertinent articles, portrays "The true situation in the Motherland so that the world, particularly our Filipine Southern may know our inglorious and miserable destiny under the Union Jack and the righteousness of our cause."

Tokyo, English, 7/27/44

Manila: Reiterating Gandhi's warnin there can be no compromise on India's demand for freedom, Karam Sigh Gill, spokesman of the Phillipines Chapter of the Indian Independence League declared people of India would not be content with anything short of independence.

Tokyo, English 8/9/44

Manila Branch Activities

Manila: A gigantic 2 day crush, Anglo American raly sponsored by the Manila Branch of the Indian Independence League was opened here this morning. Speeches were delivered by (B.B.B. Swun), President of the local chapter, Bose Vargas, Chairman of the Philippines Executive Commission, Beningo Aquire, Director General of the Kalibapi as well as by representatives of the Japanese Militaruy Administration.

Hainking, English 8/8/43

The Philippine Indian Independence League at Manila held a people's rally today. The Philippines Indian Independence League at Manila gathered together a large number of Indian representatives residing in various areas of the philippines at the Metropolitan Theater in Manila this morning in order to felicitate the establishment of the Provisional Government of Free India and held an Indian people's rally. First resolution of the Provisional Government of Free India. Then a resolution felicitating the independence of the Philippines was passed.

Tokyo, Japanese H., 10/25/43

Davao Branch: Activities

Davao, July 10: The Davao Branch of the Indian Independence League held an extraordinary meeting on the night of July 8 on the occasion of the recent nomination of Subhas Chandra Bose as President of the Indian Independence League and unanimously resolved to grant absolute support to the new President in the fight for the liberation of India from the British yoke.

Tokyo, Spanish 7/10/43

Cebu Branch: Activities

Attended by prominent Indian residents, the inauguration ceremony of the Cebu branch of the Indian Independence League was held in Cebu City last Tuesday night in conjunction with the anniversary of the establishment of the provisional government of Free India. During the ceremony, a resolution was read by chairman (Farbha) of the Indian..... Committee in the Visaya (sector). The affair was also attended by many local government and civilian leaders. *Manila, English, 3/23/44*

Cabu : With the Japanese and Indian National Army Forces having crossed the Indo-Burma border, members of the Local Chapter of the Indian Independence League gave an appreciation dinner for Japanese Filipine officials here for aid and encouragement given the Indians in their struggle for freedom from British and United States tyranny. The dinner was attended by Paulino Gullas, Commiissioner for Visayas; Jose Delgade, Governor of Cebu; Kyosabu Mogaki, Japanese Consul in Cebu; and Japanese Military Officials as well as other leading Japanese and Filipine citizens.

Tokyo, English, 4/4/44

Women's Service

Manila: About 60 Indian women residents of Manila held a meeting at the headquarters of the Indian Independence League Manila, in which they expressed their desire to participate in the National Movement. In this meeting, Mrs. Schwani, who is the wife of the President of the Indian Independence League, said that the women, shall work in the hospitals, and nurse the wounded soldiers.

Saigon, Urdu, 7/30/43

Manila: It is learned that the Indian Community in the Philippines, on the occasion of the recent visit of Subhas Chandra Bose to this city, donated 100,000 pesos to the cause of the liberation of their mother country from British tyranny.

Tokyo, English, 12/12/43

And now we bring news of the Indian Independence League in the Philippines. The (nation's) Indians have contributed (a sum of) 100,000 pesos to the Independence of Free India. Previously they had given 50,000 pesos. *Manila, English, 12/13/43*

On this day the Philippine Branch of the Indian Independence League sent a donation of 10,000 pasos to the Philippine Administration for the purpose of aiding in the increased food production program.

Tokyo, Japanese, 3/10 /44

Anti-British Demonstration

At a general meeting of the Philippines branch of the Indian Independence League on Monday, a wholehearted support of the anti-British demonstration now (appearing over all India) was expressed by the Indian residents at Manila. *Tokyo, English, 9/25/42*

A large scale anti-British demonstration will be held by members of the Indian Independence League in the Philippines on October 2 which happens to be the birthday of Mahatma Gandhi.

Manila, English, 9/30/42

All the Indian merchats on Monday closed their shops as a protest against the British Government in India and to hold a prayer meeting at the Indian temple on (name) Street for Mrs. Gandhi, who has died fighting for the independence of India side by side with her husband Mahatma Gandhi.

Tokyo, English, 10/26/42

Cooperation with Philippines

Manila: Manila revealed President Jose P., Laurel received additional messag of felicitations from branches of the Indian Independence League in Thailand, Malai and Sumatra on the occasion of the inauguraton of the Republic of the Philippines. Chairman of Thailand Branch said in part, your people have a long history of most cordial brotherly relations with the people of India. Our people very sincerely share (repoc....) Our brothers and sisters of the Philippines pray for their peace progress and prosperity." "70,000 Indians of Johore state heartly felicitations for attainment of complete independence by your excellency and the whole Philippines. Bengal for the Philippines! – read a cablegram from the Indians of Johore State, Malai. A similar message from Taise Sera, head of ...... said Indians there "Pray that the Almighty will bring happiness and prosperity to all Fillipine people in the future." Indians in Madan, Sumatra, through Mahatma, Chairman of the League branch there, stated. "andently wish the Fillipine people will forget to the goal of success under the leadership of your excellency."Manila: President Laurel sent a message to Subhas Chandra Bose acknowledgeing the gift of 125,000 pesos to the Republic of the Phillipines. This gift was given .... by Bose supporters in Manila yesterday. *Batavia, English, 12/6/43*

Manila: The entire Indian communtiy in Manila turned out this morning to senior voluntary labor service, this contributing toward winning the war, and at the same time siding the Philippines Government's food production campaign, The Indians young and old, dug the earth with determination, encouraging one another with heroic deeds of the Indian National Army on the India Front, The Indians worked side with Chinese volunteer workers, while Filipines and Japanese groups toiled nearly presenting a happy picture of GEA cooperation.

Tokyo, English, 4/23/44

Leaders

Subhas Chandra Bose

Tokyo: Surprise visit of Bose —asserted that Britain is now at War with India.

Shonan: Indian Independence has issued statement re arrival of Bose, is pleasent surprise for all Indians as well as to whole world.

Manila: Commenting on report of arrival of Bose in Japan, President of Manila Branch of Indian Independence League will be great blow to British and help to Indian fight for freedom.

Bangkok: As soon as news of presence of S. C. Bose in Japan came over either Indians in Asia rose up in body to strive now. Tomorrow mass rally.

Saigon : Receiving news of Bose visit to Tokyo residents of FIC attaching great hope of future activity talk to Tojo re Indian independence shortly after declaration that Japan would not spare efforts.

Rangoon: Upon receiving news of Bose arrival in Tokyo on Saturday called leaders into conference and sent cable of congratulations. Indian residents in Burma looking forward to leadership of Bose for liberation of India.

Tokyo, English, 6/20/43

Members of the (Manila) Chapter of the Indian Independence League numbering some 600 held a meeting at its headquarters Tuesday evening celebrating the presence of Subhas Chandra Bose in Shonan. The meeting passed a resolution: "We Indians of (Manila) great the arrival of Subhas Chandra Bose in Shonan and his resumption of leadership of the Indian Independence Movement. We hereby pledged to do our utmost to attain the final objectivity of the Indian Independence and of our fatherland."

Tokyo, English, 7/8/43

For the purpose of paying a felicitation call on the Philippine government upon its attainment of freedom, Subhas Chandra Bose, leader of the provisional government of "Free India arrived at Manila today, Nov. 22. Immediately upon arriving at the capital of the Island called for a visit upon President Laurel at the Malacanan Palace. Chandra Bose expressed his congratulations to his host for the happy birth of freedom for his national and held a conference on various matters. Following this Subhas Chandra Bose called upon the Japanese Ambassador in the Philippines, Murata, at his ambassadorial residence and extended words of greeting.

Tokyo, Japanese, H., 11/22/43

Manila: The Phillipines are proud and happy to welcome Subhas Chandra Bose, head of the Provisional Government of Free India, who arrived this afternoon as a guest of State accompanied by leading officers of the Indian National Army. *Tokyo, Japanese, 11/22/43*

Manila: More than 400 Indinas as well as hundreds of sympathizers resoundingly took up the challenge flung by Subhas Chandra Bose, head of the Provisional Government of Free India, to drive out the Anglo-Americans from E. Asia at a month rally held at the Metropolitan Theater this afternoon. *Tokyo, English, 11/23/43*

Manila: Indians in the Philippines reaffirmed their "Untarnished faith and absolute confidence" in Netaji Subhas Chandra Bose and pledged their entire resources to the aid of India's fight for freedom in a resolution passed at a ceremony held at 9:30, officially starting the local celebration of Netaji Week from July 4 to July 10. *Tokyo, English, 7/4/44*

Indian National Army

Manila, Domei: Ever since the return of the representatives of the Indian Independence League Branch in the Philippines who attended the convention which was recently held in Shonan, the sentiments for the participating in armed residence for the Indian Independence was further deepened. In the meeting, which was held day before yesterday, for making report of the meeting, which was held day before yesterday, for making report of the conference , several Indian youths.... immediately applied for volunteer service in the India National Army. President (name) of the Philippine Branch of the Indian Independence League and a certain number of youths decided of join the Indian Natinal Army. Monetary contribution for the causes of the independence movement is specially growing.

Tokyo, Japanese, 7/26/43

Davao: 14 Indian residents in Davao have volunteered for service with the Indian National Army under command of Subhas Chandra Bose. Encouraging these Indian volunteer warriors, the Davao Branch of the

Indian Independence League held a dinner party Monday, which fell on the first anniversary of the start of the Independence Movement by the All Indian National Congress and imprisonement of Mahatma Gandhi.

Tokyo. English, 8/11/43

Manila: More than 18 young Indian volunteers for the Indian National League gathered Monday afternoon at the finance building to undergo physical examination prior to their enlistment for active duty against Anglo-American oppressors of their motherland. Led by (Subhas Pagani), chief of the local volunteer corps, the volunteers expressed desire to die for their country if necessaruy to win independecne for India. die for their country if necessary to win independecne for India.

Tokyo, English, 8/31/43

Manila: Volunteers from the Philippine Chapter of the Indian Independence League who joined the Indian National Army some time ago are now undergoing rigid training to fight for the liberation of the motherland, according to reports received by the local chapter. It is undestood that even Manila Indians are admitted into the officers training school while others will fight for the Indian freedom in other capacities.

Tokyo, English, 12/12/43

Manila: "This is it, and I know we are going to win", declared D. B.Sehwani , President of the Philippine Chapter of the Indian Independence League, in commenting on the beginning of the Indian March "On Delhi". He said the local indians are enthusiastic and following closely on the news report of the progress of fighting are flooding the office with inquiries. Emphasizing it is "Indeed good news, " Sehwani asserted. " Every Indian in the Philippines feels with heart and soul that the Indian National Army's march to Delhi under the inspiring leadership of S. C. Bose will be climax with victory.

Tokyo, English 2/8/44

Appendix II

Decorations for the Azad Hind Fauj[1]

335. The following will be the order of precendence for Decorations awarded to members of the Azad Hind Fauj by the

Provisional Government of Azad Hind:—

(i) Shaheed -e- Bharat

(ii) Sher-e-Hind

(iii) Sardar-e-Jang

(iv) Vir-o-Hind

(v) Tamgha-e-Bahaduri

(vi) Tamgha-e-Shatrunash

II. In future there wil be two classes of the 'Sardar-e-Jung' Medal according to the standard of individual bravery, devotion to duty and leadership exhibited in the field.

The awards of 'Sardar-e-Jung' medal made up till now will be of Class I of that medal.

III. Members of the Azad Hind, who render meritorious and commendable service in the field, but fall short of qualifying for a decoration, will be granted the certificate 'Sanad-e-Bahaduri, by the Head of the State Provisional Government of Azad Hind.'

The award of Tamgha-e-Shatrunash is of the following classes:—

Class II : to be awarded to those members of the Azad Hind Fauj who kill or capture alive any British or American Officer or other rank either in single combat or in a group fight where

1. I.N.A. Trial Papers.

qualities of individual initiative and individual bravery come into play.

Class I : to be awarded to those members of the Azad Hind Fauj who exhibit conspicuous gallantry and devotion to duty in killing or capturing alive any British or American Officer or other rank either in single cambat or in a group fighting where qualities of individual initiative and individual bravery come into play.

Index

J

M

N

O

P